Palgrave Macmillan Studies in Banking and Financial Institutions

Series Editor: Professor Philip Molyneux

The Palgrave Macmillan Studies in Banking and Financial Institutions are international in orientation and include studies of banking within particular countries or regions, and studies of particular themes such as Corporate Banking, Risk Management, Mergers and Acquisition. The books' focus is on research and practice, and they include up-to-date and innovative studies on contemporary topics in banking that will have global impact and influence.

Titles include:

Michele Modina
CREDIT RATING AND BANK-FIRM RELATIONSHIPS
New Models to Better Evaluate SMEs

Jes Villa
ETHICS IN BANKING
The Role of Moral Values and Judgements in Finance

Dimitrios D. Thomakos, Platon Monokroussos &
Konstantinos I. Nikolopoulos (*editors*)
A FINANCIAL CRISIS MANUAL
Reflections and the Road Ahead

Elena Beccalli and Federica Poli (*editors*)
BANK RISK, GOVERNANCE AND REGULATION
LENDING, INVESTMENTS AND THE FINANCIAL CRISIS

Domenico Siclari (*editor*)
ITALIAN BANKING AND FINANCIAL LAW
Supervisory Authorities and Supervision
Intermediaries and Markets
Crisis Management Procedures, Sanctions, Alternative Dispute
Resolution Systems and Tax Rules

Dr. Fayaz Ahmad Lone
ISLAMIC FINANCE
Its Objectives and Achievements

Valerio Lemma
THE SHADOW BANKING SYSTEM
Creating Transparency in the Financial Markets

Imad A. Moosa
GOOD REGULATION, BAD REGULATION

Elisa Menicucci
FAIR VALUE ACCOUNTING
Key Issues arising from the Financial Crisis

Anna Omarini
RETAIL BANKING
Business Transformation and Competitive Strategies For The Future

Yomi Makanjuola
BANKING REFORM IN NIGERIA FOLLOWING THE 2009 FINANCIAL CRISIS

Ted Lindblom, Stefan Sjogren and Magnus Willeson (*editors*)
GOVERNANCE, REGULATION AND BANK STABILITY
FINANCIAL SYSTEMS, MARKETS AND INSTITUTIONAL CHANGES

Gianluca Mattarocci
ANOMALIES IN THE EUROPEAN REITS MARKET
Evidence From Calendar Effects

Joseph Falzon (*editor*)
BANK PERFORMANCE, RISK AND SECURITIZATION
BANK STABILITY, SOVREIGN DEBT AND DERIVATIVES

Josanco Floreani and Maurizio Polato
THE ECONOMICS OF THE GLOBAL STOCK EXCHANGE INDUSTRY

Rym Ayadi and Sami Mouley
MONETARY POLICIES, BANKING SYSTEMS, REGULATION AND GROWTH IN THE SOUTHERN MEDITERRANEAN

Gabriel Tortella, Ruiz García and Luis José
SPANISH MONEY AND BANKING
A History

Anabela Sérgio
BANKING IN PORTUGAL

Palgrave Macmillan Studies in Banking and Financial Institutions
Series Standing Order ISBN: 978–1–403–94872–4
(*outside North America only*)

You can receive future titles in this series as they are published by placing a standing order. Please contact your bookseller or, in case of difficulty, write to us at the address below with your name and address, the title of the series and the ISBN quoted above.

Customer Services Department, Macmillan Distribution Ltd, Houndmills, Basingstoke, Hampshire RG21 6XS, England

---

Banking in Portugal

Anabela Sérgio
Universidade Lusófona de Humanidades e Tecnologia, Lisbon, Portugal

palgrave
macmillan

First published 2016 by
PALGRAVE MACMILLAN

Palgrave Macmillan in the UK is an imprint of Macmillan Publishers Limited, registered in England, company number 785998, of Houndmills, Basingstoke, Hampshire RG21 6XS.

Palgrave Macmillan in the US is a division of St Martin's Press LLC, 175 Fifth Avenue, New York, NY 10010.

Palgrave Macmillan is the global academic imprint of the above companies and has companies and representatives throughout the world.

Palgrave® and Macmillan® are registered trademarks in the United States, the United Kingdom, Europe and other countries.

ISBN 978–0–230–37141–5

This book is printed on paper suitable for recycling and made from fully managed and sustained forest sources. Logging, pulping and manufacturing processes are expected to conform to the environmental regulations of the country of origin.

A catalogue record for this book is available from the British Library.

A catalog record for this book is available from the Library of Congress.

To my mother Ângela and my husband José António

Contents

Figures

Tables

Foreword

The Portuguese banking system was essentially ignored before the recent financial crisis that swept through a good part of the western world. In that respect it was like that of most small economies. Policy makers and scholars took for granted that banking systems in such economies were either too small to matter to the outside world, or that they were exactly like those elsewhere, or they even believed both propositions. Of course, any knowledge of the history of banking crises would have shown that such crises can originate in surprising places.

The Baring Crisis in London in 1890, for example, originated with Argentina. One of the best known banking failures of the nineteenth century, it came about because of links between government and a bank. Financial problems in Argentina had such an impact on Barings, a well-known international bank based in London, that prompt and skilled management by the Bank of England was required to ensure that the difficulties were contained and did not damage the rest of the British banking system and possibly also the standing of London as a financial center. The episode provides many warnings, which if heeded could have led to useful action before the recent crisis.

However, these warnings were not heeded and the result was that banks in small, open economies caused major problems that extended well beyond these economies. These problems came about and spread so widely in part because the banks in these economies were implicitly, indeed sometimes explicitly, supported by the governments of their home economies. These bank–government links, whether actual or merely hoped for, led to problems for both. In some cases the problems were of almost catastrophic seriousness. Cyprus and Greece come to mind.

But there were also problems elsewhere, for example in the Iberian Peninsula. This book will, it is hoped, contribute most usefully to the prevention of future problems in one country in that peninsula, Portugal. In addition, there are clear implications for nations elsewhere.

Its chapters, including a most useful introduction, guide us through all aspects of Portugal's banking system. We get a clear summary of its main features, together with descriptions of retail, commercial, investment, and private banking (including asset management). These chapters tell us what the system does. We also have chapters on how well it does these things, on how risk is managed in the system, and on the role of the central bank. Very usefully, and indeed essential to full understanding, we can also read about governance and how it changed over time, the expansion of these banks into former Portuguese territories, and how the crisis and sovereign debt problems interacted and thus affected the system.

This admirable short book by Anabela Sergio and her distinguished team of co-authors gives us a thorough overview of the Portuguese banking system – how it evolved, how the crisis affected it, and how it is now. It will be useful to all researchers interested in the varieties of national banking systems, and can guide and inform plans for the integration of banking systems in the eurozone, as well as any similarly ambitious plans that may exist elsewhere.

Geoffrey Wood,
Professor Emeritus of Economics, Cass Business School, London
Professor Emeritus of Monetary Economics, University of Buckingham

Contributors

Pedro Gouveia Alves is the CEO of Montepio Crédito, a leading Portuguese financial institution focused on specialized financing for SMEs from the Logistics and Transports sector and car financing for fleets and individuals. He graduated in Economics from the Catholic University of Lisbon, and completed a Master's in Corporate Finance from INDEG-ISCTE Lisbon and the Marketing Management program at Instituto Superior de Gestão Lisbon. He has been deputy director of the Strategic Marketing Department of Banco Espírito Santo, Lisbon; and Head of Marketing, Head of Strategy and Planning, and Head of SME and Corporate Banking of Montepio Bank, Lisbon. He was a member of the board of Finibanco, Porto during the merger with Montepio Bank. During his career he has worked as a Lecturer at Instituto Superior de Gestão Lisbon, Instituto Superior de Gestão Bancária Lisbon, and Catholic University Business School Porto. He is a member of ASFAC (the Portuguese Specialized Consumer Credit Providers' Association) and has been a member of the board of APPM (the Portuguese Marketing Professonals' Association).

Paulo Bandeira holds a degree in Law and a postgraduate qualification in Securities Law from the University of Lisbon. He has been qualified as a lawyer for 15 years and is a Partner in the corporate department of SRS Advogados (Portugal), with extensive experience in corporate and M&A transactions (domestic and international) and in corporate governance matters. His work in corporate governance matters mainly focuses on board structuring (he was responsible for the governance structure of the major state-owned bank, CGD) and on directors' duties and liabilities. He was a founder of the Instituto Português de Corporate Governance (Portuguese Corporate Governance Institute), a member of the Commission in charge of drafting its companies Best Practice Code, and a member of its legal commission. He is a frequent speaker at corporate governance seminars, focusing mainly on the structure of the board of directors and directors' liability. He is a member of the Governance Lab forum (Portuguese forum of governance specialists), as well as being a member of the Union Internationale des Avocats and Vice-President of its Portuguese Section.

Miguel Teixeira Coelho is an Auxiliary Professor at Lusíada University, Lisbon, where he lectures on financial markets, and is an Invited Professor in Risk Management at IDEFE/ISEG/ULisboa, Lisbon. He has a PhD in Economics and a Master's in International Economics from ISEG/ULisboa. An executive board member of Montepio Valor (mutual funds asset management company), he was a member of the board at Futuro (pensions funds management company) and MGA (asset management company) between 2009 and 2011. He held executive positions in the Financial, Research, and Risk departments at Caixa Económica Montepio Geral between 2004 and 2009. He was an Economist in the Studies Department at the Portuguese Securities Market Commission (CMVM) between 2001 and 2004 and in the Research Department in Macroeconomics and Financial Markets at Banif Investment Bank between 2000 and 2001, having also collaborated as an external consultant with the Portuguese Economic and Social Council (CES) between 1997 and 2000.

Rui Sainhas de Oliveira is an adviser in the areas of organization and audit of banks and insurance companies. He has a degree in Economics from the Technical University of Lisbon and a Master's in Business Management from the Lusíada University, Lisbon. He was director of the Finance Division of Banco Borges & Irmão and Auditor at Banco de Fomento and Banco Português de Investimento. He was a Visiting Professor at the Department of Economics at Lusíada University, where he taught economic development, international economics, and financial markets.

João Gil Pedreira is the CEO of Bridges Advisors, an advisory firm for strategic, socio-economic, management, and financial matters, which he founded after more than 15 years as a strategic consultant in McKinsey International, Diamond Cluster, and Greenwich Consulting, focused on and specializing in banking, insurance, and telecom sectors, throughout Europe, America, and Africa. He is the author of *The Bailout of Families and Companies from Chronic Over-indebtedness* (in Portuguese, 2013) and is an international lecturer on banking, finance, sustainability, over-indebtedness, and risk.

Mário Coutinho dos Santos holds a PhD from the University of Aveiro, Portugal, with a thesis entitled "Firm's Capital Structure Decisions: Theory and Empirical Evidence from Portuguese Banks." His advisor was

Professor Samuel Hayes III of Harvard Business School. He also holds postgraduate diplomas in Management and Finance from Harvard Business School, Massachusetts, and Stanford Graduate School Business, California. He is a Visiting Professor of Finance at the Catolica – Lisbon School of Business and Economics at the Catholic University of Portugal. He has taught courses on financial theory, corporate finance, money and financial markets, banking, and financial intermediation, at undergraduate, MBA, Master's, and executive education levels. His research interests in the area of banking focus on banks' capital structure, mergers and acquisitions, and performance; and in the area of corporate finance, on corporate financing and contracting, capital structure, corporate restructuring, and corporate governance. He was Associate Dean, Chair of the Finance and Accounting Department, Director of the Master of Science in Finance, and Director of the Management and Business Administration undergraduate program at the Faculty of Economics and Management of the Catholic University of Portugal, Porto.

Anabela Sérgio is Full Professor of Economics, Banking and Finance at Universidade Lusófona de Humanidades e Tecnologia (ULHT), Lisbon, where she belongs to the Research Center DREAMS. She also is a full member of CIJE (Centro de Investigação Jurídico-Económica), the Economic and Juridical Center for Research of University of Porto Faculty of Law. She developed her teaching activities at Instituto Superior de Gestão (ISG), Instituto Superior de Economia e Gestão (ISEG), University of St. Joseph-Macau (Universidade Católica), and Universidade Lusíada in both Lisbon and Porto. She is a member of the European Association of University Teachers of Banking and Finance, of Ordem dos Economistas, and of Sociedade Nacional de Geografia. She graduated from Universidade Livre de Lisboa, obtained an MSc in Economics from Nova School of Business and Economics, and her PhD in Banking and Finance is from Cass Business School, City University of London. She has spoken at conferences in Brazil, China, and the UK. Her recent research topics include the regulation and supervision of financial institutions and markets, financial crisis, Basel III, the financing of innovative small to medium-sized enterprises, and the implementation of governance models in the banking system. Among others, she is the author of *O Sistema Bancário e a Expansão da Economia Portuguesa (1925–1959)*, published by the Portuguese Central Bank.

António Rebelo de Sousa is an Associate Professor with Aggregation at the University of Lisbon (former Technical University of Lisbon) and at

Lusíada University, Lisbon. He is also Chairman of the Board of Directors of SOFID (the Portuguese Development Bank), Director of the Magazine *Energy and Future,* Vice-Chairman of OSCOT-Safety Observatory, Organized Crime and Terrorism, and Economic Advisor to the Japanese Embassy. He graduated from Instituto Superior de Economia (Higher Institute of Economics), obtained a PhD in Economics from Lusíada University, and became Aggregate Professor of International Economics at the Technical University of Lisbon. He was a Member of the Portuguese Parliament between 1976 and 1980, and then between 1983 and 1985, as well as a Member of the Parliament of Representatives of the EFTA Countries between 1977 and 1979 and between 1983 and 1985. He was assessor to the Minister of Finance (1995–99), consultant to the Minister of Finance (2001–02), assessor to the Minister of Commerce of the VI Provisional Government (Sept. 1975–April 1976), member of the Directive Council of Belém's Cultural Foundation (Lisbon), President of the Portuguese–USA Friendship Association, President of the Portuguese–Irish Chamber of Commerce, President of the Portuguese–Kuwait Mutual Friendship and Cooperation Association, and President of the Movement for Peace and Democracy in Mozambique. He was Professor of the New University of Lisbon (1976–85) and Professor of the University of Coimbra (1979–80). He is presently President of Honor for Life of the Portugal–USA Mutual Friendship Association.

1
Introduction

Anabela Sérgio

The impact of the financial crisis on various banking and financial systems has been severe, even dramatic, and has required interventions of different kinds: bailout operations by governments; regulatory and supervisory rethinking by policy makers and supervisory authorities; and, for financial intermediaries, the definition of new strategies and refocusing of their business.

The Portuguese banking system has found itself paying for the consequences of a crisis that originated in the United States, which can be traced in more general terms to the development of the typically Anglo-Saxon originate-to-distribute (OTD) model. This book aims to describe the impact of the crisis in several fields: consolidation and the evolution of governance models; supervision and regulation; risk management in financial institutions; the performance and efficiency of the banking system; retail banking for households; and corporate and investment banking. There is also an overview of the importance of Portuguese banks and their expansion.

The discussion in the second part of this chapter of the main features of the Portuguese financial system analyzes both the European banking union and the banking situation in Portugal in relation to the crisis.

The current study considers the period between May 2011 and May 2014. During that time Portugal has been through a demanding Financial Assistance Program (amounting to €78 billion and €12 billion for bank recapitalization), the repercussions of which are explained in Chapter 2. Analysis of the problem of Portuguese sovereign debt is an important step toward assessing the impact of the crisis and the measures taken by the government and the credit authorities.

The fall of Lehman Brothers and the accountability of other financial institutions for the crisis led to a recentering of corporate governance.

It is, in fact, an example illustrating that from a hazardous event a positive movement can be created. The financial crisis has demonstrated that there was a lack of governance in several financial institutions across the world, Portugal being no exception. This showed itself in a dearth of reporting, a lack of risk management, multiple failures in auditing procedures, but most of all a deep lack of knowledge by the boards of directors of several financial institutions of what products their institutions were selling, what sort of unguaranteed loans were being granted, and what risks were associated with these products/sellers. Governance models in Portugal are the subject of Chapter 3.

The purpose of Chapter 4 is to analyze and discuss issues related to the banking regulatory and supervisory framework and structures in Portugal, and the role of the country's Central Bank in that context. Banking regulation and supervision have been subject to general and ongoing concern, which has garnered considerable scrutiny and fostered a vivid debate among academics, public policy makers, regulatory authorities, supervisory agencies, the banking community, and capital market participants. Not surprisingly, an extensive body of literature has developed as a result of the attention dedicated to the topic by both scholars and practitioners.

This analysis is followed by Chapter 5, where risk management in Portuguese financial institutions is strongly linked with the idea of commitment. Methodologically, the aim is to obtain an understanding of the Portuguese financial system in several international contexts and of its particular characteristics, in which both social and political issues are important. Facing so many challenging endeavors, there is a need for awareness of the discriminating factors that would allow Portuguese institutions to cope with the several types of risks that they face. The chapter concludes by shedding light on how solvency ratios in Portugal are in line with high international standards, despite the challenges in the sector regarding efficiency and profitability.

Chapter 6 consists of a study of the performance and efficiency of the Portuguese banking system. Its main purpose is to examine account-based indicators of profitability, risk, and operating efficiency from 1993 to 2009. First, it discusses the theoretical background of banking performance measurement, before describing the empirical investigation. Its conclusion is that on average, the profitability of the banking system measured by both ROA (return on assets) and ROE (return on equity) is below the mean of the countries included in the sample, which indicates that it is underperforming. Using the capital regulatory ratio to measure the banking system's average capital adequacy, it is found that during the sampling period, for most of the time this ratio was below the mean of the other banking systems sampled, and consequently, from this standpoint, could be considered as undercapitalized. Furthermore, from 1993–2009 the Portuguese banking system was less efficient then its peers in terms of asset-liability management, measured by the interest expenses to total assets and interest expenses to total liabilities indicators. The chapter also concludes that, using the implicit income tax rate indicator, the Portuguese banking system is undertaxed.

Retail banking for households in Portugal is examined in detail in Chapter 7. In the last 25 years there have been relevant and decisive changes in the sector, and its size relative to gross domestic product (GDP) has grown significantly. The chapter aims to capture and analyze these changes and growth from two different perspectives: the main players, their strategies and evolution; and the main impacts on overall financial intermediation figures at a national level and in an international eurozone comparison. Two main subperiods are considered. Alhough it is a period during which retail banks and specialized consumer credit institutions assumed a significant role in the lives of Portuguese households, it must be divided into two different subperiods. The first one – which may be called "the rise of the empire" – will lead us through the 1990s and almost the entire first decade of the new millennium, until the outbreak of the financial crisis; and the second – which may be called "the fall of the empire" – will tell us the unfinished story from the outbreak of the financial crisis to the present day.

Corporate and investment banking in Portugal is the subject of Chapter 8. Corporate banking in Portugal in the mid-1980s is related to commercial banking, which looked after the regular needs of small and medium enterprises (SMEs), mainly from the manufacturing and services sectors. The offer portfolio was mainly composed of products and services for short-term financial loans (based on working capital needs, such as overdrafts or very short-term loans) and commercial loans (based on trade financing needs, such as factoring or similar instruments). The main players in the Portuguese market were banks with a strong tradition of short-term loans.

Until the end of the 1980s, there were several restrictions on housing loans and only three financial institutions were allowed to offer them. In the early 1990s the Portuguese financial market was liberalized, with the end of the privatization phase of banks that were nationalized following the 1974 revolution. Based on market mechanisms, the model encouraged banks to broaden their offers to housing loans and construction on a large scale. The scarcity of housing in Portugal, with very restrictive letting laws, opened the door to a period of rallying real estate leverage.

After the market liberalization in the late 1980s, a new bank emerged as a disruptive player proposing a new distribution model based on segments for corporates (small business, SMEs, and large corporates). Thus the first account managers appeared specializing in dealing with corporate customers. The model that was widely adopted by the Portuguese banking system up to the end of the 1990s, although with some variations, was a dedicated account manager in the universal branches, or middle-office facilities reserved for corporates (mainly small businesses and SMEs) with centralized back offices.

In the mid-1990s, the bank loans market became more dynamic and attractive due to the expansionist budget and monetary policies of the western economies. Large companies, related to public investments and large-scale private investments in facilities and infrastructure, demanded more specialized services, such as structured loans adjusted to the project's characteristics or financial solutions with longer maturities, requiring new structures of funding (not only classic loans, but structured high-grade debt and raising funds on capital markets). This brought corporate and investment banking closer to what we know today.

The final chapter concludes the survey by identifying the strengths and weaknesses of the Portuguese banking system when expanding its activities all over the world, focused on Portuguese-speaking countries. It also outlines the possible strategies still available for surviving the great financial crisis.

Main features of the Portuguese financial system

Evolution of the world economy and the role of central banks

The speech that Ben Bernanke, Chairman of the US Federal Reserve, gave on May 22, 2013 signaled a softening of quantitative easing (QE) and inverted the normal mode in which financial markets operated. This led to corrections in various asset classes and generated high volatility in emerging economies, which were affected by the adjustment impact of expectations concerning American monetary policy.

Emerging markets received large inflows of US capital, the so-called carry trade, due to the abundant liquidity and low interest rate policy created by the American QE program. However, the tapering in prospects opened the way to capital repatriation, the "flight for quality," with the consequent direct depreciation of local currencies (Brazilian real, Indian rupee, Indonesian rupiah, South African rand, and Turkish lira).

In the meantime, the European Central Bank (ECB) has issued assurances that the low interest rate policy will remain unchanged for a long period, since economic recovery in the eurozone continues to be subdued.

Financial integration in Europe and the role of the ECB

The fragmentation of eurozone financial markets increased during the first half of 2012, due to the risk of a euro breakup and the consequent risk of redenomination into national currencies.

During the second half of 2012, the prospects for a European banking union and the ECB's announcement of unconventional monetary policy measures – that is, three-year funding (long-term refinancing operations or LTRO), assignment of liquidity to commercial banks (credit easing) to prevent a credit crunch in Europe, and direct monetary transactions (DMT) – restored confidence in the eurozone, but did not eliminate the segmentation of these markets reflected in the sovereign public debt risk premiums of peripheral countries. This implies that in these countries, including Portugal, interest rates remained high in comparison to Germany and the center of Europe. Interest rate spreads were stronger in sovereign debt markets than in corporate markets.

Essentially, the ECB's policy would buy some time until European political leaders took decisions regarding progress toward some form of political union that would stabilize the eurozone (far from an optimal monetary zone and the political union of the United States). The biggest design flaw in the current EU is the lack of the large central budget and transfer union that make monetary unions and federal currencies, such as the dollar, work. Obviously, this weakness can only be addressed by a movement toward something closer to a political union.

European banking union

A European banking union would require a single supervisor on a European scale, which would be the ECB. For Portugal domestically, this role was played by Banco de Portugal. There would also be a need for a European regulator, the European Banking Authority (EBA). In the Portuguese case, Banco de Portugal played the role of regulator.

A deposit guarantee fund would be required on a European scale to cover deposits up to €100,000, which already occurs nationally. Furthermore, there would have to be decision-making mechanisms on bank closure and rescue on a European scale, with the consequent European rescue funds. In Portugal assurances were issued by the Portuguese government and treasury, as has been seen with the cases of the country's banks BPN, BPI, BCP, and BANIF, which were financed by contingent convertible bonds (COCOS) funded by the Troika Program cooperation between the International Monetary Fund (IMF), the European Commission, and the ECB.

However, agreement has only been achieved on the European supervisory agency, the ECB, since the EBA was already, to a certain extent, performing this regulatory role on a European scale.

The financial crisis and the Portuguese banking system

When Portugal joined the eurozone, its banking system started to use European wholesale funding markets for its needs arising from insufficient internal savings, which are expressed in the retail market through the deposits of residents. The Portuguese external deficit reflected a national savings gap in relation to investment. In other words, we could say that the Portuguese banking system was the agent that went to the external market to seek the external savings required to finance the country.

Based on this funding model, the Portuguese banking system grew in terms of mortgage loans and consumer credit, in real estate and construction, following credit facilities linked to the dramatic decrease in interest rates. This led to a loan-to-deposit ratio well over 100%, which implied that internal savings, in the form of deposits in the Portuguese banking system, were insufficient to fund the necessary credit, whereby the banks resorted to external savings/debt. The closure of the Portuguese economy to financing from external markets also dramatically affected external funding to the banking system.

Due to the deterioration of the economic situation, the financial crisis caused an increase in loan defaults by companies, as well as by individuals who became unemployed and required fresh capital.

The Economic and Financial Assistance Program, following the guidelines that Banco de Portugal had been issuing for some time, led to a deleveraging of the Portuguese banking system, with loan-to-deposit ratios having shifted from 143.2% in 2010 to 128% in 2011 and 117.4% in 2012. It is important to note that this has been an extremely difficult period for Portuguese banks, since this was, additionally, carried out in the context of the required strengthening of Core Tier 1. This forced the banks to sell assets, restrict credit to the economy, and compete for deposits, leading, in fact, to exaggerated increases in deposit interest rates.

Hence, this period also resulted in liquidity problems for the economy and the threat of a credit crunch, which were mitigated by the ECB's assignment of liquidity to the Portuguese banking sector, approximately €48.742 million up to May 2013.

The significant reduction in leverage, capital strengthening, and the impressive growth of deposits in the Portuguese banking system (remarkable in the context of the peripheral countries in difficulties, such as Spain and Greece) have contributed to a notable adjustment of the balance sheet of the country's banks. However, profitability remains a serious concern.

A credit pricing problem also persists. At the moment there is no serious problem of liquidity for the banking system in terms of credit lines for good companies, namely those producing and selling tradable goods. The real issue is the credit risk of companies with very weak equity, which unfortunately covers a large majority of Portuguese non-exporting SMEs.

On the other hand, the success of the Adjustment Program in terms of the country's external position, with the elimination of the current and capital account deficits, has considerably improved the perception of Portuguese risk. This will also facilitate the path for large companies and banks to return to external markets, with a softening of their funding costs, which will be good for credit pricing.

In 2012, the non-financial private sector generated savings that exceeded investment, both due to increased individual savings, reflected in higher deposits, and as a result of low business investment, which is very negative for the future growth of the economy. Nevertheless, the public deficit offsets private savings.

Net interest income will continue to be subject to strong pressure derived from a series of factors, namely low demand for credit; weak profitability of mortgage loans, with bank refinancing costs well above the lending rates applied and whose spread cannot be changed; the continuation of high funding costs in relation to the center of Europe; as well as low short-term interest rate levels and the squeezing of net interest income associated with demand deposits. Additionally, the banking sector has downsizing costs due to the lower demand for credit, which is particularly evident in mortgage loans and consumer credit.

In this context, the banks must continue to implement rigorous management of credit risks and a prudent policy of recognition of non-performing loans (NPL).

Thus in the forthcoming scenario, the banking system will continue to experience difficulties because of the economic situation and the ongoing adjustment policy. It is also important to emphasize that macroeconomic constraints will persist during the post-Troika period.

Acknowledgments

The author wishes to thank Engº Luís Mira Amaral, CEO of Banco BIC Portugal, for his valuable contribution to the structure of this chapter. Any remaining errors are my own.

2

The Impact of the Financial Crisis on Portuguese Banks: The Problem of Portuguese Sovereign Debt

Anabela Sérgio and António Rebelo de Sousa

This chapter aims to analyze the effects of the 2008 financial crisis on the Portuguese financial system. The impact was twofold. On the one hand, the expansionary tax policy that followed increased the need for government funding and there was a trend toward recourse to the wholesale credit market. On the other hand, banks' usual resources dried up (e.g., the interbank monetary market), pushing these institutions into much more expensive funding (for instance, bond issues), therefore squeezing financial intermediation rates. The huge increase of Portuguese government debt (well above 100%) led to a crisis of sovereign debt.

In order to mitigate this situation, Portuguese banks decided to take advantage of the special credit lines (both in terms and amounts) put in place by the European Central Bank (ECB). However, there remained the problem of the quality of securities encompassing these repo (or repurchase) transactions.

Between 2010 and 2011, this led banks in Portugal to become aware of the need for new capital in order to reinforce their own funds. At the beginning of 2012, doubt remained over whether some more significant potential losses still existed (implying further recapitalization procedures in addition to those previously estimated). In June 2012, the government published a law making available €12 billion for banks to be able to strengthen their own funds.

A broad question was then addressed. This concerned the ability to reverse the "crisis cycle," thus obtaining a more sound equilibrium of public finance within a framework of a relatively inefficient "export-led growth model" in the Portuguese economy.

As a result of the 2008 crisis, the Portuguese financial system faced a particularly difficult situation, not only due to the existing international financial instability, but also as a consequence of the strong structural disequilibria that the national economy was facing. The international financial crisis was also the root of an economic crisis. This led the Portuguese government to implement countercyclical policies and to deepen their public expenses (and, naturally, to increase the public debt), thus contributing to the appearance of a sovereign debt crisis. It was this sovereign debt crisis that led to an increase in the associated risk premium . This, in turn, generated negative consequences regarding access to funding by the Portuguese financial system (with an increasing difficulty in obtaining "buffers").

Thus, the disequilibrium that occurred in the Portuguese public finances, with the corresponding worsening of interest rates and the public debt, together with increasing difficulty in accessing the international financial wholesale markets, became more and more problematic and associated with an economy in recession.

The requirements to reduce expenses, promote savings, and deleverage the financial sector (which, meanwhile, faced an increasing asset liability quality transformation) led to recession in the Portuguese economy.

Curiously, during 2010, when the deleveraging process had already begun, the Portuguese economy was not facing a credit crunch. The economy's financing conditions remained largely acceptable, thanks to the adoption of the ECB's monetary policy.[1]

Additionally, the granting of credit to the public sector accelerated from 2009 until the beginning of 2010, substantially reinforcing the portfolio of public debt held by banks (and therefore increasing their assets). This public debt could be used as collateral in repo transactions with the ECB (in this way facilitating banks' acquisition of funding). Nevertheless, this method of funding became harder and harder considering the risk of the sovereign debt, which led to a lack of interest in holding this kind of asset in banks' own portfolios. Conditions were then created so that the government could choose alternative ways of financing, namely using the EU's European Financial Stability Facility and loans from the International Monetary Fund (IMF).[2]

This has been the context against which the global problems of liquidity in the banking system have deteriorated. The situation implied increasing funding of banks' clients through deposits, combined with time deposits experiencing a deceleration (more precisely since the third quarter of 2010, which contributed significantly to an already existing problem). Additionally, the system began to experience more severe breaches of contracts, and in the course of 2010 default ratios increased dramatically, especially concerning loans to non-financial companies as well as for individual consumption.

The negative evolution of the national economy, in the sense of a contraction of the cycle with the corresponding increase in the unemployment rate, allowed a continuous worsening of default levels to be foreseen as early as 2010, which, in turn, would always result in the reinforcement of funds allocated to deal with the increasing disparities experienced by credit institutions.

This development (together with other factors arising from the need to improve the asset quality transformation ratio) contributed to a decrease in Portuguese banks' profitability, not only in 2010 but also during 2011. The banks had to refocus on their balance sheets, reinforcing them with complementary reserves in order to increase their own funds and, therefore, improve the ratios for Core Tiers 1 and 2.[3]

From the Keynesian pact to a new Laffer curve

The international financial crisis, in fact, makes evident the fragilities of countries with less sound or sustainable public finance situations.

It is common to accept that in a situation of recession or pre-recession, the Keynesian pact advocates both the utilization of liquidity injections to the financial system and the implementation of public investment programs. These procedures are adopted through "credit easing" and "quantitative easing" policies.

Starting with the equation $M^*V = P^*Y$, where M is the money supply, V the velocity of money's circulation, and where P stands for the level of prices and Y for the real income, the trend is for monetarists to consider that V is a constant variable and Y is unchangeable, at least in the short run, allowing these two variables to change in the medium and long term. Thus, an increase in M would always imply a variation in the level of prices P of the economy, not promoting a positive transmission mechanism into the level of economic activity in the economy represented by Y.

Notwithstanding this, New Keynesians, such as N. Gregory Mankiw and Olivier Blanchard, have advocated that neither prices nor wages will immediately adjust (or automatically adjust) to variations in the quantity of the money provided and, therefore, to variations in demand, considering that there exists a certain level of resilience in the level of prices and rigidity in wages. Price stickiness would be explained mainly thanks to the existence of "menu costs," the externalities of aggregate demand, and the absence of coordination between prices. Rigidity of wages (in the short and medium term) was a result of institutional factors (as explained by Robert C. Lieberman) as well as of factors of inaction, which regulate both employers' and employees' behaviors.

From what has been explained, liquidity improvements in the economy may be considered within a countercyclical policy. Nevertheless, this framework of providing liquidity to the financial system and resorting to public investment, in order to avoid recession and recovering the expansion of an economy, is hindered by two important constraints: budget constraints, and foreign disequilibrium budget constraints.

Indeed, if adopting an expansionary policy within this framework implies a deepening of the budget deficit (BD) and of the public debt (PD), and/or a deepening of foreign disequilibrium (FD), this means that, in the short run, it will cause effects in the premium risk of Portuguese sovereign debt. Therefore, the ability to be able to obtain the funding required either by the economy or by the financial system is compromised.

That is why we argue that the idea of belonging to a monetary area with a strong currency, by itself, is not enough to set aside problems in obtaining funding and in terms of international payments made by this economy. Both the interest in and the capacity for adopting a strategy of reverting to public investment are somehow associated with the dimensions of the state or, in other words, associated with the weight of the state in such an economy.

Moreover, this may address the issue of the optimal size of the state in the economy, which is synonymous with the correlation between the relative weight of the state and the welfare state in the economy.

The first issue to overcome is the selection of which indicators to use to enable "measurement" of the relative weight of the state in the economy. Indeed, several methodologies may be adopted.[4]

By analytical simplification, we may consider the expenses of the "SPA – Sector Público Administrativo," or the Portuguese public sector administration, in relation to gross domestic product (GDP). Nonetheless, we are facing a methodology with limitations, since it does not consider the relative importance of the "SEE – Sector Empresarial do Estado," or the state-owned company sector.

An underdeveloped economy needs, in principle, more of a state, more investments in infrastructure for state-financed schools, as well as other framework infrastructure. However, a developed economy may reach a level where an increase in public expenditure does not lead to an improvement in the level of collective welfare. Instead, a decrease in the welfare level may be observed, considering that self-initiative is hindered and the future of new generations is compromised by issuing this excessive level of debt.

Adjustments have unavoidable signals

During 2010, countries with higher profitability rates with 10 years of maturity, related to the benchmark of Germany, were Greece, Ireland, and Portugal. It is also true that these differentials reflected a larger demand for such assets of refuge by investors, in a context of risk aversion.[5]

Disturbances in the market for sovereign debt gave rise to negative externalities in the banking sector through several channels.

First, one must bear in mind that for a long period banks were the most important investors in sovereign debt. Therefore, the wide variations and volatility experienced in prices produced substantial losses in the portfolios held by banks.

Secondly, we may state that there is a positive correlation between funding conditions in the international markets and the cost of funding supported by the public sector.

Thirdly, we know that the value of the collateral in the form of guarantees assigned by the state decreases with the increase in sovereign risk. This situation means that the financial system experienced increasing difficulties in obtaining funds in the interbank monetary market. We must add that in particular, in what concerns the Portuguese economy, there was a huge external deficit, with savings and investment rates at historical minima.

Thus, it was evident in 2010, and at the beginning of 2011, that the required macroeconomic adjustments should be based on the reduction of expenses, therefore allowing for an increment in the savings rate and a decrease in the excessive leverage of many economic agents.

Furthermore, it was known that such an adjustment policy would lead to a non-expansionary effect in the level of economic activity. On the contrary, a contraction in the Portuguese economy was observed.

Moreover, it was also known that investments should primarily be channeled to duly proven production activities, granting privilege to the sector of tradable goods.[6]

Finally, the impact of the recessionary adjustment had several outcomes: an increase in the unemployment rate; a downgrading of Portuguese banks' rating; and an increase in the spreads of credit granted to companies, hampering their ability to meet principal and interest installments.

On the other hand, it is important to recognize that the consolidation of public finance is a sine qua non for the most suitable adjustment in the national economy. In fact, any expressive disturbance in the markets, even if exogenous in origin, may always question the possibility of a gradual inversion in the current "crisis cycle."

Additionally, this inversion would to a large extent have to go through a successful implementation of an "export-led model," which, in its turn, would depend on the evolution of the global economy in general and the European economy in particular.

From Basel II to Basel III and the evolution of the banking sector

The Basel Committee on Banking Supervision made an announcement in September 2010 about the revision of minimum capital requirements to higher levels. A transition period for the adoption of the new levels was also established.

Reinforcement of the required capital is essentially linked with the Core Tier 1 ratio. Simultaneously, new improvements were introduced concerning the items eligible for this measure in what, conventionally, was termed own funds' positive elements.

We may add that, meanwhile, the Basel Committee suggested the creation of two distinctive buffers; namely, the buffer for capital conservation and the countercyclical buffer. The former aims at having the capacity to absorb potential losses in the banking system within a framework of financial stress,[7] while the latter should perform a complementary role during periods of excessive credit growth or in moments of excessive accumulation of risks.

Furthermore, the Tier 1 ratio, as a percentage of assets (which is, incidentally, linked with leverage), should be transformed at the level of 3%, allowing for an observation period between 2013 and 2015.

Basel III also aims to insert prudential requirements related to liquidity risk; namely, using two indicators, the ratio of liquidity cover and the ratio of stable net financing.

Meanwhile, non-conventional monetary policy measures, adopted by the ECB, allowed the financing of the Portuguese banking system to be guaranteed by replacing the financing of wholesale international debt markets. This, in turn, made possible the growth of credit granted to families and companies during 2010. During this period public-sector financing was, to a large extent, underpinned by the resident banks and by acquisitions under the Eurosystem's "Securities Markets Programme."

Until the beginning of the second semester of 2010, activity in the Portuguese banking system registered a variation of 4.3% compared with the end of the previous year.[8] This evolution was the result of incremental values in the financial asset portfolios available for selling (highlighting public debt securities) and in the growth of the portfolio of credit to clients (thanks to loans granted to the state central public administration and to non-financial companies).

Afterwards a different development was registered. From the third quarter of 2010 onward, there was a negative trend in the registration of loans granted to the public administration and to non-financial companies by the resident Portuguese banking sector.

At the end of the first semester and the beginning of the second semester of 2010, the value of the external assets of Portuguese banking groups, on a consolidated basis, corresponded to around 30% of the total assets of domestic institutions.

As regards the profitability indicators of the Portuguese banking system, after a less positive evolution during the first quarter of 2010, the banking sector experienced a recovery during the second quarter of the same year. A cost-cutting policy explains this positive progress.

In 2010 it was also necessary to consider the policy of mitigating operational costs. This policy counterbalanced, although only partially, the reduction in the financial margin. Nevertheless, the "cost to income"[9] ratio at the level of 57% showed some deterioration when compared to the same period in the previous year. On the other hand, the results of international activities exhibited significant expansion during the first half of 2010.

Concerning own funds adequacy, we should underline that, in July 2010, the global adequacy ratio of the Portuguese banking system (on a consolidated basis) attained 10.1%, while the adequacy ratio of own funds, on the Tier 1 ratio basis, reached 8%.[10]

Nevertheless, in accordance with the Bank of Portugal's Financial Stability Report,[11] "disturbances in the sovereign debt markets would not reveal significant impacts in capital requirements during the first half of 2010."

We must confess that the international financial crisis displayed some fragility in the regulation of the financial system in global terms. As a result, the Basel Committee on Banking Supervision introduced several proposals, as has already been mentioned, trying to intensify the quality of banks' own funds, inserting measures of a countercyclical nature into the regulation of the financial system. The corresponding aim was to mitigate the risks resulting from excessive leverage and to adopt more demanding regulations in the framework of the Own Funds Requirements Directive. One of the most relevant issues implied the imposition of additional capital buffers ("countercyclical capital buffers").[12]

In a geographical approach to risk exposure, dominance goes to the developed countries, in particular to those countries belonging to the euro area. As is well known, both 2010 and 2011 were marked by a crisis in sovereign debt markets, which led to a significant increment on the profitability rates of public debt in several countries, Portugal included. As a corollary, the banks started facing an increasing country risk, with the consequent greater difficulty in accessing the wholesale international debt markets. Portuguese banks obtained their funding from the ECB. It was within this framework that the portfolio of Portuguese state sovereign debt increased dramatically.

On the other hand, and considering the need for deleverage and Portuguese state budgetary consolidation,[13] the majority of assets held in Portuguese banks' portfolios were bonds and other instruments issued by Portuguese companies. This led to negative consequences with respect to their ability to grant more credit to the Portuguese economy.

Notwithstanding this, the existence of sovereign risk has always had some impact on the profitability and solvability of Portuguese banks. This impact was somewhat limited, since the existence of sovereign debt held by banks did not generate potential losses, because Portugal avoided a situation of default.

We must underline that, due to the evolution of Portuguese sovereign risk, banks registered a strong increase in the profitability rates of bonds issued by banks in the secondary market, together with the constraints that occurred in wholesale debt markets.

From the financing conditions of banking activity to the recapitalization of credit institutions

During 2010 – and even during 2011 – the banking sector's asset weight in Portuguese GDP was below the ratio of the euro area, notwithstanding the relevant role played by this sector in the Portuguese economy. We should underline that, during the 2008 financial crisis, the activities developed by financial services, including insurance and pension funds, corresponded to around 8% of the country's gross value added. This percentage is above the corresponding relative weight observed for the euro area (slightly below 5%).

In December 2011, approximately 50% of the banking sector's total assets corresponded to credit granted to clients (against 36.7% in the euro area). We must also add that the annual average rate of credit expansion between December 2005 and December 2008 was 10%, which subsequently started to soften and stopped its decrease from the second quarter of 2011 onward. However, although the reduction of the ratio of credit to GDP began decreasing from 2011, in 2012 it was still at a high level when compared with the euro area.

Another issue to bear in mind is that at the end of 2011, both individuals and non-financial companies revealed a greater dependence on banking credit when compared with the euro area. State-owned companies represented almost 10% of the total debt of non-financial companies to the resident financial sector. With respect to credit to individuals, this corresponded mainly to developers and to the real estate sector.[14] Moreover, it should be noted that in 2011, in the euro area itself, the sector absorbing the greatest proportion of credit granted to non-financial companies was the real estate sector. Default credit in this sector underwent an incremental increase during 2008.

It is important to recognize that, between December 2008 and December 2010, wholesale financing by Portuguese banks experienced expansion at a higher rate than that of the euro area (19.2% per year against 10% per year). We should also consider the deposit side of banking activities. Until December 2011, time deposits with a maturity below one year represented a greater relative weight. This follows a substantial increase in the transformation ratio between 2000 and 2009, from 115% to 161% in September 2011, and actually closer to 120%.

Likewise we should register the fact that, in the euro area in general and in Portugal in particular, debt titles issued by banks were predominantly long-term financial instruments. In fact, between 2006 and 2010, "covered bonds" showed a remarkable increase in Portugal (116% per year). These financial instruments were very similar to "asset-backed securities" as a result of securitization processes, but still kept their status as issuers' bonds.

With increasing constraints in the monetary interbank markets, Portuguese banks became more dependent on the European Central Bank. Therefore there was a substantial increment in Portuguese banks' relative weight in the ECB's liquidity disposal transactions. This weight was slightly below 2% in December 2004 and attained 9% in June 2011.

As far as solvability is concerned, Portuguese banks registered a considerable increase in their Tier I ratio between 2008 and 2010, with an annual average growth rate of 4.4%.

It is important to stress that Portuguese banks' capital levels have been well above the legal minimum required. We underline in this connection that the Core Tier 1 ratio increased from 8% in 2010 to 9% in 2011.[15] However, as regards the framework of the Financial Assistance Program to Portugal, banks started facing new minimum capital requirement levels.[16]

In December 2011, the European Banking Authority proceeded with the presentation of the outcomes of the assessment conducted in banks under the stress tests regime (tests performed during June 2011). The Authority determined that the need for additional capital for the 12 European banks was €114,685 million (€6,950 million in the case of Portugal).

In the specific case of Portugal, the capital needs that banks had to face were the result of two circumstances, namely the exposure to sovereign debt, and the increase in the required ratio referring to Core Tier 1. As a matter of fact, for the four biggest Portuguese banks, the new requirements in terms of capital required an increase in their capital of 40%.

Portuguese banks tried to overcome the financial crisis without government support in relation to recapitalization, although six credit institutions used the Government Guarantee Regime until the end of 2011, amounting, during this first phase, to €4,875 million. Afterwards, in June/July 2011, these six banks used the same Guarantee Regime for new financing operations to the amount of €8,880 million. Therefore, in December 2011, the guarantees available (in cumulative terms) amounted to €12,505 million.

Meanwhile, there was a relevant increase in commission costs resulting from the increase in the volume of guarantees, and the price effect stemming from the increment of the average rate of guarantee commissions applied to new transactions. Thus, the total cost with guarantee commissions reached €500.4 million at the end of 2011. The total cost for the overall operations performed until the end of 2011 is estimated at €381.3 million for the years 2012, 2013, and 2014.

Finally, the 2008 financial crisis was the origin of the implementation of expansionary policies and consequently led to a worsening of budgetary deficits and to the sovereign debt crisis. The latter crisis affected the Portuguese financial sector and it became evident that several financial institutions needed to be recapitalized.

Several questions remained after 2012. Would there be additional difficulties for the financial system arising from default on credit granted due to the non-expansionary policies that had been adopted, together with the stagnation of European markets, making it difficult to strengthen the Portuguese "export-led model"? Would there be additional difficulties arising from disparities related to housing credit and to credit granted to public works and to the real estate sector?

Notes

1. In fact, during 2010 the European Central Bank kept on making funding available for Portuguese banks and buying the euro area's public debt in the markets.
2. In this regard refer to the Bank of Portugal's "Financial Stability Report," November 2010.
3. In the last few years the Portuguese banking sector's international activity significantly contributed to its profitability. This international activity explains, for instance, one third of the results generated during the first semester of 2010. Nevertheless, Portuguese financial institutions had to improve their capital and liquidity ratios within the framework of Basel III. This fact would always imply a negative effect, in the short run, on profitability levels.
4. See A. Rebelo de Sousa (2013) *Da Economia Política*, 2nd edn, Loures: Diário de Bordo.
5. The ten-year rates for Germany, the USA, and the UK were at historical minima, below 3%.
6. Although we should recognize that the tradable goods sector does not generate employment in a significant way, because this sector is mainly capital intensive.
7. This would refer to an additional requirement to the common equity ratio, demanding a minimum value of 2.5% (this means that total requirements for the common equity ratio should be at the level of 7%).
8. Assessed by total assets on a consolidated basis.
9. Bank of Portugal (2010) "Financial Stability Report," p. 63.
10. If we eliminate the values for BPN and BPP, it should be 8.8%.
11. Bank of Portugal (2010) "Financial Stability Report."
12. Own capital margins allow for the absorption of losses that not too big, distinguishing between capital conservation buffers and countercyclical buffers.
13. We should also consider the fall in Portuguese companies' rating due to the evolution of the rating of Portuguese sovereign debt.
14. See Associação Portuguesa de Bancos (2012), "Síntese do Sistema Bancário Português," March.
15. If we consider the average for the four biggest Portuguese banks.
16. Consequently the requirements for the Core Tier 1 ratio attained 9% on December 31, 2011 and 10% on December 31, 2012. On the other hand, on September 30, 2011, a new capital buffer to deal with the exposure to sovereign debt was put in place.

Bibliography

Amaral, Luís Mira (2010) *E Depois da Crise? Cenários para a Evolução da Economia Mundial e Portuguesa*, Lisbon: Bnomics.

Associação Portuguesa de Bancos (2010) "Síntese do Sistema Bancário Português," March.

Bank of Portugal (2010) "Financial Stability Report," November.

Sousa, A. Rebelo de (2009) *Manual de Economia do Desenvolvimento*, Lisbon: ISCSP.

Sousa, A. Rebelo de (2013) *Da Economia Política*, 2nd edn, Loures: Diário de Bordo.

3

Consolidation and the Evolution of Governance Models in Portuguese Financial Institutions

Paulo Bandeira

Discussion of corporate governance in financial institutions (namely banks) has been recentered in the last five years and the fall of Lehman Brothers and other financial institutions is to be accounted liable for that event.[1] It is, in fact, an example that shows us that from an hazardous event a positive movement can be created.

What the financial crisis has demonstrated is that there was a lack of governance in several financial institutions across the world (Portugal was no exception). This lack of governance was manifest in a dearth of reporting, a lack of risk management, multiple failures in auditing procedures, but most of all a deep lack of knowledge by the board of directors of several financial institutions of what products their institutions were selling, what sort of unguaranteed loans were being granted, and what risks were associated with these products/offers. There could only be one result: the failure of the system and a very profound intervention by the regulators worldwide.

The regulators' intervention was mainly driven by two factors: the systemic risks associated with the fall of one or more great banks; and the fact that it was necessary to inject government money (people's money) into the system to solve existing and prevent further systemic problems. Notwithstanding that, all these situations created a huge opportunity to rethink several governance issues of financial institutions.

A document with major relevance in this area that was updated due to the crisis was "Principles for Enhancing Corporate Governance," issued by the Basel Committee on Banking Supervision in March 2010. This paper addressed relevant matters such as:

- the role of the board;
- the qualifications and composition of the board;
- the importance of an independent risk management function, including a chief risk officer or equivalent;
- the importance of monitoring risks on an ongoing firm-wide and individual entity basis;
- the board's oversight of compensation systems;
- the board and senior management's understanding of the bank's operational structure and risks.

The principles also emphasize the importance of supervisors regularly evaluating the bank's corporate governance policies and practices, as well as its implementation of the Basel Committee's principles.

The same opportunity has also materialized in Portugal and was seized by the regulators worldwide to touch on governance models, risk management, compliance, directors' remuneration, auditors' liability, and so on.[2]

To discuss corporate governance in banks properly one should analyze every one of these subjects, as they all are extremely relevant and each allows part of each cause of the financial crisis to be explained. Notwithstanding the relevance of all of these matters, we will focus this chapter on the evolution of governance models in financial institutions, as well as offering concrete examples of Portuguese banks that have profoundly changed their governance model and board structure and the reasons underlying such decisions.

Portuguese governance models

To understand Portuguese banks governance models fully, one must be familiar with the governance models permitted and ruled by the Portuguese Companies Code.[3]

Governance models up to 2006

Governance models in Portugal are defined in the Companies Code. The legal regime applicable to the incorporation and licensing of financial institutions (RGICSF)[4] does not establish any specific regime applicable to these entities, indicating solely that credit institutions must "foresee solid mechanisms of corporate governance, including a clear organizational structure, with accountability rules well defined, transparent and coherent."[5]

The concept of "solid mechanisms of corporate governance" is better explained subsequently,[6] it being established that a financial institution must provide for:

a) Clear organizational structure with accountability rules well defined, transparent, and coherent.
b) Effective procedures for identification, management, control, and communication of risks to which it is or may be exposed.
c) Adequate mechanisms of internal control, including solid administrative and accounting procedures and policies of remuneration that promote and are coherent with sound and prudent risk management.

The legal regime for financial institutions mainly focuses on the prevention of risks and the remuneration of members of corporate bodies.[7] There is nothing on governance models and board structure.

Governance models foreseen in the Companies Code suffered a dramatic review and update in 2006, when the CMVM (the Portuguese Securities Market Commission)[8] and the Portuguese government seized the opportunity granted by the review and transposition of the auditors Directive[9] to amend the existing models and integrate a new one.

Up to June 2006, Portuguese companies could be established in accordance with one of two governance models:

- The classic or Latin model – a one-tier model comprising a board of directors and an audit board (one of the members of which was a chartered accountant).
- The German model – a two-tier model comprising an executive board of directors, a supervisory board, and a chartered accountant (as a separate corporate body).

The differences between the two models were significant.

The one-tier model was (and still is) the most broadly used in Portugal, in both listed and non-listed companies. It is a governance model whereby the powers and strengths of the most significant corporate bodies (the shareholders' meeting and board of directors) are very clear and well balanced. The shareholders understand their role in the company as holding the power and competence to appoint or dismiss the directors, approve the annual accounts, and resolve on relevant changes such as share capital increases or amendments to the articles of association, among others that are less relevant. On the other side, directors do have significant autonomy, being legally empowered to manage the company without having to consult the shareholders, except for structural changes to the company's activity.

This model also comprises an audit board or a sole auditor, being the corporate body in charge of the supervision of the board of directors' activity and review of the company's annual accounts.

The two-tier board was a rather complex and very rarely used model in Portugal. The reason for that was a combination of factors that turned it into an unattractive model.

The first difficulty was that this model was solely suited to big companies. This observation derives from the fact that all the members of the supervisory board (with a minimum of five members) had to be shareholders of the company.

The second difficulty was the fact that the supervisory board had significant powers over the board of directors, which created an important distance between the directors and the shareholders' meeting. In fact, it was the supervisory boards that had the competence to appoint and dismiss the board of directors' members and approve the annual accounts, and they also had a right of veto over some of the board of directors' resolutions.

Both of these situations were suited to empower the supervisory board and diminish the board of directors' role within the company.

Looking back to the governance models adopted by financial institutions in Portugal up to 2006, it was very clear that none felt comfortable with the German model, as it was not adopted by any of them. In fact, all of the Portuguese banks adopted the Latin governance model with a one-tier board, with two having foreseen variations to this model in their articles.

The first of these banks was Banco Espírito Santo (BES). BES was a traditional, family-controlled bank that had years ago taken the opportunity to be listed on the New York Stock Exchange. This listing obliged BES to adopt the governance and listing rules of the NYSE. Such rules forced it to embed in its board of directors an audit commission, composed of non-executive independent directors. This corporate body created by the articles of association was not recognized in Portuguese law, which determined that the supervision of the board of directors was to be performed by an external audit board. On the other hand, in the USA no one recognized this audit board as a relevant corporate body.

The second bank that adopted the Latin model was Banco Comercial Português (BCP). BCP created a governance model whereby along with the board of directors there was a superior board (also elected by the shareholders' meeting), which had the competence to issue opinions on several management actions and effectively, despite not electing the board of directors, had significant influence over that board. The BCP model was kind of a *tertium genus* governance model providing a synthesis of the Latin and German models, as it was formally a one-tier model with a two-tier board. Following 2006 and the legal amendments to the governance models framework, BCP effectively changed its governance model to the German one, assuming finally what was already in its DNA.

Governance models from 2006 onward

From June 2006 the governance models of Portuguese companies have undergone very relevant amendments. Although the Latin model was only slightly touched by the legislator, the German model went through significant changes and, furthermore, there was the establishment of a new, third model, the Anglo-Saxon.

The changes to the Latin model were just those necessary to foresee a segregation between the supervision of the board of directors and the auditing of the annual accounts, applicable to listed companies, as determined by Directive 2006/43/EC.

More significant amendments were foreseen in the German model. The idea was to revitalize this model, creating the conditions for major companies to use it as a true alternative to the others. For this purpose the shareholders' meeting was empowered and the supervisory board lost part of its powers. This was achieved through a curious methodology in which the legislator allowed the shareholders to determine whether some important rights should be exercised by the shareholders' meeting or by the supervisory board. In fact, the shareholders' meeting regained the right to appoint the members of the board of directors (if this was provided for in the articles) and the right to approve the annual accounts. On the other hand, the supervisory board lost part of its characteristic as a corporate body strictly representative of the shareholders, as currently it may include non-shareholders, but also the loss or transfer of powers to the shareholders' meeting may turn it into a corporate body more similar to an audit board.

The supervisory board in the German model is nowadays a kind of strategy board with the ability (although not commonly used, one should say) of having veto rights over some matters.

All of these amendments have made this board closer to the two-tier governance model used and interpreted in the Netherlands rather than that in Germany.

In any event, the significant novelty was the establishment of a new governance model known in Portugal as Anglo-Saxon. Despite the name given by the legislator, we are not convinced that UK and US doctrine would find many similarities between this model and the governance model in place in those countries.

It was mainly called Anglo-Saxon due to the fact that the supervision of the board of directors is not carried out by an external body but by itself, through an audit committee composed solely of non-executive directors. The main task of these board members is to supervise the activity of the executive committee, but as they are board members like any others they have, of course, the right and duty to discuss and approve the strategy to be adopted by the company, as well as other major issues within the overall competence of the board.

This model has an obvious advantage over the classic model, which is the fact that the audit committee members have full and immediate access to the information provided to other board members, thus empowering them with more tools to perform their supervisory work. On the other hand, it might have a disadvantage, which is the theoretical risk that its members might be "captured" by the executive members of the board due to the fact that they are working closer together, thus creating the chance for executive members to influence the others.

As a summary, one could synthesize the different models in accordance with Figures 3.1–3.3.

Governance models adopted by Portuguese banks

Currently Portugal has seven major banks[10] that are worthy of mention:[11] Caixa Geral de Depósitos (CGD), BCP, BES,[12] Banco Português de Investimento (BPI), Montepio Geral, Banif, and Caixa Central. One is fully state owned (CGD), four are listed on the Euronext Lisbon stock exchange (BCP, BES,[13] BPI, and Banif), and the other two are organized

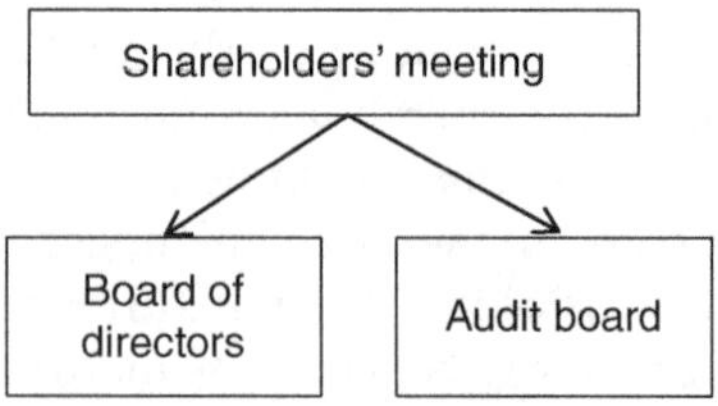

Figure 3.1 Latin model

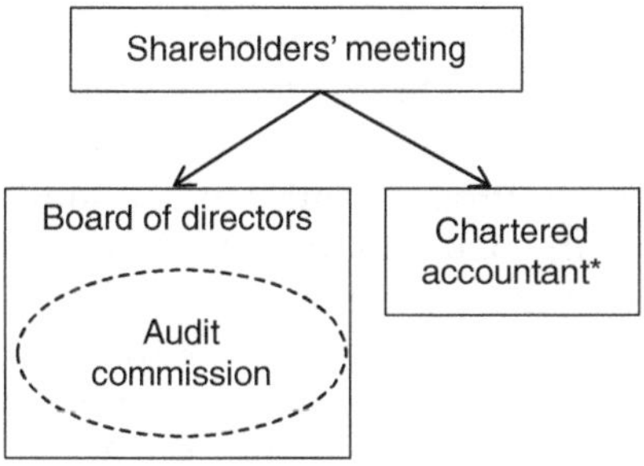

Figure 3.2 Anglo-Saxon model
Note: *The chartered accountant is appointed by the shareholders' meeting following a proposal by the audit commission.

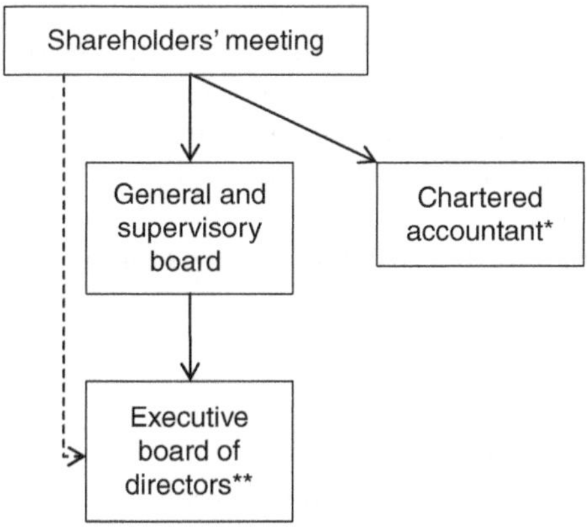

Figure 3.3 German model
Notes: *The chartered accountant is appointed by the shareholders' meeting following a proposal by the general and supervisory board.
**The executive board of directors may be directly elected by the shareholders' meeting if the articles of association so determine.

in alternative legal forms to the company model (Montepio is a mutual savings bank and Caixa Central is a cooperative).

Considering for analysis the state-owned and the four listed banks, of these five, two adopted the Latin model (BPI and Banif) and the other three the Anglo-Saxon model (CGD, BCP, and BES). Currently no bank embraces the two-tier model. This is due to a variety of facts that should be analyzed.

We believe that it is interesting to analyze the governance choices of BES, CGD, and BCP, as these banks have introduced relevant changes in their governance models in the last ten years.

BES's governance model

BES was probably the bank that underwent the fewest changes in its governance paradigm and philosophy. As already outlined, BES was a traditional, family-controlled bank with a subsidiary that several years ago had taken the opportunity to have some stock listed on the New York Stock Exchange (up to June 2004[14]). This listing obliged BES to adopt the governance and listing rules of the NYSE and to embed in its board of directors an audit commission, composed of non-executive independent directors. Accordingly, once the Anglo-Saxon model was adopted in Portuguese legislation, BES naturally seized the opportunity to amend its articles of association, thus extinguishing the (external) audit board and formalizing in the articles the audit commission as the corporate supervisory body.

Up to the Bank of Portugal's intervention, the board of directors had 25 members, with 10 in the executive commission. The board also incorporated the corporate governance commission (three independent directors) and a remuneration commission (with the same three independent directors).[15]

Compliance, risk, and internal auditing departments were dependent hierarchically on the executive committee, although with reporting obligations to the audit commission.

CGD's governance model

CGD has a different background and governance story. As stated earlier, it is a state-owned bank, historically the biggest bank in the market, and has a profile as *the* Portuguese savings bank.

Historically, state-owned companies in Portugal adopted the Latin model. The underlying reasons for such a choice are easily understandable. There is a very strong political orientation in state-owned companies and major decisions are often discussed directly with the relevant ministry or secretary of state (thus being – materially, although not formally – subtracted from the board of directors) as the company follows a state-oriented strategy for a specific sector. Furthermore, companies tend to have smaller boards solely comprising executive members, due to the direct political orientation and the need to contain costs in public companies. Thus, it was common sense for CGD (as for any other state-owned company) to have established in its articles of association the Latin model.

That situation changed in 2011. Due to the international crisis of sovereign debt and the possibility of a Portuguese default, Portugal decided to ask for financial assistance from the International Monetary Fund (IMF), the European Central Bank (ECB), and the European Union (EU). As is commonly known, the exposure of Portuguese banks to Portuguese sovereign debt, the severe economic crisis (with consequences such as an increase in the number of bankruptcies and devaluation of real estate assets), and the tightening up of sustainability ratios determined by Basel III pushed the banks in several countries (not only Portugal) to a reinforcement of their own capital that, in most cases, would only be possible through the adoption of lines of credit provided by the ECB.

All of these situations also pushed the banks to refocus their strategy on purely financial-sector services and to sell assets that were not directly linked to financial activity (whose sale would finance the main operations).

CGD also faced such demands from the IMF, the ECB, and the EU. It seized the opportunity to rethink its strategy in the market, which assets to retain and to sell,[16] and, most of all, which group governance structure to adopt and which governance model to implement.

On this subject, it must be borne in mind that CGD is a flagship company in Portugal with millions of clients, with a huge presence in the national economy, and that any action it takes can have huge repercussions in the market. Accordingly, CGD, despite being a state-owned company, is widely seen as a "listed" company in which every Portuguese has a stake (notwithstanding that it does not have any kind of direct shareholding). The benchmark should, in accordance, be the rules applied to listed banks in Portugal, enhancing the transparency and the perception of the market (all the stakeholders) regarding the independence of the management from the political environment.

Against this background, the classic governance model and its results were revisited and CGD decided to change to the Anglo-Saxon model. Its main reasons were the following:

- By 2011 this was a governance model with a track record in Portugal, adopted by important Portuguese banks and proven to function adequately.
- It is a model that integrates an internationally recognized corporate supervisory body (an audit commission), thus making it easier for any international counterpart and regulator to understand the fundamentals of the governance model.
- Supervision is performed by non-executive directors (and not outsiders to the board), thus providing a better knowledge of the files, a

better flow of communication between executive directors and supervisors, and a greater comprehension of the objectives and company activity; this is, in fact, an advantage in the process of supervision and evaluation of the work of the executive directors.
- The integration of a sufficient number of non-executive directors has the ability to make the board of directors more efficient, as it will allow for the incorporation of various board commissions (governance, risk, remuneration, etc.).
- The inclusion of non-executive board members should entail greater independence regarding possible political influence.

Accordingly, CGD adopted a board of directors with the following structure:

- Executive and non-executive members, as well as an audit commission.
- An executive committee.
- The appointment of non-executive members with knowledge of the business areas in which CGD was operating and, whenever possible, including the management of relevant subsidiaries.
- An audit commission comprising three independent and non-executive board members.
- A non-executive chairman.
- Independent board members forming at least one quarter of the board.

The institution of such a model in CGD was broadly discussed in Portugal and in the media, with various misinterpretations and negative public feedback concerning the need for non-executive board members in a fully state-owned company and the cost of such appointments. As a response to public opinion, the bank's shareholder (the state) decided not to increase the global remuneration of the board.

Currently the board of directors comprises fourteen members, including seven non-executives, of which three form the audit commission. The board of directors also comprises a risk commission and a strategy, governance, and evaluation commission.

BCP's governance model

Of the three Portuguese banks specifically analyzed here, BCP is the one that has gone through the most major changes in its governance model.

As identified previously, up until 2006 BCP had adopted a mixed governance model, whereby along with the board of directors there was a superior board (also elected by the shareholders' meeting), which had the competence to issue opinions on several management activities and effectively, despite not electing the board of directors, had significant influence over that board and was empowered by the articles to supervise the board's activity. This was a sort of *tertium genus* governance model, providing a synthesis of the Latin and German models, as it was formally a one-tier structure, but materially with a two-tier board. This was mainly due to the fact that BCP wanted to assume the advantages that a two-tier model entails, but not to be constrained by the German model as it was designed in the Portuguese Companies Code.

Following the implementation of the Companies Code in 2006 and the legal amendments to the framework of governance models, BCP began a profound reflection on its corporate governance model and effectively decided to change to the refurbished two-tier model, assuming finally what was already in its DNA.

Accordingly, in 2006 BCP formally changed to a two-tier board, thus appointing an executive board of directors and above that a supervisory board (with the functions and powers previously attributed to the superior board). In this model, the shareholders' meeting elected both the board of directors and the supervisory board, but the supervisory board retained the power to pronounce regarding the definition of strategy and the general policies of the company; the corporate structure of the group; and any decisions that may be deemed strategic due to the amount involved, risk, or any other special characteristics.

This dual governance model was only followed in Portugal by one other listed company (EDP, an energy company) and lasted for six years, until 2012, the year in which BCP adopted the Anglo-Saxon model.

There were several reasons for the failure of the two-tier model in BCP, but it mostly had to do with a traumatic experience of the appointment of the previous CEO (Jardim Gonçalves) as chairman of the supervisory board and the nomination of his successor as CEO. This was a classic story of a power struggle in a large institution, but was mainly a clear misinterpretation of the roles and powers reserved for the chairman and CEO of such an institution. This misinterpretation was in fact magnified by the governance structure that the bank adopted and the fact that the supervisory board was empowered to approve the strategy that the company should follow.

In fact, the two-tier system that was in place until 2006 was clear in the sense that the board of directors was then a corporate body completely subordinated to the supervisory board, which appointed it. Accordingly, the board of directors obtained its legitimacy and authority from the supervisory board. Furthermore, it was common for the articles of association to grant veto powers to the supervisory board for some categories of actions, which was in line with the legitimacy of this corporate body to appoint the board of directors.

From 2006 onward, the flexibility included in the law determining that the board of directors could be appointed by the shareholders' meeting or by the supervisory board brought greater adaptability to the model, but, on the other hand, put the two corporate bodies in the same hierarchical position within the company. When the board of directors is appointed by the shareholders' meeting, both boards have the same legitimacy, which means that if the articles of association do not clearly establish the powers within the sphere of the board of directors and those lying with the supervisory board, there might be a dispute over the definition of the corporate strategy. In this regard, if one sums up the difficulty of a former CEO in letting go of that function and assuming his new function as chairman of the supervisory board, then the company may have within itself a recipe for disaster.

It was mainly the dissension between the chairman of the supervisory board and the CEO that led later on to the replacement of both. Furthermore, it was one of those situations in which one could see that a lack of proper governance could destroy the value of the company when the market decided to divest itself of BCP stock, causing a tremendous loss of market value on the stock exchange.[17] This situation was then magnified by the crisis of the financial sector, which brought BCP share values to unprecedently low levels.

It was the echoes of this traumatic experience that led BCP shareholders in 2012 to propose and vote for a dramatic change in the governance model. In fact, the proposal to the resolution expressly stated that "in 2006 the shareholders opted for the institution of a two-tier model, which has originated dissension among the corporate bodies, with prejudice to the stability and development of BCP."[18] It further said: "the two-tier model adopted in 2006 does not have a tradition in Portugal and was not adopted by the generality of the financial institutions in Portugal, not even among the majority of the listed companies." It concluded by recommending that BCP should adopt a model that enabled greater efficiency and internal cohesion, maintaining the auditing and supervisory mechanisms at a higher level, objectives achieved by the adoption of the Anglo-Saxon model (just as was adopted by BES and CGD).

Accordingly, currently BCP has a board of directors with twenty members, comprising as corporate bodies an executive committee with seven members and an audit committee with four members (one exceptionally appointed by the state due to the financial assistance regime from which BCP has chosen to benefit).

Furthermore, the board of directors also comprises as bodies provided for in the articles of association an appointment and evaluation commission, a governance commission, a risk evaluation commission, and an ethics commission. All of these commissions are composed of non-executive members, the majority of which are independent (except for the appointment and evaluation commission, for which such an independence rule is not prescribed).

Conclusion

It must be noted that, notwithstanding the path that each bank has decided to take, the three biggest banks in Portugal have reached the same material conclusion, that the Anglo-Saxon model is the one that most enhances the supervision of the company and has a better balance between managerial and supervisory powers and competences.

This is all the more remarkable if one considers the situation of shareholder control at each of these three banks. In fact, CGD is a fully state-owned bank (thus with a sole shareholder); BES had a family stakeholding of more or less 36% and a very important shareholder with almost 11% (Crédit Agricole, SA),[19] which granted two shareholders effective control of the company (in fact, institutional entities controlled around 60% of the shares); and BCP has a more undefined situation with a shareholder with almost 20% (Sonangol) and five other shareholders ranging between 2% and 4%, which means that six shareholders control roughly 35%.

Concerning the functioning of the board of directors, all of the three institutions segregate the roles of chairman and CEO and integrate further board commissions other than the mandatory audit commission, highlighting the importance of the governance and risk commissions.

The perceived advantages of the model are mainly those identified earlier:

- international recognition;
- internal cohesion;
- easier and deeper access to information by the supervisors;
- the same level of importance in the structure for executive directors and supervisors (as they are both members of the board of directors);

- more efficiency for the board and its commissions;
- greater independence in the performance of supervisory work.

The impact of the Financial Assistance Programme on banks' governance models

One of the immediate reactions to the 2008 crisis was the need perceived by the regulators to reinforce the financial strength and stability of banks, thus increasing the Core Tier 1 ratio demanded.

This tightening up required banks to reinforce their own capital, demanding share capital increases from shareholders. Not all of the banks were in a position to successfully request from their shareholders new apportions of capital, mainly due to the fact that their accounts and financial status would not allow new shares to be subscribed at par value (in Portugal it is not permitted to subscribe shares below their nominal value). Accordingly, the only possible solution would be a recourse to state investment.

There were obvious precautions to take when adopting this measure. From a national standpoint, it was important that this investment did not operate to nationalize the banks. From an EU standpoint, it was crucial that it was not a mechanism distorting competition among financial institutions (in fact, the recapitalization plan for Portuguese banks was discussed and approved by the European Commission).

In Portugal there were several institutions that took advantage of this recapitalization opportunity[20] and indeed requested it (BCP, CGD, BPI, and Banif[21]). In any event, if it is not requested, the law grants the Bank of Portugal the possibility of forcing a bank to ask for such recapitalization measures. A breach of such an obligation by the financial institution grants the Bank of Portugal the power to appoint provisional management for the institution or to revoke its operating license.

Apart from the financial conditions of such loans, recapitalization using state funds is subject to obligations of a corporate governance nature. The first obligation for financial institutions is the adoption of generally accepted principles of corporate governance. Publicly listed companies already adopt such principles, as they are subject to regulation by the CMVM and its code of best practice, with which they have to comply or explain why not in an annual governance report. Non-listed companies do not have to comply with any code of best practice, being subject solely to the Bank of Portugal's regulations, which have only a limited set of rules on governance, mainly focused on risk.

The second obligation is to comply with specific remuneration policies established in the legal regime for financial institutions, whose main purpose is to strongly limit the payment of variable remuneration. In fact, a Ministry of Finance ruling established in 2012 that in financial institutions benefiting from recapitalization, the global amount of remuneration paid to members of corporate bodies cannot be more than 50% of the average remuneration of the previous two years.[22]

The third obligation is to accept the appointment by the state of a non-executive board member (which happened at BCP and Banif) and/or a member for the corporate supervision body (e.g., audit commission or "external" audit board – which happened at BPI).

The functions of the non-executive board member appointed by the state is to verify the fulfillment of the recapitalization plan and of the financial institution obligations established in the recapitalization legal regime, bearing in mind the financial stability and the patrimonial interest of the state. Furthermore, the non-executive board member and/or the supervisory board member are obliged to report monthly to the Bank of Portugal and the Finance Ministry on the conclusions of their evaluation and, at any time, to inform them of any fact deemed relevant that comes to their knowledge in the performance of their functions.

The state's effort to recapitalize Portuguese banks uses EU funds and can assume the form of a subscription of shares (which grant the right to a priority dividend) or bond-type securities (namely contingent convertible bonds, also known as CoCos, which can be converted into shares whenever there is a material breach of the obligations and milestones determined in the recapitalization program).

Due to the fact that it is an exceptional regime, whenever it occurs by share subscription, Portuguese law provides that regardless of the percentage of voting rights held, the state can only vote as a shareholder in resolutions addressing amendments to the articles of association, mergers, demergers, transformation or dissolution of the company, or in any other resolutions for which the law or the articles of association require a qualified majority. Whenever the voting rights hold by the state are in excess of 50% of the total, then the reported suspension of voting rights will not be applicable, as the state is able to participate in any resolution.

Some of the Portuguese banks that have used this recapitalization instrument are currently promoting share capital increases to obtain the necessary funds to repay the state's financial assistance in advance. It was likely that BPI would end its financial assistance program in 2014 and that BCP would also do so before its term, thus leaving Banif as the most difficult and long-lasting situation.

Notes

1. The event that is commonly accepted as the beginning of the global financial crisis is the bankruptcy of Lehman Brothers in 2008 (which at the time was the fifth largest investment bank in the USA). The fall of Lehman Brothers gave rise to a systemic effect of the fall of several other institutions. Immediately after it the Federal National Mortgage Association (Fannie Mae) and the Federal Home Loan Mortgage Corporation (Freddie Mac) were put under the control of the US government. Subsequently, the Bank of America acquired Merrill Lynch and JP Morgan Chase acquired Bear Stearns.

   In Europe, Northern Rock was nationalized by the UK government, Fortis by the joint efforts of the Dutch and Belgium governments, and several other banks received massive amounts from governments to regain liquidity and avoid falling into bankruptcy.

   In Portugal, Banco Privado Português was financed with €450 million by six Portuguese financial institutions (with a state guarantee as collateral) and Banco Português de Negócios was nationalized due to an imminent situation of bankruptcy, which the government understood as potentially having a systemic effect.
2. For some examples see David Walker (2009) "A review of corporate governance in UK banks and other financial industry entities – final recommendations," November, http://webarchive.nationalarchives.gov.uk/+/http:/www.hm-treasury.gov.uk/d/walker_review_261109.pdf; and European Commission (2010) "Green Paper – Corporate Governance in Financial Institutions and Remuneration Policies" (COM(2010)284 final), June, http://ec.europa.eu/internal_market/company/docs/modern/com2010_284_en.pdf, both accessed July 27, 2015.
3. Approved by Decree-Law 262/86 of September 2, 1986 and subsequently amended.
4. Regime Geral das Instituições de Crédito e Sociedades Financeiras, approved by Decree-Law no. 298/92 of December 31, 1992, amended several times and available in a consolidated version in Portuguese at http://www.bportugal.pt/pt-PT/Legislacaoenormas/Paginas/DL298ano92.aspx, accessed July 27, 2015.
5. RGICSF, Article 14, paragraph 1, subparagraph f.
6. RGICSF, Article 17, paragraph 2.
7. An annex to RGICSF (approved by Decree-Law 104/2007 and further amended in 2010 and 2011) identifies the following risks: (i) credit and counterpart, (ii) residual, (iii) credit concentration, (iv) titularization, (v) market, (vi) interest rates, (vii) operational, and (viii) liquidity.
8. Comissão do Mercado de Valores Mobiliários.
9. Directive 2006/43/EC of the European Parliament and of the Council of May 17, 2006.
10. Ordered by value of net assets in 2012, data collected from APB, Portuguese Banks Association website, http://www.apb.pt/associados/dados_dos_bancos. The net asset values in 2012 were: CGD, €102 billion; BCP, €85 billion; BES, €68 billion; BPI, €44 billion; Banco Santander Totta, €38 billion; Barclays Bank, €27 billion; Montepio, €24 billion; Banif, €15 billion; Caixa Central, €13 billion; Banco Popular, €8 billion.

11. In addition to the banks referred to one should also mention four branches of foreign financial institutions (Barclays, Deutsche Bank, Bank of Brazil, and Bank of China), three subsidiaries of Spanish institutions with no autonomy in Portugal and following governance instructions from their Spanish headquarters (Santander Totta, BBVA, and Popular), and five other small Portuguese banks (Carregosa, BIG, BIC, Finantia, and Invest).
12. Between this article being started and finished, in August 2014, due to the imminent bankruptcy of BES, the Bank of Portugal (the regulator) was forced to adopt an innovative solution untested in the whole of Europe, which was to segregate assets from BES to create a new bank (literally named Novo Banco, S.A.) and to leave BES as a bad bank. It is likely that shareholders and junior bond holders of BES will assume full losses in this process.

    It is not within the nature or the purpose of this article to analyze the regulator's intervention, but only the governance models adopted in Portugal. Accordingly, any facts depicted in this article refer to the situation existing prior to the intervention of the Bank of Portugal in BES. That notwithstanding, one must say that BES's bankruptcy is a clear situation of a lack of governance (to say the least). The bank had in theory a solid governance model, with properly drafted internal regulations, audit mechanisms, and internal commissions, but it falled due to excessive credit exposure to the main shareholder company group and to several malpractice situations that are still under investigation.
13. BES was delisted in August 2014 following the intervention of the Bank of Portugal.
14. BES Governance Report of 2004 (part of the annual management report), p. 242, which prior to the regulator's intervention was available for consultation at https://www.bes.pt/sitebes/cms.aspx?plg=4e3c1b50-93b2-4f37-88e0-b5b6ce7a1bd5.
15. BES Governance Report of 2012, which prior to the regulator's intervention was available for consultation at http://www.bes.pt/sitebes/cms.aspx?plg=8a83552b-2815-4c85-a151-63629a22be29.
16. It is public information that CGD has sold its hospital health business to Brazil's AMIL (concluded in 2013) and its insurance operation to Chinese's Fosun (concluded in 2014). Other less important divestitures were also undertaken.
17. It should be noted that in July 2007, while the institutional war between the CEO and the chairman of the supervisory board was still active, BCP traded at a share market value of €3.90. Since then the market value has been decreasing and in October 2014 was trading at around €0.09.
18. The text of the proposal to the February 28, 2012 shareholders' meeting of BCP is available at http://ind.millenniumbcp.pt/pt/Institucional/investidores/Documents/AssembGeral/Proposta_ponto_1_440916a.pdf, accessed July 27, 2015.
19. BES went through a share capital increase in June 2014 and both shareholdings have been diluted.
20. The recapitalization regime was established by Law 63-A/2008, of November 24, 2008, and subsequently amended by Law 3-B/2010, of April 28, 2010; Law 55-A/2010, of December 31, 2010; and Law 4/2012, of January 11, 2012.

21. The state injected €1.65 billion into CGD, €3.5 billion into BCP, and €1.5 billion into BPI in 2012. It further injected €1.1 billion into Banif in 2013, holding a share capital of 98%.
22. Article 12 of Portaria 150-A/2012, of May 17, 2012.

Bibliography

Abreu, Coutinho de (2006) *Governação de Sociedades Comerciais*, Coimbra: Almedina.

Borges, Sofia Leite (2011) "O Governo dos Bancos," in Paulo Câmara (ed.), *O Governo das Organizações – A Vocação Universal do Corporate Governance*, Coimbra: Almedina, 251–317.

Cadbury, Adrian (1995) *Report of the Committee on the Financial Aspects of Corporate Governance: Compliance with the Code of Best Practice*, London: Gee & Co.

Câmara, Paulo (2001) "O Governo das sociedades em Portugal: Uma introdução", *Cadernos MVM*, 12: 46–55.

European Commission (2003) *Modernising Company Law and Enhancing Corporate Governance in the European Union – A Plan to Move Forward*, com/2003/284, Brussels: European Commission.

European Commission (2010) *Green Paper: Corporate Governance in Financial Institutions and Remuneration Policies*, Brussels: European Commission.

Pierce, Chris (2010) *Corporate Governance in the European Union*, London: Global Governance Services.

Pinto, José Costa (2014) *A Emergência e o Futuro do Corporate Governance em Portugal*, Coimbra: Almedina.

4

Banking Supervision and Regulation in the Euro Area: The Case of Portugal

Mário Coutinho dos Santos

The purpose of this chapter is to analyze and discuss issues related to the banking regulatory and supervisory framework and structures in Portugal, and the role of the Portuguese Central Bank (henceforth and interchangeably Portuguese Central Bank, Banco de Portugal, and BdP) in that context.

Banking regulation and supervision have been matters of generalized and ongoing concern, which has garnered considerable scrutiny and fostered a vivid debate among academics, public policymakers, regulatory authorities, supervisory agencies, the banking community, and capital market participants. Not surprisingly, an extensive body of literature has developed as a result of the attention dedicated to the topic by both scholars and practitioners.[1]

Driven by powerful global forces of market integration, economic liberalization, financial innovation, regulation/deregulation, and technological progress, financial markets in general, and banking markets in particular, became more integrated, concentrated, and interconnected, and, most likely, more vulnerable to a large spectrum of risks.[2] Additionally, periods of significant build-up in risk taking by financial market participants will tend to increase the likelihood of a financial crisis developing, endangering both the financial and economic performance of a country and its stability.[3] Therefore, we have witnessed, at both national and international levels, an array of regulatory proposals to try to curb excessive bank risk taking.

Given the market and technological changes that banking systems in particular have been experiencing, it is evident that regulatory and supervisory structures from the end of the twentieth century might well be unable to achieve adequate levels of banking safety, soundness, and stability.[4]

Before the Single Supervisory Mechanism was in place, financial services supervision in the European Union (EU) exhibited a fragmented institutional and functional architecture, where several committees were endowed with advisory powers, mostly issuing guidance and recommendations that were not mandatory and, typically, were determined and interpreted at the level of each country.[5] In these instances, banking supervision might tend to evidence episodes of random casuistry, such as excessive dependence on self-ruling, which may end up amplifying harmful developments in banking markets in adverse states of the world.[6]

The remainder of the chapter is organized as follows. The next section presents a brief discussion of the economic rationale for banking regulation and supervision, and banking regulatory and supervisory institutional structures, and delves into the roles, functions, and responsibilities of central banks in that context. The following section presents a brief characterization of the Portuguese financial and banking system, and then there is an examination of the Portuguese regulatory and supervisory institutional structure. The last section summarizes and offers concluding remarks.

Economic rationale for financial services regulation and supervision

This section provides the economic rationale for governmental market intervention, particularly through regulation and supervision, in the financial services industry in general and the banking system in particular.

Is it necessary to regulate and supervise markets?

Adam Smith's "invisible hand" metaphor is a well-known tenet of the laissez-faire proposition of neoclassical economics, which recognizes a self-regulating role for competitive markets and efficient allocative behavior.[7] Under this framework, "invisible hand" markets would be able to self-regulate, making government regulatory intervention in free markets not only redundant but also harmful, because regulators may "lack the expertise and the incentives to regulate,"[8] and consequently "fail to produce socially desirable outcomes."[9]

However, government intervention may yield positive social welfare effects in cases of antitrust laws and economic agents' protection in general, and "to ensure the safety and soundness of the banking system" in particular.[10]

Why does the financial services industry need to be regulated and supervised?

There is a broad consensus among academics that a well-functioning, stable, and safe financial system is an important requirement for promoting economic development and improving social welfare.[11] Ill-functioning financial systems can hinder a country's economic development, and consequently undermine its social welfare. Well-functioning financial systems promote economic growth, which in turn alleviates poverty.[12] Therefore, government intervention in real-world financial markets can be justified and predicated by public interest aiming at attaining first-best efficiency and welfare when there are market frictions, imperfections, or failures.[13] Among those can be included market power abuses, fraudulent practices, and asymmetric information problems.

Market failures can make perfectly competitive financial markets equilibrium unattainable, inhibiting allocative efficiency and affecting the safety and soundness of the financial system. In these instances, financial markets regulation can be justified to mitigate the effects of suboptimal operation. The costs generated by this intervention are less onerous than those that would be generated by the full manifestation of all those market failures.

Financial system regulation can be justified to protect market participants, for example preventing, suppressing, and punishing abuses of market power and fraudulent practices, and promoting the confidence of economic agents in financial markets and institutions, are justified concerns for the law and regulatory institutions devoted to minimizing the liquidity and solvency risks to which financial intermediaries are exposed.

Banks, like non-banking organizations, are prone to asymmetric information problems. In fact, banks experience uneven distribution of information between insiders and outsiders. Furthermore, banks become involved in a panoply of informational problems in performing some of their financial intermediation activities, including collecting and processing private information; providing delegated monitoring services; and carrying opaque assets and liabilities on their balance sheets. Moreover, banks enjoy non-negligible economies of scale as information producers, and they have access to private information on their counter parties, which is not publicly available.

In banking organizations, asymmetric information problems arise from both sides of the balance sheet. Whatever the circumstances, those problems are a manifestation of the different forms of opportunistic contracting behavior: *ex ante* (the so-called adverse selection/hidden information); *interim* (the so-called moral hazard/hidden action); and *ex post* (the so-called costly state verification).[14]

The notion that a bank is an informationally opaque entity is well established in the literature, and enjoys compelling empirical support.[15] Understandably, a bank's asset allocation decisions, as well as the risk and return characteristics of a significant part of its assets, are unobservable by outsiders. It is also believed that financial intermediation can be helpful in mitigating asymmetric information problems in financial contracting. In screening and monitoring borrowers, banks acquire an informational advantage. This informational superiority, however, becomes in itself a source of informational asymmetry between banks and financial market participants.[16]

The nature of the financial intermediation activities performed by banks and other financial services institutions makes them prone to innate asymmetric information problems. Associated with these kinds of problems, mostly in the form of moral hazard and adverse selection behavior, are negative externalities intrinsic to failures of institutions, panics, systemic crises, and other phenomena of a similar nature. Thus, both the financial system in general and banking systems in particular have traditionally been heavily and extensively regulated, with the aim of providing stability to mitigate the main negative economic effects of financial systemic crises.

Supervisory agencies and regulatory authorities engage in bank monitoring activities to gather information to assess the individual financial condition and performance of the banks they are examining, as well as to promote the overall safety, soundness, and stability of the banking system.

Although all of these arguments seem valid, they do not respond to some fundamental questions. What is wrong with financial markets' functioning that requires protection for market participants? Why is it necessary to monitor and curb financial institutions' behavior? Why the market's "invisible hand" work cannot work out these problems?

There is a well-known argument among academics, public policymakers, supervisory agencies, regulatory authorities, and banking community participants that banks are *special*.[17] The argument goes that this attribute of banking *specialness* arises from the unique functions that banks perform in the economy. Among those functions are the supply and administration of transaction and payment services; the provision of liquidity and credit; and the transmission of monetary policy impulses to the economy. These pivotal roles of banks in most national financial systems are a conspicuous motivation for governments in many countries to exert supervisory and regulatory discipline over the banking industry.[18] Therefore, banking regulation should primarily aim at protecting the economy from systemic risk.[19]

It is widely recognized that in adverse states of the world, information asymmetries tend to induce opportunistic behavior from superiorly informed parties in a binding financial transaction, threatening the safety and soundness of the banking system, and even the financial stability of the country. The likelihood of such an outcome creates an extra motivation for most governments worldwide to take action in extensively and heavily regulating and supervising banks to prevent disruption in the provision of banking payment and liquidity services; and to curb the burden of potential negative externalities on taxpayers, in the form of the deadweight costs of financial distress.[20] However, the pervasive informational opacity of many of the financial assets that banking organizations typically carry in their balance sheets may hinder regulatory and supervisory efforts to monitor banks' economic performance and financial condition.

Banking regulation and supervision: Is there a role for central banks?

Most contemporary central banks are among the most powerful institutions in the financial systems of market economies, power that comes, among other factors, from the role that they perform as "public policy agencies for central banking functions."[21] It is well recognized that across the globe, central bankers enjoy special prerogatives in terms of both independence and autonomy vis-à-vis the established governmental power. Among such prerogatives is the issuing of bank notes, the control of the quantity of money available in the economy, and resorting to a wide spectrum of monetary policy mechanisms, aimed at influencing the performance of economic variables such as the inflation rate, interest rate levels, and economic growth. Therefore, the actions of central banks play a decisive role in promoting social welfare, and indirectly affect the redistribution of income and wealth. Additionally, central banks also play a role in the oversight of banks' conduct, performance, and financial condition, and in that capacity they are heavily and extensively involved in regulating and supervising the banking system to promote its soundness and safety, as well as national financial stability.

Since it was set up, the European Central Bank (ECB) has adopted the so-called German central bank model of separating monetary policy and banking supervisory functions, rather than combining them, as in the case of the Bank of England.

Banking regulation and supervision: Some worldwide experiences

The turbulence associated with the 2008 global financial crisis made it clear that the stabilization of financial and banking markets should make it to the top of public policymakers' action priority list.[22] Aditionally it should create awareness that it is imperative to start fixing the current challenges and threats to banking and financial regulatory and supervisory jurisdictions; namely, its fragmentation; the excessive domestic market focus; and the effect of the shadow banking system on the rise of systemic risk levels.[23]

According to a recent Financial Stability Board (FSB) assessment, in 2013 the global shadow banking system reached US$71 trillion of assets, representing "on average about 24% of total financial assets, about half of banking system assets and 117% of GDP" of the 25 jurisdictions included in the sample.[24] Recently the International Monetary Fund (IMF) encouraged "policymakers to address the continued expansion of finance outside the regulatory perimeter through a more encompassing approach to regulation and supervision that focuses both on activities and on entities and places greater emphasis on systemic risk."[25] Therefore, there is a natural need for urgent reform in the existing supervisory institutional set-up, in order to address the challenges and threats faced by economies worldwide.[26]

The architecture of banking regulatory and supervisory institutions developed around three models:

- a traditional model in which the central bank conducts monetary policy and also supervises banks;
- a second model where regulatory and supervisory functions are segregated from the central bank and assigned to an independent authority;
- a third model where banking supervisory responsibilities are shared between the central bank and one or more independent supervisory agencies.[27]

In both the first and third models the central bank, with sole responsibility for conducting monetary policy, also assumed responsibility for supervising banks.

For example, in the United States the Federal Reserve System conducts monetary policy and is involved in banking supervision. However, in the pre-euro era, the German central bank, the Bundesbank, conducted monetary policy, but the banking supervision function was already assigned to an independent agency, the Federal Banking Supervisory Office. In the United Kingdom and Japan, banking and financial market supervisory responsibilities were assigned to a single authority. In the euro area, where the European Central Bank conducts monetary policy, banking supervisory responsibilities are assigned either to national central banks or to other national supervisory agencies. Various other institutional arrangements exist around the world, including the more traditional model in which the central bank also serves as a supervisor of the banking system.

The empirical literature documents that in a sample of 24 Organization for Economic Cooperation and Development (OECD) countries, central banks are either directly responsible for the banking supervision function or share that responsibility with an independent authority; and that the 24 countries included in the sample cluster almost evenly between the two models.[28]

Using more recent data drawn from the Bank of International Settlements (BIS), we developed a sample of regulatory authorities and supervisory agencies of 171 states and territorial entities, shown in Table 4.1.

In 77.8% of the states and territories included in the BIS sample, banking supervision is conducted by central banks, either on their own (the central bank model) or in conjunction with a supervisory agency (combined model). Only in 22.2% of the sample observations is supervision handled by an independent agency.

Analyzing a subsample of countries that are members of the eurozone, Table 4.2 demonstrates that the percentage of countries where banking

Table 4.1 Distribution of regulatory authorities and supervisory agencies

Central Bank	Independent Agency	Combined	Total
105	38	28	171
61.4%	22.2%	16.4%	100.0%

Data source: http://www.bis.org/regauth.htm, accessed August 12, 2014.

Table 4.2 Distribution of regulatory authorities and supervisory agencies in eurozone countries

Central Bank	Independent Agency	Combined	Total
16	2	10	28
57.1%	7.1%	35.7%	100.0%

Data source: http://www.bis.org/regauth.htm, accessed on August 12, 2014.

supervision is conducted by central banks, either on their own or in conjunction with a supervisory agency, goes up to 92.8%.

This finding is explained by both the 4.3% drop in the central bank model when compared to the BIS sample results, and the preference in 35.7% of eurozone countries for the so-called combined model of banking supervision.

From the recent financial crisis we certainly learned that banking markets are increasingly integrated and interconnected. Therefore, it seems somewhat counterintuitive that banking supervisory institutional jurisdiction still exhibits such an atomized architecture.

In some countries central banks are also involved in oversight of the financial system, and in that capacity they are heavily and extensively involved in regulating and supervising the banking system to promote its soundness and safety, as well as national financial stability. However, to the best of our knowledge, there is not yet such a thing as a fully defined general specification of the functions, role, and responsibilities with which a prototypical central bank should be endowed to conduct its monetary policy role, while promoting banking system safety and stability.

In abstract, banking supervisory functions typically include both micro- and macro-prudential supervision.

Key elements of the micro-prudential supervisory function usually include:

- on-site inspections and off-site examinations of the safety and soundness of individual banks;
- mandatory compliance with accounting standards, financial reporting standards, and financial disclosure requirements;
- internal financial control systems in place;
- financial statements externally audited;
- supervisory systemic assessments.[29]

The macro-prudential supervision activities include:

- monitoring of systemic risk exposure;[30]
- detection of potential threats to stability driven by macroeconomic or financial market risk factors, which is typically conducted by the central bank.

Therefore, it is not surprising that intense international debate about the institutional governance architecture of financial systems regulation and supervision in general, and of banking systems in particular, is still ongoing. Despite broad agreement about the pivotal responsibility of central banks in conducting monetary policy, their role in banking supervision still seems, to say the least, controversial. A central question remains unanswered: "Are there good *economic* reasons for combining or separating monetary policy and bank supervision?"[31]

Public and academic debate is continuing in the following areas:

- national supervisory institutional scope and structures;
- whether or not there is an appropriate balance between markets' self-regulatory behavior and government regulatory and supervisory intervention;
- whether the efficient and effective functioning of a financial market requires the presence of an adequate regulatory and supervisory framework;
- regulatory and supervisory governance structure/institutional design of regulation and supervision.[32]

In many countries worldwide, supervisory agencies engage in extensive examination programs to monitor and assess banking organizations' financial performance and condition, while performing their supervisory and regulatory roles. That is, bank capital regulators and deposit insurance administrators are among the entities that regularly, extensively, and closely appraise banks' compliance with, among others, safety net mechanisms, capital adequacy standards, and deposit insurance provisions.[33]

In the United States, the Federal Reserve System, the Office of the Comptroller of the Currency (OCC), the Federal Deposit Insurance Corporation (FDIC), the Office of Thrift Supervision (OTS), and the banking departments at state level are the entities most often involved in bank surveillance.[34] In Japan, the Bank of Japan also conducts on-site examinations and off-site monitoring as bank surveillance tools. In the United

Kingdom, similarly, banking supervisory responsibility is assigned to a single supervisory agency.

Sahajwala and Van den Bergh's review of banking supervisory practices in place or under development in the G10 countries[35] points out that "supervisory authorities, which do not have the mandate or resources to carry out periodic on-site examinations, rely extensively on this method [off-site monitoring] to monitor the financial condition and performance of banks."[36]

In several continental European countries, Polizatto notes that "a legalistic approach was developed that was less 'hands-on' than in the United States and delegated much of the verification and inspection of bank records to external auditors."[37] The prevailing bank supervisory approach in continental Europe "stipulates various ratios that the banks must observe." Polizatto also indicates that "in Belgium, special auditors are appointed and paid by the authorities. In Switzerland, the auditors are licensed by the Federal Banking Commission and are subject to special statutory duties. In Germany, general auditors perform the examinations of banks and must inform the authorities if they discover facts which justify the qualification of an audit."[38]

Despite the fact that the United States and continental Europe, in the past decades, have experienced similar occurrences in terms of financially distressed banks, in continental European countries bank monitoring seems to be a less extensive and widespread practice. Frequent supervisory inspections and extensive off-site examinations do not appear to be as common in continental Europe as they are in the United States.

What can we learn from US banking supervisory practice?

In the United States, assessment of a bank's overall financial condition is primarily based on private information collected during periodic on-site inspections and reviews of banks' operations. These inspections are complemented by analysis supported by publicly available information, such as banks' financial statements. Since 1975, US supervisory and regulatory agencies alike are resorting to off-site analytical examination tools, not only to complement on-site inspections, but also to increase the frequency of supervision and regulatory scrutiny of bank conditions.[39]

The assessment of the safety, soundness, and financial performance and condition of banks is conducted through on-site bank inspections; supervisory ratings assignment – CAMELS ratings[40] for individual banks, and BOPEC ratings[41] for individual bank holding companies (BHC) – to summarize overall financial condition and the level of supervisory concern; and off-site monitoring.[42]

Despite the fact that banking supervisory examiners gather private information about banks' opaque financial assets, a growing strand of the literature suggests that the supervisory ratings assigned based on the private information gathered during on-site bank inspections may have a useful information content.

Typically, US federal and/or state supervisory agencies conduct periodic on-site inspections of individual banks every 12–24 months. While the rating notations issued on completion of those inspections are shared with banks' top management, they are not publicly disclosed.[43]

However, although individual banks' supervisory ratings are not publicly available information, time series comparison of them across banks can potentially provide useful information about the aggregate safety, strength, and soundness of the banking system as a whole.

Contrasting the observed periodicity of on-site inspections of both BHC and individual banks in the United States with the increased volatility in general economic and financial conditions may lead assigned supervisory ratings to become outdated, and consequently inaccurate, before a new examination is due. Empirical findings "suggest that the information content of examination ratings begins to decay after two quarters."[44] Therefore, we should expect the information content of a supervisory banking rating assigned at the end of an on-site inspection to suffer from time erosion and soon become an inadequate reflection of the bank's financial condition associated with that assigned rating.

Aimed at resolving this problem, the US Federal Reserve Board developed the System for Estimating Examiner Ratings (SEER), an off-site monitoring tool. Among other features, this was designed as a way of forecasting next-quarter CAMELS ratings.[45]

Furthermore, US banking supervisors adopted the SCOR monitoring system (Statistical CAMELS Off-site Rating) to assess whether a bank's financial condition had experienced some material degradation since its last on-site inspection that might lead to a CAMELS downgrade in a future on-site examination.[46]

In 1993 the Federal Reserve System implemented the Financial Institutions Monitoring System (FIMS), aimed at being more accurate than previous off-site surveillance tools at identifying and gauging banks' financial performance and condition.[47]

Supervisory agencies also use financial markets information in their surveillance process to complement the information gathered through other monitoring mechanisms. Therefore, financial markets data can be seen as signaling individual bank riskiness, because of the strong correlation of that data with supervisory examination results.[48]

Market discipline and banking supervisory monitoring may be seen as complementary devices for assessing banks' financial condition and therefore overtime, a variable combination of both may be optimal in determining compliance with and enforcement of the applicable regulatory apparatus.[49]

Regulation and supervision in Portugal

This section presents a brief characterization of the Portuguese banking system, highlighting the major milestones and developments related to its regulation and supervision.[50]

Overview of the Portuguese banking system

Banking markets across the world have undergone significant changes in the last few decades. As national economies and financial markets became increasingly integrated and liberalized, the volatility of financial markets surged, and competition steadily evolved to higher thresholds.

Neither the Portuguese economy in general nor its financial and banking systems in particular were immune to the significant transformations experienced by economies worldwide.[51] Specifically, the confluence of global forces of change and internal idiosyncratic factors, such as entry to the European Economic Community (EEC), adhesion to the European single market, and entry into the third phase of Economic and Monetary Union (EMU), submitted the Portuguese banking industry to significant pressure for structural readjustment and reorganization.

First, in the aftermath of the political unrest of April 25, 1974, the Portuguese banking industry experienced a period of dramatic change that culminated in 1975 with the nationalization of all privately owned Portuguese banks and insurance companies. Additionally, entry to the financial intermediation industry by private investors was prohibited, and the management of all state-owned banks became mostly politically motivated.

By the mid-1980s, and coinciding with Portugal joining the EEC, a strong trend of economic liberalization led to significant modernization of the Portuguese financial and banking systems in terms of their regulation and supervision. The major milestones in that process included:

- the reopening of the banking industry to private investors, and the consequent authorization of setting up new banking ventures led by Portuguese private investors;
- permission for the establishment of new branches of foreign banks;
- progressive abolition of administrative rulings on interest rates, as well as restrictions on bank lending;
- progressive elimination of capital movements control;
- enforcement of banking-specific mandatory accounting standards, principles and practices, and financial reporting;[52]
- the beginning of the reprivatization of the formerly nationalized banks;
- joining the European single market for financial services;[53]
- the conclusion of the reprivatization of the nationalized banks;
- joining the third phase of EMU.[54]

During this time the Portuguese stock exchange, which was virtually inactive after the 1974 revolution, was revamped and restarted its operations in a new regulatory and operating framework.

Overview of the Portuguese banking supervisory framework

Banco de Portugal was assigned the role of central bank of the Portuguese Republic on July 1, 1931. It was nationalized in September 1974, and since January 1, 1999 it has been part of the European System of Central Banks (ESCB).[55]

Although it was informally involved in regulating and supervising the banking system from 1925, responsibility for the supervision of Portuguese credit institutions, financial companies, and payment institutions was only formally assigned to BdP with the 1975 "Organic Law" (Decree-Law No. 644/75 of 15 November), with the purpose of promoting and preserving the safety, soundness, and stability of the banking system.[56]

Until the country joined the third stage of EMU on January 1, 1999, the Portuguese central bank was assigned both monetary policy and banking supervision functions. After joining EMU, when the ECB took over as the euro area monetary policy authority, Portugal adopted a banking supervisory separated model, with BdP ascribed exclusive banking supervisory responsibilities.[57] During this period there were some problematic supervision episodes, involving BCP – Banco Comercial Português (2007), BPN – Banco Português de Negócios (2008), BPP – Banco Privado Português (2008), and Banco Espírito Santo (2014).[58]

Up to November 2014, when the European Central Bank assumed its new banking supervision responsibilities, BdP was in charge of "the prudential and market conduct supervision of credit institutions, financial companies and payment institutions with a view to ensuring the stability, efficiency and soundness of the financial system, as well as the compliance with rules of conduct and transparency."[59] Within its prudential banking supervision legal framework, BdP "monitors the activities of the institutions in a systematic and continuous manner, by resorting to a range of prudential rules and supervisory procedures (for instance, on-site inspections and analysis of the information regularly reported by the institutions)."[60] Under the Portuguese banking conduct supervision legal framework, it "has the power to establish rules of conduct for credit institutions and financial companies, ensuring transparency of information during the pre-contractual and contractual stages."[61]

It seems appropriate to emphasize that in Portugal, banks are also monitored by antitrust and stock market regulatory authorities, entities statutorily independent from BdP. Because until now there has been no developed legal doctrine regulating the interaction of those agencies, their regulatory provisions and actions can potentially be redundant, overlapping, or even contradictory, imposing on supervisees inefficient deadweight costs of compliance.

Analyzing supervisory practices in Portugal, it remains unclear whether or not the BdP at the conclusion of its supervisory on-site inspections really does assign any type of composite measures (ratings) to individual banking organizations, as, for example, the US and the Bank of Japan's supervisory agencies do.[62] We also donot know whether the BdP, between successive on-site inspections of a specific bank, does perform off-site routine examinations aimed at mitigating the well-known information decay problems.

The Single Supervisory Mechanism (SSM)

Starting in November 2014, the Single Supervisory Mechanism (SSM) has created a new financial supervision institutional framework for euro area countries,[63] which participate automatically in the SSM, while non-euro area[64] participating countries have the option to take part. The declared main aims of the SSM are to promote and ensure the safety and soundness of the European banking system, and to increase financial integration and stability in Europe.[65]

The ECB will be responsible for the effective and consistent functioning of the SSM, cooperating with the national competent authorities of participating EU countries. Under the SSM there will be directly and indirectly supervised institutions. Significant credit institutions will be directly supervised by the ECB. In participating countries, at least the three most significant credit institutions will also be directly supervised, regardless of their absolute size.[66] All other credit institutions in the participating countries will continue to be supervised by the national competent authorities. The ECB can decide at any time to exercise direct supervision of any one of these credit institutions.

A final list of credit institutions was published in September 2014 and will be regularly updated.[67]

Acknowledgments

Valuable comments and helpful suggestions from Aníbal Santos and Nuno Garoupa on an early draft are gratefully acknowledged. Any remaining errors are my own.

Appendix 4.1 Milestones of Portuguese financial system regulatory reform

Year	Summary
1975	• Portuguese privately owned banks were nationalized.
1977	• Portugal entered an International Monetary Fund (IMF)financial assistance program.
1983	• Portugal entered an IMF financial assistance program.
1984	• Private investment and ownership in banking were legalized.
1985	• Mutual funds and fund management rules were approved. • Treasury Bills were created. • Interest rates were liberalized: minimum rates were set for over 180-day term deposits, and maximum rates were set for 90 to 180 days, and over 2 years' banking credit. • Regulation of pension funds and pension funds management. • The foreign exchange spot market was introduced.
1986	• Portugal joined the European Economic Community (EEC). • The charter of Banco de Portugal (BDP) was revised. • Venture capital was regulated. • Money market brokers were allowed to establish and operate in the interbank market. • The privatization of state-owned banks was made legally possible. • Banks were allowed to invest in international money markets.
1987	• Certificates of Deposit were created. • Rules and regulations for the Interbank securities market were changed to allow BDP to absorb excess liquidity, and to introduce an open market policy.

Appendix 4.1 (Continued)

Year	Summary
	• The exchange rate stopped being established by BDP. The Foreign Exchange market was liberalized. Operations in the forward exchange market started, although restricted to Portuguese legally resident banks. • New security markets regulations were introduced. A securities exchange auditor was appointed. Later, the securities exchange auditor was replaced by a Securities Exchange Commission. • Fixed-rate treasury bonds were launched and started being traded in the secondary market.
1988	• Revolving credit facilities to the public sector (CLIPs) were introduced. • Major changes related to the modernization of the security markets were introduced, including bonds with warrants; dematerialized equity securities; regulation of Initial Public Offerings and Public Offers of Acquisition; and closed-end funds. • Interbank money market brokers were allowed to operate in the foreign exchange market. • Banks were allowed to own brokerage and dealing houses. • Limits on banking credit rates were fully removed.
1989	• A new minimum limit for banks' equity capital was established. • The bank privatization program was initiated. • The ceiling on check deposits was raised to one third of the minimum rate on term deposits under 180 days.
1990	• Limits on banking credit were fully eliminated. • A privatization law was passed, allowing the privatization, at most, of 49% of formerly nationalized equity capital. • Investment in foreign securities markets was allowed. • The Portuguese escudo started being monitored against the currencies of the Exchange Rate Mechanism (ERM). • The definition, enforcement, and oversight of banking accounting standards was assigned to BDP. • Non-residents were allowed to buy foreign currency in the forward exchange market. Restrictions on the selling of foreign exchange against escudos to residents were kept in place. • Banking capital adequacy requirements were introduced.
1991	• The leasing industry was authorized to expand into real estate. • The foreign exchange market was regulated. • Brokers and dealers were allowed to offer securities custody services. • The Securities Exchange Code was approved. • Transitory fiscal benefits were established to foster the development of securities exchanges. • The Securities Exchange Commission and its internal regulations were formally approved.

1992	• EEC Directive No. 86/635/CEE, including accounting consolidation principles and rules for financial institutions, was transposed to the Portuguese legal system. • The Portuguese currency joined the ERM of the European Monetary Union. • Bank deposit rates were liberalized. • Control of capital movements was eliminated. • Commercial paper issuance was regulated.
1993	• New rules were introduced into the interbank money market
1996	• The bank privatization program was concluded.
1999	• Portugal joined the third phase of Economic and Monetary Union (EMU).
2008	• The legal framework of credit institutions and financial companies was revised.
2011	• Portugal entered an IMF/European Central Bank/European Commission financial assistance program.
2014	• Portugal exited the IMF/European Central Bank/European Commission financial assistance program.

Notes

1. In this context, financial and banking systems regulation relates to rule making, and supervision refers to the oversight of financial institutions' behavior, performance, and condition, first and foremost in terms of risk taking and regulatory compliance. See, among others, Kahn and Santos (2005) and references therein.
2. One of most consequential manifestations of those changes in banking markets worldwide was the replacement of the "traditional originate-to-hold model of lending with the so-called originate-to-distribute model." See Bord and Santos (2012: 21) for more details.
3. There is an non-negligible body of literature that reports evidence consistent with the notion that the roots of a country's legal system, and the institutional arrangements of its financial system, can affect its performance in terms of economic growth and social welfare. See, among others, Stulz (2001); Levine (1999); Laporta et al. (1997, 1998); Gertler (1988).
4. See Benink and Benston (2005) for more details.
5. According to European Commission (2010), such "fragmented supervision undermines the Single Market, imposes extra costs for financial institutions, and increases the likelihood of failure of financial institutions with potentially additional costs for taxpayers."
6. Boot (2007: 15) suggests that "the fragility of the financial system is a key public policy concern. It is widely acknowledged that stability concerns and systemic risks in banking are real and warrant regulatory scrutiny. These issues have become more pertinent with the further integration of financial markets and the increasing cross-border footprint of financial institutions."
7. The "invisible hand" argument still is a source of debate among academics. For example, Joseph Stiglitz, a 2001 Nobel Prize winner, argues that "Adam

Smith's invisible hand – the idea that free markets lead to efficiency as if guided by unseen forces – is invisible, at least in part, because it is not there"; Stiglitz (2002). See also Stiglitz (2009); LeRoy (2010).

8. De Grauwe (2008).
9. Stiglitz (2009).
10. See also Kilinc and Neyapti (2012).
11. See Barth et al. (2001). Benston and Kaufman (1996) suggest that "the appropriate role of bank regulation, or whether banks should be regulated at all, has long been a matter of controversy."
12. Barth et al. (2004).
13. Market failures in the financial markets can be originated by anti-competitive practices originating inefficient asset pricing and deadweight transaction costs; market misconduct; information asymmetries; and systemic risk.
14. See, among others, Freixas and Rochet (2008).
15. Ross (1989) argues that "loan organizations are opaque" because they only allow market participants a blurred "view" of their financial assets' true risk and return characteristics. One of the reasons that banking firms' assets are characterized by a significant amount of opacity is that "banks know more about the quality of their assets than do outside investors"; Lucas and McDonald(1992). For further details see also Iannotta(2006); Flannery et al. (2004) and references therein.
16. According to Slovin et al. (1993), banks produce private information on informationally opaque borrowers through the loan contracting process. This conjecture is rooted in the idea that there is relationship-specific private information in bank credit activities.
17. Olson (2006).
18. Throughout the chapter we use the terms bank, banking organization, depository institution, and financial institution interchangeably. All of the designations refer to commercial banks, bank holding companies, savings banks, and thrifts.
19. Herring and Santomero (2000).
20. See Flannery (1994, 2001).
21. See, among others, Archer (2009) for further details.
22. Barth et al. (2004) argue that "the staggering scope of recent banking crises coupled with strong evidence on the beneficial effects of well-functioning banking systems for economic growth underscore current efforts to reform bank regulation and supervision."
23. Barth et al. (2004) argue that "the staggering scope of recent banking crises coupled with strong evidence on the beneficial effects of well-functioning banking systems for economic growth underscore current efforts to reform bank regulation and supervision."
24. Evidence is from Argentina, Australia, Brazil, Canada, Chile, China, Hong Kong, Indonesia, India, Japan, Korea, Mexico, Russia, Saudi Arabia, Singapore, Switzerland, Turkey, the United Kingdom, the United States, South Africa, and the euro area as a whole. See Financial Stability Board (2013) for further details. For a review on shadow banking see Claessens and Ratnovski (2014) and references therein.
25. International Monetary Fund (2014).

26. According to Bart et al. (2003),"ongoing changes in the structure and nature of banking, as well as banking crises across the globe have focused the attention of policy makers on the appropriate structure, scope, and degree of independence of banking supervision."The European Banking Federation (2007) claims that "the lag in designing an adapted supervisory structure to accommodate the needs and concerns of an integrated banking industry is a matter of considerable concern." For more details see http://ec.europa.eu/internal_market/finances/index_en.htm, accessed July 27, 2015.
27. See, among others, Lima et al. (2012); Whelan (2012); Vives (2001); Di Noia and Di Giorgio (1999); Goodhart and Schoenmaker (1993, 1995).
28. See Haubrich (1996) and Goodhart and Schoenmaker (1995).
29. For further discussions on banking regulation and supervision see, among others, Peláez and Peláez (2009); Freixas and Rochet (2008); Llewellyn (2006); Bhattacharya et al. (1998); Dewatripont and Tirole (1993).
30. As argued in Goodhart (2005), central banks should have a special regulatory and supervisory focus on the "overall systemic stability in the financial system."
31. See Haubrich (1996).
32. According to Stiglitz(2009),"well-designed regulatory structures and systems should take into account: (a) asymmetries of information between the regulator and the regulated; (b) that a regulator's behavior is consistent with social welfare (for example, the potential moral hazard associated with the capture of the regulator by the regulated); and (c) human limitations, namely in implementing and enforcing regulations."
33. See Dahl et al. (1998).
34. See Bernanke (2007).
35. The so-called G10 include Belgium, Canada, France, Germany, Italy, Japan, the Netherlands, Sweden, Switzerland, the United Kingdom, and the United States. The Bank for International Settlements, the European Commission, the International Monetary Fund, and the Organization for Economic Cooperation and Development are official observers of the activities of the G10.
36. See Sahajwala and Van den Bergh (2000).
37. See Polizatto (1990).
38. See also CEBS (2010) for a set of guidelines "for implementing a common European framework for supervisory disclosure."
39. The Bank of Japan seems to have adopted an approach similar to that of the United States.
40. The uniform individual bank rating system known under the acronym of CAMELS was the first supervisory rating tool used in the United States, created in 1979. Under the CAMEL model a bank is assessed in relation toCapital, Asset quality, Management, Earnings, and Liquidity. In 1997 an "S," standing for market risk and interest rate risk Sensitivity, was added. CAMELS ratings are assigned on a scale from 1 (best) to 5 (worst). Banks with a rating of 1 or 2 are considered non-problematic from a supervisory standpoint, while banks assigned with ratings from 3 to 5 are viewed as increasingly problematic.
41. The BOPEC supervisory rating system was adopted in 1979 as an instrument to summarize bank holding companies' safety and soundness of financial

condition in the form of a rating. Under the BOPEC rating, known as BOPEC/F-M, a bank is evaluated and rated in relation to its condition on BHC subsidiaries; Other BHC (non-bank) subsidiaries; BHC Parent company; BHC Earnings; and BHC Capital. "F" represents the financial composite rating, and "M" the management composite rating. The BOPEC rating system was in place from 1979 to 2004. From January 1, 2005 onward, the Board of Governors of the Federal Reserve System made effective a revised supervisory rating system for BHCs and FHCs (financial holding companies). Each of the BOPEC rating components is evaluated and rated on a scale from 1 (lowest degree of supervisory concern) to 5 (highest degree of supervisory concern). For further details see Kini (2004).

42. See Deyoung et al. (2001); Berger and Davies (1998).
43. According to the *Bank Supervision Process Comptroller's Handbook* (Office of the Comptroller of the Currency, 2005, updated 2013), "the CAMELS composite and component ratings . . . are formally communicated to the bank's board of directors and management."
44. Cole and Gunther (1995).
45. See Krainer and Lopez (2002);*Do Supervisory Rating Standards Change Over Time?* Working paper available at: http://www.bis.org/bcbs/events/cbrworkshop09/krainerlopez.pdf. Cole et al. (1995).
46. According to Collier et al. (2003), "the SCOR model is very similar to the SEER rating model," although "SCOR does not use past CAMELS ratings to forecast future ratings." The SCOR system bench marked the Capital, Asset quality, Earnings, and Liquidity (CAEL) off-site monitoring system developed during the 1980s. The authors also indicate that the FIMS model was the predecessor of the SEER rating system.
47. See Cole and Gunther (1995).
48. According to Furlong and William (2006), however, "[t]he evidence on the extent to which market signals can augment the information set of bank supervisors is more subtle."
49. See Flannery (1998).
50. Amaral (2010); Pereira and Lains (2010); Lloyd-Jones (2001) provide interesting discussions on Portuguese recent economic history.
51. For a comprehensive overview of European banking see, among others, Schoenmaker and Peek (2014); Dermine (2003); and comments by Harry Huizinga and Eric Rosengren in Gaspar et al. (2003: 97, 109).
52. After aninitial attempt to implement banking accounting standards in 1959 (Decree of Law No. 42641), those standards were finally introduced in 1978 (Decree-Law No. 455/78), which were applied until 1989. In 1990 the responsibility to define, enforce, and oversee banking accounting standards was assigned to Banco de Portugal (Decree of Law No. 91/90, of March 17). Following the transposition to the Portuguese legal jurisdiction of the European Union (EU) 7th Directive in 1991 (Decree of Law No. 238/91, of July 2), new mandatory accounting consolidation rules were enforced for banks (Decree of Law No. 36/92, of March 28, 1992).
53. See Murphy (2000) for a discussion of the single market in banking.
54. See Appendix 4.1 for a summary of the milestones in the process of regulatory reform of the Portuguese financial and banking systems.

55. The European System of Central Banks (ESCB), known as the "Eurosystem," has no legal personality of its own and because of differentiated levels of integration in EMU, the main actors are the European Central Bank and the national central banks of the countries belonging to the euro area. See Scheller (2006) for further details.
56. See Valério (2010)for an account of the "evolution of banking at both a world level and a European level, presenting the political, economic and monetary framework governing the evolution of the Portuguese banking system, analysing the main facts of this evolution and discussing the relationship established between the banking system and the Portuguese economy and society in general."Barata (1995) provides an overview of the Portuguese banking system during the 1986–92 period.
57. "The powers and responsibilities of Banco de Portugal as supervisory authority are stipulated in its Organic Law, in the (revised) Legal Framework of Credit Institutions and Financial Companies (published in Decree-Law No 1/2008 of 3 January), and in the Legal Framework of Payment Institutions and Payment Services." This Organic Law, following the French legal tradition, is a supe rmajority law. See http://www.bportugal.pt/en-US/Supervisao/Pages/default.aspx for further details, accessed July 27, 2015.
58. For more details in the cases of the Banco Português de Negócios and the Banco Privado Português, see Banco de Portugal (2008)"Financial Stability Report,"Box 4.1, p. 131.
59. See http://www.bportugal.pt/en-US/Supervisao/Pages/default.aspx for further details, accessed July 27, 2015.
60. See http://www.bportugal.pt/en-US/Supervisao/SupervisaoPrudencial/Pages/default.aspx for further details, accessed July 27, 2015.
61. See http://www.bportugal.pt/en-US/Supervisao/SupervisaoComportamental/Pages/default.aspx for further details, accessed July 27, 2015.
62. In the United States, federal and state banking supervisors and regulators have engaged in extensive surveillance of banks, mainly through a combination of on-site inspections and off-site examinations, in order to monitor and appraise their financial performance and condition. For more details see http://www.federal reserve education.org/about-the-fed/structure-and-functions/banking-supervision/, accessed July 27, 2015. The Bank of Japan also conducts on-site inspections and off-site examinations; for further details seehttp://www.boj.or.jp/en/finsys/exam_monit/, accessed July 27, 2015.
63. Eurosystem countries that are members of the euro area are Austria, Belgium, Cyprus, Estonia, Finland, France, Germany, Greece, Ireland, Italy, Latvia, Luxembourg, Malta, the Netherlands, Portugal, Slovakia, Slovenia, and Spain.
64. Euro system countries that are not members of the euro area are Bulgaria, Croatia, Czech Republic, Denmark, Hungary, Lithuania, Poland, Romania, Sweden, and the United Kingdom.
65. For the legal regulation assigning, under Article 127(6) of the Treaty on the functioning of the European Union, to the European Central Bank specific tasks concerning policies relating to the prudential supervision of credit institutions, see http://eur-lex.europa.eu/legal-content/EN/TXT/?&uri=CELEX:32013R1024, accessed July 27, 2015.

66. The significance of credit institutions will be based on the total value of their assets; the importance for the economy of the country in which they are located or the EU as a whole; the scale of their cross-border activities; and whether they have requested or received public financial assistance from the European Stability Mechanism (ESM) or the European Financial Stability Facility (EFSF).
67. The list of the significant entities that on August 6, 2015 were directly supervised by ECB's SSM can be found at: https://www.banking supervision.europa.eu/ecb/pub/pdf/list_sse_lsi.en.pdf?492828653da06f7b24babd65e9e3077c

Bibliography

Amaral, Luciano (2010) *Economia Portuguesa, as Últimas Décadas*, Lisbon: Fundação Francisco Manuel dos Santos.

Archer, David (2009) "Roles and Objectives of Modern Central Banks," in G. Ortiz (ed.), *Issues in the Governance of Central Banks*, Basel: Bank for International Settlements, Chapter 2.

Banco de Portugal (2008) "Financial Stability Report," Lisbon: Banco de Portugal.

Barata, José (1995) "O Sector Bancário em Portugal: Evolução e Análise Estratégica (1986–1992)," *Revista da Banca*, 33: 17–60.

Bart, James, Nolle, Daniel, Phumiwasana, Triphon, and Yago, Glenn (2003) "A Cross-Country Analysis of the Bank Supervisory Framework and Bank Performance," *Financial Markets, Institutions and Instruments*, 12(2): 67–120.

Barth, James, Caprio, Gerard, Jr., and Levine, Ross (2001) "Banking Systems around the Globe: Do Regulation and Ownership Affect Performance and Stability?," in F. Mishkin (ed.), *Prudential Supervision: What Works and What Doesn't*, Chicago, IL: University of Chicago Press, 31–96.

Barth, James, Caprio, Gerard, Jr., and Levine, Ross(2004),"Bank Regulation and Supervision: What Works Best?" *Journal of Financial Intermediation*, 13(2): 205–248.

Benink, Harald, and Benston, George (2005) "The Future of Banking Regulation in Developed Countries: Lessons from and for Europe," *Financial Markets, Institutions and Instruments*, 14(5): 289–328.

Benston, George, and Kaufman, George (1996) "The Appropriate Role of Bank Regulation," *Economic Journal*, 106(436): 688–697.

Berger, Allen, and Davies, Sally (1998) "The Information Content of Bank Examinations," *Journal of Financial Services Research*, 14(2): 117–144.

Bernanke, Ben (2007) "Central Banking and Bank Supervision in the United States," speech at the Allied Social Science Association Annual Meeting, Chicago, IL, January 5, http://www.federalreserve.gov/newsevents/speech/bernanke20070105a.htm, accessed July 27, 2015.

Bhattacharya, Sudipto, Boot, Arnoud, and Thakor, Anjan (1998)"The Economics of Bank Regulation," *Journal of Money, Credit, and Banking*, 30(4): 745–770.

Boot, Arnoud (2007) "Supervisory Arrangements, LOLR, and Crisis Management in a Single European Banking Market," in Douglas Evanoff, George Kaufman, and John LaBrosse (eds.), *International Financial Instability: Global Banking and National Regulation*, Danvers, MA: World Scientific Publishing, 387–406.

Bord, Vitaly, and Santos, João (2012) "The Rise of the Originate-to-Distribute Model and the Role of Banks in Financial Intermediation," *Economic Policy Review*, 18(2): 21–34.

CEBS (2010)"Guidelines on Supervisory Disclosure – Revised," January, London: Committee of European Banking Supervisors.

Claessens, Stijn and Ratnovski, Lev (2014) "What Is Shadow Banking?" International Monetary Fund Research Department, Working Paper No. WP/14/25, Washington, DC: IMF.

Cole, Rebel, and Gunther, Jeffrey (1995) "A CAMEL Rating's Shelf Life. Federal Reserve Bank of Dallas," *Financial Industry Studies*, December: 13–20.

Cole, Rebel, Cornyn, Barbara, and Gunther, Jeffrey (1995) "FIMS: A New Monitoring System for Banking Institutions," *Federal Reserve Bulletin*, January: 1–15.

Collier, Charles, Forbush, Sean, Nuxoll, Daniel, and O'Keefe, John(2003) "The SCOR System of Off-Site Monitoring: Its Objectives, Functioning, and Performance,*FDICBanking Review*,15(3): 17–32.

Dahl, Drew, O'Keefe, John and Hanweck, Gerald(1998)"The Influence of Examiners and Auditors on Loan-Loss Recognition," *FDICBanking Review*,11(4): 10–25.

De Grauwe, Paul (2008) "The Banking Crisis: Causes, Consequences and Remedies," Centre for European Policy Studies, No. 178 (November), Brussels: CEPS.

Dermine, Jean (2003) "Banking in Europe: Past, Present, and Future," in V. Gaspar, P. Hartmann and O. Sleijpen (eds.),*The Transformation of the European Financial System*, Frankfurt: European Central Bank, 31–95.

Dewatripont, Mathias, and Tirole, Jean(1993)*The Prudential Regulation of Banks*, Cambridge, MA: MIT Press.

Deyoung, Robert, Flannery, Mark, Lang, William, and Sorescu, Sorin (2001) "The Information Content of Bank Exam Ratings and Subordinated Debt Prices," *Journal of Money, Credit and Banking*, 33(4): 900–925.

Di Noia, Carmine, and Di Giorgio, Giorgio (1999) "Should Banking Supervision and Monetary Policy Tasks Be Given to Different Agencies?"*International Finance*, 2(3): 361–378.

European Banking Federation (2007) *Report on Integration of European Financial Services Markets*, December, Brussels: EBF.

European Commission (2010) *Financial Supervision Package – Frequently Asked Questions*, MEMO/10/434, 22 September, Brussels: European Commission.

Financial Stability Board (2013) *Global Shadow Banking Monitoring Report*, November, Basel: Financial Stability Board.

Flannery, Mark (1994) "Corporate Finance, Market Discipline and Bank Supervision," in *30th Annual Conference on Bank Structure and Competition Proceedings*, Chicago, IL: Federal Reserve Bank of Chicago, 313–330.

Flannery, Mark (1998) "Using Market Information in Prudential Bank Supervision: A Review of the U.S. Empirical Evidence," *Journal of Money, Credit, and Banking*, 30(3): 273–305.

Flannery, Mark (2001) "The Faces of 'Market Discipline.'" *Journal of Financial Services Research*,20(2–3): 107–119.

Flannery, Mark, Kwan, Simon, and Nimalendran, M. (2004) "Market Evidence on the Opaqueness of Banking Firms' Assets," *Journal of Financial Economics*, 71(3): 419–460.

Freixas, Xavier, and Rochet, Jean-Charles (2008) *Microeconomics of Banking*, 2ndedn., Cambridge, MA: MIT Press.

Furlong, Frederick, and Robard, William (2006) "Financial Market Signals and Banking Supervision: Are Current Practices Consistent with Research Findings?"*Federal Reserve Bank of San FranciscoEconomic Review*, 2006: 17–29.

Gaspar, V., Hartmann, P., and Sleijpen, O. (eds.) (2003) *The Transformation of the European Financial System*, Frankfurt: European Central Bank.

Gertler, Mark (1988) "Financial Structure and Aggregate Economic Activity: An Overview," *Journal of Money, Credit, and Banking*, 20(3, Pt. 2): 559–588.

Goodhart, C.A.E. (2005) "The Future of Central Banking," Financial Markets Group Special Paper No. 162, London: London School of Economics.

Goodhart, Charles, and Schoenmaker, Dirk(1993)"Institutional Separation between Supervisory and Monetary Agencies," Financial Markets Group Special Paper No. 52, London: London School of Economics.

Goodhart, Charles, and Schoenmaker, Dirk (1995) "Should the Functions of Monetary Policy and Banking Supervision Be Separated?"*Oxford Economic Papers*, 47(4): 539–560.

Haubrich, Joseph (1996) "Combining Bank Supervision and Monetary Policy," *Federal Reserve Bank of Cleveland Economic Commentary*, November.

Herring, Richard, and Santomero, Anthony (2000) "What Is Optimal Financial Regulation?" in Benton Gup (ed.), *The New Financial Architecture: Banking Regulation in the 21st Century*, Westport, CT: Quorum Books, 51–84.

Iannotta, Giuliano (2006) "Testing for Opaqueness in the European Banking Industry: Evidence from Bond Credit Ratings," *Journal of Financial Services Research*, 30(3): 287–309.

International Monetary Fund (2014) "Shadow Banking around the Globe: How Large, and How Risky?" in *Global Financial Stability Report: Risk Taking, Liquidity, and Shadow Banking – Curbing Excess while Promoting Growth*, Washington, DC: IMF, 65–104.

Kahn, Charles, and Santos, João (2005) "Allocating Bank Regulatory Powers: Lender of Last Resort, Deposit Insurance and Supervision," *European Economic Review*, 49(8): 2107–2136.

Kilinc, Mustafa, and Neyapti, Bilin (2012) "Bank Regulation and Supervision and Its Welfare Implications," *Economic Modelling*, 29(2): 132–141.

Kini, Satish (2004) "New Bank Holding Company Rating System Revises the Focus of the Federal Reserve's Supervisory Practices," *Banking Law Journal*,121(9): 784–790.

Krainer, John, and Lopez, Jose (2002) "Do Supervisory Rating Standards Change over Time?"working paper, http://www.bis.org/bcbs/events/cbrworkshop09/krainerlopez.pdf, accessed July 27, 2015.

Laporta, Rafael, Lopez-de-Silanes, Florencio, Shleifer, Andrei, and Vishny, Robert (1997) "Legal Determinants of External Finance," *Journal of Finance*, 52(3): 1131–1150.

Laporta, Rafael, Lopez-de-Silanes, Florencio, Shleifer, Andrei, and Vishny, Robert (1998) "Law and Finance," *Journal of Political Economy*, 106(6): 1113–1155.

LeRoy, Stephen (2010) "Is the 'Invisible Hand' Still Relevant?"*Federal Reserve Bank of San Francisco Economic Letter*, 14(May): 1–4.

Levine, Ross (1998) "The Legal Environment, Banks, and Long-Run Economic Growth," *Journal of Money, Credit, and Banking*, 30(3, Pt. 2): 596–613.

Levine, Ross (1999) "Law, Finance, and Economic Growth," *Journal of Financial Intermediation*, 8(1–2): 8–35.
Lima, D., Lazopoulos, I., and Gabriel, V. (2012)"Monetary Policy and Banking Supervision: Is There a Conflict of Interest?" Working paper, https://www.surrey.ac.uk/economics/files/dpaperspdf/Conflict%20interest_Dec%202012.pdf, accessed July 27, 2015.
Llewellyn, David(2006)"Institutional Structure of Financial Regulation and Supervision: The Basic Issues," World Bank seminar, "Aligning Supervisory Structures with Country Needs," Washington, DC.
Lloyd-Jones, Stewart (2001) "Portugal's History since 1974," CPHRC Working Papers, Series 2, No. 1, November, http://www.cd25a.uc.pt/media/pdf/portugal-since-1974.pdf, accessed July 27, 2015.
Lucas, Deborah, and McDonald, Robert(1992)"Bank Financing and Investment Decisions with Asymmetric Information about Loan Quality," *Rand Journal of Economics*, 23(1): 86–105.
Murphy, Neil (2000) "European Union Financial Developments: The Single Market, the Single Currency, and Banking," *FDICBanking Review*, 13(1): 1–18.
Office of the Comptroller of the Currency (2005) *Bank Supervision Process Comptroller's Handbook*, September (updated 2013), Washington, DC: OCC.
Olson, Mark (2006) "Are Banks still Special?" speech at the Annual Washington Conference of the Institute of International Bankers, Washington, DC, March 13.
Peláez, Carlos M., and Peláez, Carlos A. (2009) *Regulation of Banks and Finance: Theory and Policy after the Credit Crisis*, Houndmills: Palgrave Macmillan.
Pereira, Álvaro Santos, and Lains, Pedro (2010) "From an Agrarian Society to a Knowledge Economy: Portugal, 1950–2010," Universidad Carlos II de Madrid Working Paper in Economic History No. 10-09, http://e-archivo.uc3m.es/handle/10016/9361?locale-attribute=en, accessed July 27, 2015.
Polizatto, Vincent (1990) "Prudential Regulation and Banking Supervision: Building an Institutional Framework for Banks," World Bank Policy Research Working Paper No. wps340, http://documents.worldbank.org/curated/en/1990/01/700348/prudential-regulation-banking-supervision-building-institutional-framework-banks, accessed July 27, 2015.
Ross, Stephen (1989) "Institutional Markets, Financial Marketing, and Financial Innovation," *Journal of Finance*, 44(3): 541–556.
Sahajwala, Ranjana, and Van den Bergh, Paul (2000) "Supervisory Risk Assessment and Early Warning Systems," Basel Committee on Banking Supervision Working Paper No. 4, http://www.bis.org/publ/bcbs_wp4.pdf, accessed July 27, 2015.
Scheller, Hanspeter(2006)*The European Central Bank: History, Role and Functions*, 2nd rev. edn., Brussels: European Central Bank.
Schoenmaker, Dirk, and Peek, Toon (2014) "The State of the Banking Sector in Europe," OECD Economics Department Working Papers No. 1102, http://www.oecd-ilibrary.org/economics/the-state-of-the-banking-sector-in-europe_5k3ttg7n4r32-en, accessed July 27, 2015.
Slovin, Myron, Sushka, Marie, and Poloncheck, John (1993) "The Value of Bank Durability: Borrowers as Bank Stakeholders, "*Journal of Finance*, 48(1): 247–266.

Stiglitz, Joseph (2002) "There Is No Invisible Hand," *The Guardian*, 20 December, http://www.theguardian.com/education/2002/dec/20/highereducation.uk1, accessed July 27, 2015.
Stiglitz, Joseph (2009) "Regulation and Failure," in D. Moss and J. Cisternino (eds.) *New Perspectives on Regulation*, Cambridge, MA: Tobin Project, 11–23.
Stulz, René (2001) "Does Financial Structure Matter for Economic Growth? A Corporate Finance Perspective," in A. Demirgüç-Kunt and R. Levine (eds.)*Financial Structure and Economic Growth. A Cross-Country Comparison of Banks, Markets, and Development*, Cambridge, MA: MIT Press, 143–188.
Valério, Nuno (ed.)(2010) *History of the Portuguese Banking System: From the Bank of Portugal's Role as a Central Bank to the European Monetary Union – 1831–1998*, Vol. II, Lisbon:Banco de Portugal.
Vives, Xavier (2001) "Central Banks and Supervision," in A. Santomero, S. Viotti, and A. Vredin (eds.)*Central Banks and Supervision: Challenges for Modern Central Banking*, Norwell, MA: Kluwer Academic, 95–113.
Whelan, Karl (2012) "Should Monetary Policy Be Separated from Banking Supervision?" Policy Department A: Economic and Scientific Policy, Strasbourg: European Parliament.

5

Risk Management in Portuguese Financial Institutions

Anabela Sérgio, Miguel Teixeira Coelho, and Rui Sainhas de Oliveira

This chapter is, by its nature and content, defined by the idea of commitment. Methodologically, the aim is to obtain an understanding of the situation of the Portuguese financial system in several international contexts and of its own characteristics, in which both social and political issues are important. The question to be addressed is: Facing such challenging endeavors, which discriminating factors would allow Portuguese institutions to cope with the several risk types they face?

In order to understand the evolution of the Portuguese banking system in relation to risk management, we need to look, on the one hand, at nationalization and reprivatization processes. On the other hand, the latter is the explanation for why Portugal has one of the most up-to-date automated teller machine (ATM) systems among western banks. This network encompasses all banks in the Portuguese financial market, with corresponding links to their foreign peers.

The chapter ends by shedding light on the evidence of how solvency ratios in Portugal are in line with high international standards, despite the challenges the sector faces regarding efficiency and profitability.

From uncontrolled political risk to the (unsurprising) declaration of disaster

The Carnation Revolution in April 1974 ended with the so-called *Estado Novo* of Salazar's regime. The outcome of riots on the streets and corresponding political turmoil led to strong structural transformations in Portuguese society, including, as will be described, in the Portuguese banking system.

In order to better understand what follows, we stress at this point of historical reference two brief but important conclusions. First, the April 25, 1974 coup d'état in Portugal refers to the definite disappearance of the Portuguese Corporativist Regime, instead of the emergence of a revolutionary movement. Secondly, Portugal, with 10 million inhabitants at that time, received and had to absorb more than 500,000 people (e.g., 5% of the population) coming from Portuguese former colonies that became independent in the meantime.

Hazard or need: Portuguese banking system nationalization

Before the nationalization of the Portuguese banking system that took place on March 11, 1975, its structure was characterized by several informal aspects, namely:

- demand deposit interest rates settled above the legally authorized level;
- interest-free lending to some bank managers;
- commissions paid to those in charge of channeling funds to Portuguese banks from Portuguese emigrants;
- securities price manipulation on the exchange market;
- "window dressing" of banks' account books;
- sporadic occurrences of corruption.

This framework led to the process of nationalization. Privately owned banks (with Portuguese-owned shares) became state-owned ones.

A better understanding of this period can be gained from the brief macroeconomic glance in Tables 5.1–5.3.

Request for EEC accession: Domestic political conflict and new levels of stability

Nationalization of both the banking system and insurance companies obtained unanimity among the most important political forces, ranging

Table 5.1 Portuguese economy debt level (1973–77)

Year	1973	1974	1975	1976.000	1977.000
Credit/GDP	0.924	0.930	0.976	1.108	1.127

Source: Annual Reports of Bank of Portugal.

Table 5.2 Foreign exchange situation of the Portuguese economy (1973–75)

	1973	1974	1975
Net claims toward the rest of the world (1)*	387	310	192.5
Imports (2)*	466	701	605
(1)/(2)	83.0%	44.2%	31.8%
GDP (current prices)*	1402.5	1689	1907.5

*in million euros.
Source: Annual Reports of Bank of Portugal.

Table 5.3 Emigrants' foreign exchange Inflows (1975–78)

Year	Amount*	Δ %	Δ CPI% (without housing)
1975	104.6		15.2
1976	137.8	31.7	20.0
1977	224.3	62.8	27.4
1978	369.7	64.4	22.7

*in million euros.
Source: Pordata (www.pordata.pt).

from parties on the right to those on the extreme left. We should add that, on the eve of the first free elections in Portugal by universal suffrage (which took place on April 25, 1975), the issue of "anti-monopoly strategy" had been withdrawn from the political agenda. Therefore, democratic forces won the elections, inflicting a severe defeat on the communist parties.

Simultaneously with the process of nationalization, a transitional structural form was created to aid in the revitalization of the Portuguese economy. Two main issues were addressed to deal with the twin main problems faced by banks, lack of efficacy and lack of profitability, as follows:

- On the one hand, keeping on dismantling spurious corporativist links remaining inside former financial conglomerates where the bank was the corresponding financial arm.
- On the other hand, dismantling the structural chain of central planning: Serviços de Coordenação da Actividade Bancária (coordination of banking services), Conselho Coordenador da Política de Crédito (coordinating council of credit policy), and its Comissão Executiva

(executive committee), to name a few. All of these institutions were set aside from the framework of the new Organic Law of the Portuguese Central Bank (Banco de Portugal), Decree-Law nr. 644/75, dated November 15, 1975.

This course of action led the Portuguese authorities to formally ask, on March 28, 1977, for the integration of Portugal into the European Economic Community (EEC).

The most relevant impacts of EU integration on the Portuguese banking system

Negotiations for accession to the EEC, followed by the final agreement in 1985 (implemented in 1986), were based on Portugal's acceptance of both Treaties that supported the Communities[1] and those that, afterward, supported future enlargements.

Notwithstanding that agreement, barriers to inflows of capital originating in other member states destined for the banking system (in the form of foreign direct investment or FDI) were not completely dismantled and were subject to the following derogations:

- For seven years the Portuguese authorities had the power to adopt a preemptive authorization for new credit institutions in the country, always bearing in mind the non-discretionary principle.
- Only in the third year after accession were those authorized credit community institutions able to open an additional branch and, after five years, two more additional ones.
- Referring to the liberalization of funding obtained outside the banking system, a progressive pattern was adopted with a length of seven years, ending the discrimination between national and European institutions after this time.

Membership of the EEC was in fact a guarantee that the course of the Portuguese economy would not follow that of socialism, because it involved the abolition of constitutional provisions such as those that prevented the opening to private firms of the banking and insurance sectors, whose nationalization was considered irreversible in the 1976 Constitution.

Community support funds were, in fact, very effective in smoothing over some political positions that led to such a policy reversal enshrined in the constitutional revision of 1989, which, inter alia, recognized the end of the irreversible nature of nationalization, ameliorating the political risk that hung over the majority of activity sectors.

Beyond pre-accession funds support, European Cohesion and Social Funds channeled to Portugal, designed to be over four periods,[2] were aimed at a structural transformation in the Portuguese economyand reached €156 billion in 2011[3] (annual average of 4% of GDP in 2011).

Such a huge amount of funds helped to reconfigure and reshape the Portuguese economyboth economically and socially. We are going to shed light on this issue by referring to a study of the Fundação Francisco Manuel dos Santos.[4] That study highlights the following aspects concerning the minimization of political risks and also banking risks:

- The Portuguese currency, the escudo, was brought into the Exchange Rate Mechanism (ERM) of the European Monetary System (EMS) on April 6, 1992, leaving the"crawlingpeg" exchange rate adjustment system adopted until 1989.(Between 1989 and 1992 the Portuguese Escudo had been inserted in a "shadow" mechanism of the European Exchange Rate Mechanism, with the aim of analyzing whether the Portuguese currency could cope with the European Monetary System before it joined formally.)Portugal experienced a significant reduction in exchange rate risk with the corresponding benefits in liberalization of capital movements, increasing competition in the banking system, and convergence toward average European inflation and interest rates.
- It follows that cheap credit together with an abundance of resources in the system gave way to an (unwise) lowering of credit risk monitoring by lenders.
- When trying to maximize funding from the European Community, illusions can occur. National economic players, both private and public, simply relaxed external deficit constraints.
- More generally, the same concern created the illusion of a virtuous character of indebtedness.
- In addition, asignificant allocation of structural funds, in order to finance cohesion politics, led to a perverse effect: on the one hand, it reduced competitiveness in the global market regarding domestic transaction goods; on the other hand, the sustainability of progress in cohesion improvements was compromised.

To conclude, despite the crisis, the Portuguese banking system survived and improved its defenses, as will be illustrated in Chapter 6.

The efficacy of Basel I within the framework of disruption of the former institutional model

In 1988, the Cook Committee, the global Banking Supervision Committee (also called the Basel Committee), proposed a new methodology to address banking soundness and sustainability. This proposal was centered on the requirement of minimal capital amounts for credit institutions and was ratified by more than 100 countries. Formally, the proposal is expressed in Directive 89/647/EEC. Its transposition to Portugal can be found in Aviso do Banco de Portugal no. 12/90.

At this point we should stress the benefits of the Basel Committee's work to improve the achievement of the internal market for financial services.In fact, this idea is mirrored in the metamorphoses of the framework of banks' behavior and performance, more significant after the end of the Bretton Woods Agreement in 1971. The developments that occurred are outlined chronologically in what follows.

Internationalization

American banks were the first to begin operating internationally worldwide. They were followed by both European and Japanese banks, which step by step abandoned traditional domestic transactions (and those originating in domestic branches and headquarters, even when their nature was intentional), demonstrating the importance of internationalization and diversification). The aim was to follow and comply with their clients' needs. World financial hubs became more important and it follows that international banking was reshaped. The main and most important transformations involved concentration; non-specialization, e.g., general characteristics of the products supplied; and disintermediation.

Securitization

For non-investment-grade securities banks adopted the behavior of opening credit lines, at the level of the wholesale market, to their clients. Securitization was one way of obtaining funding, and banks were able to diminish their assets, therefore reducing their credit exposure.

Deregulation

Within the above mentioned framework one can understand the existing pressure on governments to deregulate. Competition was far from the required "level playing field" and inequalities between banks were a reality (between banks operating domestically and those developing their activities internationally). That is why the process of financial markets deregulation evolved.

These developments in internationalization, securitization, and deregulation went along with increasing risk taking by banks. We may shed light on some of these risks:

- Risks undertaken in the international markets by bank branches, which should be assigned to the parent company (the latter is in charge of group solvability).
- Off-balance-sheet risks, namely counterparty risks, which arose from securitization and disintermediation.
- Risks referring to government and/or state-owned companies' financing, which concern developing countries.

These new types of problems began to create a new type of concerns over the reinforcement of supervision measures. Accordingly, in May 1983 the Central Bank Governors of the Group of 10 issued a proposal, based on the Cook Committee's recommendation, that supervision of credit institutions should be undertaken on a consolidated basis. With the same orientation and worries, Directive 83/350, dated June 23, 1983, was enforced in all EEC countries, Portugal included.

The accounting innovation of off-balance-sheet registration on banks' books, and the corresponding new risks, was the result of a constraint. This arose from the mandatory allocation of prudential coefficients linked to transactions on the asset side of banks' books in order to cover credit risks. Progressively, the conclusion was that risks associated with the majority of off-balance-sheet transactions were similar, in nature, to those registered on the asset side of the balance sheet. It follows that they should have the same prudential approach and control.

That is why the methodology proposed in June 1988 by the Basel Supervision Committee (Basel I) was aimed at unifying the solvability ratio, covering both on- and off-balance-sheet operations. It was meant to reassure depositors that their own bank's funds were sufficient to cover any losses arising from both on- and off-balance-sheet operations. We may add that this represents a further step toward the creation of a truly international "level playing field" where banks could compete by the same rules.

Directive 89/647/EEC, dated December 18, 1989, and its corresponding transposition to the Portuguese system, Aviso do Banco de Portugal no. 12/90, dated December 4, 1990, define the solvability ratio of a bank as the relation between the value of own funds and the sum of asset values together with off-balance-sheet values, weighted by the level of risk, established at 8%but following the following schedule:

- 4% from December 31, 1990.
- 6% from December 31, 1991.
- 8% from December 31, 1992 (inclusive).

Aviso do Banco de Portugal no. 12/90 states that the solvability ratio should be calculated on a consolidated basis as far as regulation of the consolidated accounts of Portuguese credit institutions is concerned.

We may stress that, in the early 1990s and for the Portuguese financial system, the solvency ratio of 8% was met in almost all the private banks, but unfortunately in only a few state-owned banks due to the high number of underperforming loans registered by these banks.[5] Nevertheless, this was the moment when the privatization process began. The new private banks (former state-owned banks) were able to obtain the required solvability ratios.

The regulation of solvability at once took on an important role in Portuguese banks' management, namely:

- A stronger focus on the study of increasing own capital opportunities as a step and condition to increase business.
- To restrain the number of transactions registered off balance sheet (since they also began to be weighted by coefficient risks).
- To weight the return of asset-side and off-balance-sheet transactions regarding the corresponding level of risk.

In the 1990s, Portuguese credit institutions went far beyond the solvency ratio. These institutions, in addition to Directive 89/647/EEC, also met other ratios and boundaries concerning own funds:

- Ratio of fixed assets to own funds.
- Ratio aimed at hedging foreign exchange risks.
- Limits concerning financial participations.
- Limits concerning huge credit risks.[6]

Table 5.4 depicts the evolution of the own capital of Portuguese banks between 1986 and 1989.

Table 5.4 Net worth of Portuguese banks as a percentage of assets (1986–89)

	1986	1987	1988	1989
Total	4.90	6.44	8.10	8.90
State-owned banks	4.60	5.80	7.10	7.90
Nationally owned private banks	7.80	11.50	14.30	13.10
Foreign banks	11.50	12.80	15.5	17.6

Source: Associação Portuguesa de Bancos (APB), newsletter, June 1990.

Basel II Accords: The evolution of risk management in a framework of national emergency

The initial revisions to the Agreements on Capital (1988), and the corresponding improvements that were incorporated (the last of which was dated January 1996 and concerned market risk), began in 1999. They are expressed in a document from the Basel Banking Supervision Committee, published in June 2004 and enforced in 2006, entitled "International Convergence of Capital Measurement and Capital Standards: A Revised Framework," also known as "Basel II."

In Portugal, these ruleswere expressed in Decreto-Lei no. 103/2007 and Decreto-Lei no. 104/2007, dated April 3, 2007. These Decree-Laws are complemented by a range of announcements and instructions from Banco de Portugal concerning the implementation of the corresponding contents.[7]

In general, most Portuguese banks began their preparation for Basel II before its implementation. On the one hand they were trying to reassure regulators that they could meet the requirements; on the other hand they were aiming to adopt the most sophisticated tools and methodologies to assess risk. As a result, in 2007 some of the most important banks began to prepare files to be presented to the Portuguese Central Bank.

In this context, it was possible for most of the Portuguese banks to obtain the required authorization to apply the IRB (Internal-Based Approach) method for credit risk and the Advanced Approach to monitor market risk. In regard to operational risk, refer to Appendix 5.1, which depicts the almost unanimous adoption of the Standard Method (TSA).

Notwithstanding further significant improvements in managing credit risk by Portuguese banks, the Portuguese macroeconomic deterioration since 2008 had a significant impact on credit risk outcomes for

Table 5.5 Credit risk percentages (2008–13)

		2008	2009	2010	2011	2012	2013
Ratio of credit in risk (1 and 2)	Global ratio	3.61	5.06	5.19	7.74	9.80	10.56
	Resident non-financial private sector	4.11	5.52	5.63	8.33	10.35	11.58
	Public administration residents	1.04	0.66	0.83	2.49	3.32	3.65
	Non-residents	2.00	3.83	4.39	6.69	9.13	8.59
Ratio of credit in default (1 and 3)	Global ratio	3.61	5.06	5.19	7.74	9.80	10.56
	Resident non-financial private sector	2.24	3.53	3.84	5.19	6.93	8.14
	Public administration residents	1.00	0.50	0.71	1.56	2.13	1.81
	Non-residents	1.28	2.31	2.65	3.40	4.60	4.85

(1) Credit values reported on a consolidated basis by the aggregate of the Portuguese banking system, excluding branches in Portugal of credit institutions with headquarters in countries belonging to the European Union. Includes credit to residents and non-residents, as well as loans granted by foreign subsidiaries of Portuguese banks. Derecognized securitizations were not considered.
(2) Credit risk, defined according to the Instruction of Banco de Portugal #22/2011, includes the total amount due: credit that has installments of principal or interest overdue by more than 90 days; restructured loans, whose payments of principal or interest, having been overdue for a period exceeding 90 days, have been capitalized, refinanced, or arrears payment date agreed, without having been adequately strengthened by collateral security or accrued interest and other charges fully paid by the debtor; and credit installments of principal or interest overdue by less than 90 days, but on which there is evidence to justify its classification with credit risk.
(3) Non-performing loans include credit and interest overdue by more than 90 days and other doubtful loans, referring to future payments of credit when there are questions regarding its collection, as is established in the Announcement of Banco of Portugal #3/95.
Source: Bank of Portugal Statistical Bulletin and Data Package (www.bportugal.pt/pt-PT/.../VisaoSistemaBancarioPortuguesDadosPT.xls).

the banking system. Credit risk increased more than twofold between 2008 and 2011, as depicted in Table 5.5.

Simultaneously, Portugal faced a significant deterioration in the rating of its most important banks, even though they were investment grade until the end of 2010, as shown in Table 5.6.

In a context in which credit risk was increasing, bank solvability was weakening, and the public finances were bankrupt, on April 7, 2011 Portugal had to submit a request for financial support from the International Monetary Fund (IMF), the European Commission (EC), and the European Central Bank (ECB). A loan of €78 billion was granted to Portugal to readdress its macroeconomic situation, in what was termed the Financial and Economic Assistance Programme (FEAP).

Table 5.6 Long-term rating

Bank	Rating agencies	2005	2006	2007	2008	2009	2010	2011
CGD	Fitch	AA–	AA–	AA–	AA–	AA–	A	BB+
	Moodys	Aa3	Aa3	Aa1	Aa1	Aa2	A1	Ba2
	S&P	A+	A+	A+	A+	A+	A–	BB+
BCP	Fitch	A+	A+	A+	A+	A+	BBB+	BB+
	Moodys	A1	A1	Aa3	Aa3	A1	A3	Ba1
	S&P	A–	A	A	A	A–	BBB+	BB
BES	Fitch	A+	A+	A+	A+	A+	-	-
	Moodys	A1	A1	Aa3	Aa3	A1	A2	Ba2
	S&P	A–	A–	A	A	A	A–	BB
BPI	Fitch	A+	A+	A+	A+	A+	A	BB+
	Moodys	A2	A2	A1	A1	A1	A2	Ba2
	S&P	A–	A–	A	A	A	A–	BB–

Source: Annual reports.

Implementing FEAP had a strong positive impact on the Portuguese banking system. This was for three reasons:

- It demanded a process of deleverage (asset/liabilitytransformation of 120%), to be achieved by 2014. This was clearly achieved before the end of 2013 (Table 5.7), with severe consequences for Portuguese financing activities.
- It demands strong requirements for liquidity. Assets available as collateral with the ECB credit lines were reinforced.
- The banking system was able to issue bonds to a maximum of €35 billion with a government guarantee. Therefore, the liquidity gap substantially improved after 2011.[8]

Beyond the imposition of liquidity levels, FEAP established a greater follow-up of the banking system as well. Simultaneously this program was aimed at both anticipating occasional risks and reinforcing its credibility. In this context we may contrast it with the so-called OIP, On-site Inspections Programme of June 30, 2012. For the eight banking groups being analyzed, this estimated the necessity of reinforcing by €861 million the potential losses registered in banks' exposure to risks, so that a greater level of robustness provisions could be achieved (about 2.2% of the global amount of exposure under scrutiny).[9]

Due to the FEAP, the Portuguese Central Bank began to ask the eight big banks for quarterly plans concerning funding and average levels of medium-term capital until 2015. These plans contained information

Table 5.7 Liquidity and financing

		2010	2011	2012	2013
Total amount of resources obtained from ECB (1)		49.160*	50.720*	56.180*	51.130*
Transformation ratio (2)		157.85%	140.20%	127.88%	116.97%
Liquidity ratio (3)	3 months	−3.80%	−2.80%	5.00%	8.40%
	6 months	−7.30%	−6.30%	2.20%	6.20%
	12 months	−11.50%	−9.60%	−0.30%	2.20%

*million euros.
(1) Monetary policy operations at the Central Bank and other resources obtained in the Central Bank.
(2) (Net loans to customers + not derecognized securitized loans) / (Customer funds and other loans).
(3) (Net assets – Volatile Liabilities) / (Total Assets – Net Assets). Instruction #13/2009. Until 2008, the calculation of this indicator was based in Instruction #1/2000 and since then Instruction #13 / 2009, which are applicable only to financial institutions that take deposits.
Source: Bank of Portugal Statistical Bulletin and Data Package (www.bportugal.pt/pt-PT/.../VisaoSistemaBancarioPortuguesDadosPT.xls).

concerning measures adopted for deleverage and strategies to comply with the new capital requirements. Simultaneously, BdP established minimum regulatory levels concerning the Core Tier 1 ratios: 9% by the end of 2011, and 10% by the end of 2012.[10] Nevertheless, if banks were unable to obtain these goals during the stipulated period, they could obtain financial support from the recapitalization fund to the aggregated amount of €12 billion.

Therefore, on December 8, 2011, the European Banking Authority (EBA) issued a recommendation for capital reinforcement, so that by June 30, 2012, banks had a Core Tier 1 ratio of 9% (about €6,950 million).[11] Facing the market needs of capital strengthening, the recapitalization program[12] was used by three Portuguese financial institutions in June 2012.[13] It should be stressed that, in order to avoid a nationalization process, at the beginning of 2012 BdP authorized the public recapitalization of banksby means of hybrid instruments (CoCo bonds)[14] instead of share issues.

As a result of both the recapitalization program (under which the state bought CoCosto the amount of €5,800 million)[15] and public financing, the soundness and solvability of the Portuguese banking system increased significantly. At the end of 2013 its average level of Core Tier 1 ratio was 12.25%, clearly above the level of 10% required by the FEAP (see Table 5.8).

Table 5.8 Solvability percentages

	2010	2011	2012	2013
Core Tier 1/Total Assets (1)	4.53	5.16	6.74	6.91
Core Tier 1	7.39	8.73	11.50	12.25
Solvability Ratio	10.33	9.80	12.64	13.31

(1) All institutions under analysis determined the ratio of capital adequacy according to Basel II regulation, which mainly affected the calculation of capital requirements.
Source: Bank of Portugal Statistical Bulletin and Data Package (www.bportugal.pt/pt-PT/.../VisaoSistemaBancarioPortuguesDadosPT.xls).

Basel III Accord: The challenge of profitability

The Basel III Agreement has a very similar structure to Basel II. Above other things (like capital requirements), Basel III is strongly committed to banking liquidity concerns, which were brought to the fore by the financial crisis that began in 2007. Accordingly, it is engaged in requiring banks to increase their own quantitative and qualitative capital. Moreover, leverage ought to be reduced, together with a better management of liquidity and the decrease of pro-cyclical measures. These measures will be implemented progressively by 2020.

Very high and demanding requirements regarding liquidity and capital levels are a challenge to the Portuguese banking system. In fact, and notwithstanding the above mentioned goals established by FEAP, Portuguese financial institutions showed a strong position with reference to compliance with these new regulatory requirements. However, applying Basel III will still demand strong and significant endeavor, since it requires the restructuring of banking entities' balance sheets. Eventually, the outcome will be settled by developing new forms of business models. Strong evidence for this argument is shown in the negative evolution of the activity performance and profitability of the Portuguese banking system during the recent past (Table 5.9).

The following should be noted concerning the challenges that the Portuguese banking system will face in the near future:

- In relation to capital requirements it is in good health.
- Demanding liquidity requirements will raise the stress on the main performance and profitability indicators, which is reinforced by less friendly market conditions.
- Institutions will have to adopt more flexible business models, squeezing costs and increasing operational efficiency.

Table 5.9 Performance and profitability percentages (2008–13)

	2008	2009	2010	2011	2012	1S 2013
Annual growth rate of total assets	7.54	7.07	4.15	−3.59	−3.21	−6.68
ROE – Return on Equity (1)	5.65	7.57	7.71	−6.34	−5.49	−8.40
ROA – Return on Assets (1)	0.34	0.45	0.48	−0.37	−0.32	−0.54
Financial Margin (% of total assets)	1.92	1.62	1.49	1.52	1.31	1.05
Net commissions (% of total assets)	0.73	0.70	0.72	0.71	0.73	0.74
Ratio between operating costs and gross income	55.58	56.83	57.58	61.52	58.78	68.79

(1) For purposes of calculation, return on asset and return on equity were considered as income before taxes and minority interests, using period averages for the variables of stock.
Source: Bank of Portugal Statistical Bulletin and Data Package (www.bportugal.pt/pt-PT/.../VisaoSistemaBancarioPortuguesDadosPT.xls).

- Eventually, banking activity will be readdressed, moving from financing housing, real estate, and domestic firms toward channeling funds to the export sectors.

Conclusion

In this chapter, we have tried to shed light on the issues, situations, and events related to risk management, in particular in the specific Portuguese context. These can be synthesized as follows:

- Historical judiciousness and the Portuguese population's political sensibility meant that, during the most critical moments of the aftermath of the revolution, risk assessment was the most valuable externality in closing the gap in hostilities, according to Daniel Goleman. For example, the ability to absorb and harmoniously integrate into the society and the economy 500,000compatriots arriving from former Portuguese colonies with no goods or wealth demonstrates how expressive and relevant cohesion has been, as well as the high standards of social compromise in Portugal that have arisen during its 900 years of history.

- Since the 1974coup d'état, the Portuguese banking sector has performed a very important and decisive role in managing and stabilizing the socio-political process in the country, even though it has faced increasing difficulty in its intermediation function between saving and investment; that is, between present and future. Banking nationalization was the solution to safeguard the shaky social compromise. The subsequent peaceful process of re-privatization was the necessary solution to obtain commitment between the present and the future.
- The structural and cohesion funds channeled to Portugal from the EEC boosted the political reorganization of the country, providing a democratic choice for readdressing both its democratic regime and its economic paradigm.
- Portugal has been able to overcome the huge challenges associated with globalization. Its market shares have increased and its external equilibrium has improved. Therefore, national economic agents (families, firms, and the state) can rely on the Portuguese revival and recovery from the crisis.
- Finally, rebalancing of the Portuguese banking system, as the outcome of the efforts undertaken under the FEAP, will provide reassurance that it possesses the financial means and technical support required to consolidate the good results that have already been achieved.

The bailout of Banco Espirito Santo (BES)

While this chapter was being finalized, the bankruptcy of BES took place. It is therefore worth making some remarks concerning this matter. Although information is still scarce and misleading, we are able to offer the following.

BES had its origins in 1869 as a Casa de Câmbios (exchange rate firm). On May 14, 1975, together with all Portuguese privately owned banks, it was nationalized.

Between 1975 and 1991, the Espirito Santo group reorganized its activities abroad, in association with Crédit Agricole, and became once again the leader of the new Banco Espirito Santo (then called Banco Espirito Santo e Comercial de Lisboa). The chairman remained in place from 1991 until July 2014. At that time he was withdrawn from his position by the governor of BdP, who stated that there had been "malpractice and wrong management decisions, damaging the bank's needs and in the opposite direction to Banco de Portugal directives concerning increasing exposures toward other entities of the Group."

Some milestones in the BES resolution were:

- In May 2014 an external audit referred to a serious financial situation when asked to express its remarks concerning the disclosure of an increasein the bank's own capital.
- On July 30, 2014, the bank's accounts displayed a loss of €3.577 billion in the first quarter.
- On August 3, 2014, the chairman of the board of Banco de Portugal decided to apply to BES the first measure of its kind ever known in Portugal (and in Europe), a resolution determining that "good assets" should immediately be transferred to a new institution, termed the "New Bank," funded by a "Resolution Fund" with €4.9 billion. All remaining losses were due to be the responsibility of the shareholders and creditors of BES.
- The Associação Portuguesa de Bancos (APB) supported Banco de Portugal's decision to agree to provide the necessary money in order to reinforce the success of this measure.
- We should stress the importance of the pioneering behavior, both in Portugal and in the EU, that, during the first weekend of August, succeeded in designing and implementing the first bank bailout.

Appendix 5.1 Methods of calculating operational risk capital charges (BCP, CGD, BES, and BPI)

Bank	Methods	2008	2009	2010	2011	2012	2013
BCP	Credit risk	TSA	TSA	IRB	IRB	IRB	IRB
	Market risk	TSA	TSA	TAD	TAD	TAD	TAD
	Operational risk	TSA	TSA	TSA	TSA	TSA	TSA
CGD	Credit risk	TSA	TSA	TSA	TSA	TSA	TSA
	Market risk	TSA	TSA	TSA	TSA	TSA	TSA
	Operational risk	BIA	TSA	TSA	TSA	TSA	TSA
BES	Credit risk	TSA	IRB	IRB	IRB	IRB	IRB
	Market risk	TSA	TSA	TSA	TSA	TSA	TSA
	Operational risk	BIA	TSA	TSA	TSA	TSA	TSA
BPI	Credit risk	TSA	TSA	TSA	TSA	TSA	TSA
	Market risk	TSA	TSA	TSA	TSA	TSA	TSA
	Operational risk	BIA	BIA	BIA	BIA	BIA	BIA

Notes: TSA – The Standardized Approach; IRB – Internal Rating-Based Approach; TAD – The Advanced Approach; BIA – Basic Indicator Approach.
Source: Market Discipline Reports (BCP, CGD, BES, and BPI).

Notes

1. The concept of "Communities" means the European Coal and Steel Community (ECSC); the European Economic Community (EEC); and the European Atomic Energy Community (Euratom). According to the Maastricht Treaty, these now correspond to the European Union.
2. From 1989 to 1993 – Quadro Comunitário de Apoio I; from 1994 to 1999 – Quadro Comunitário de Apoio II; from 2000 to 2006 – Quadro Comunitário de Apoio III; and from 2007 to 2013 – Quadro de Referência Estratégico Nacional.
3. Augusto Mateus & Associados (2013).
4. Ibid.
5. "Livro Branco sobre o Sistema Financeiro: 1992,"http://purl.sgmf.pt/COL-MF-0021-1/1/, accessed July 27, 2015.
6. A group of risks undertaken by one institution toward one client or group of clients with links between them and that represents 10% or more of the institution's own funds (Aviso 10/94 of Bank of Portugal).
7. Announcements 4,5,7,8,9, and 14 dated 2007; 6,8, and 9 dated 2008; 1,2,10, and 12 dated 2009; 3,6,7, and 8 dated 2010; 2,3,6,7,8, and 9 dated 2011; 1,2,4,5,8,10, and 11 dated 2012; 2,3,4, and 6 dated 2013.
8. Maintaining high levels of funding from the ECB does not result exclusively from actual liquidity needs. Indeed, many banks have decided to obtain funding at low interest rates with the ECB to purchase government bonds with attractive remuneration, and thus significantly improve their financial margin, with a consequent effect on profits and strengthening of capital.
9. On June 30, 2012, the impact of the results of the OIP on aggregate Core Tier 1 of the set of eight banking groups would lead to a slight revision of its value, from 11.2% to 11.1%, well above the minimum required of 9%.
10. This measure strengthened the level of capital imposed previously by the Bank of Portugal (Core Tier 1 of 8% by the end of 2011).
11. Of which €3,718 million resulted from assessment at market prices of sovereign debt exposures.
12. According to Law No. 63-A/2008, of November 24, 2008, the regime of Portuguese public capitalization is temporary, has a subsidiary role in reinforcing capital compared to the role of shareholders, and involves the commitment of institutions to strengthen their capitalization through market solutions.
13. The first institutions to use the line of capital were CGD, BCP, and BPI.
14. The so-called CoCo bonds (contingent convertible bonds), accepted by the European Banking Authority (EBA), are a debt security that converts immediately into equity when the level of Core Tier 1 of a bank falls below a certain level.
15. CGD (€900 million), BCP (€3,000 million), BPI (€1,500 million), and BANIF (€400 million).

Bibliography

Associação Portuguesa de Bancos (several years and several numbers) "Revista da Banca."

Augusto Mateus e Associados (2013) "A Economia, a Sociedade e os Fundos Estruturais – 25 Anos de Portugal Europeu,"Lisbon: Fundação Francisco Manuel dos Santos.
Banco de Portugal (2011) "Programa de Assistência Económica e Financeira – Medidas para assegurar a estabilidade do sistema bancário," Lisbon: Banco de Portugal.
Banco de Portugal (2013) "Comunicado – Programa de Inspecções On-Site à Exposição das Instituições Financeiras aos Sectores da Construção e Promoção Imobiliária," Lisbon: Banco de Portugal.
Banco de Portugal (several years)"Relatórios do Conselho de Administração."
BCP (2009, 2010, 2011, 2012) "Market Discipline," Porto: Banco Comercial Português.
BES (2009, 2010, 2011, 2012) "Market Discipline," Lisbon: Banco Espírito Santo.
BPI (2009, 2010, 2011, 2012) "Market Discipline," Porto: Banco Português de Investimento.
Cardoso, M. (2013) "O Impacto de Basileia III na Oferta de Crédito – O Caso dos Grupos CGD, BCP, BES, BPI, BST e BANIF," MA dissertation, Faculdade de Economia da Universidade do Porto.
CGD (2009, 2010, 2011, 2012) "Market Discipline," Lisbon: Caixa Geral de Depósitos.
Goleman, Daniel (2006) *Inteligência Social – a Nova Ciência das Relações Humanas*, Lisbon: Círculo dos Leitores. (Portuguese translation of *Social Intelligence*.)
Ministério das Finanças, Conselho para o Sistema Financeiro (1991) "Livro Branco sobre o Sistema Financeiro: 1992," Lisbon: Ministério das Finanças.
Sérgio, Anabela (2001) *Portuguese Financial Regulatory Reform: An Assessment*, London: British Library.

6

Performance and Efficiency of the Portuguese Banking System

Mário Coutinho dos Santos

The main purpose of this chapter is to examine accounting-based indicators of profitability, risk, and operating efficiency for the Portuguese banking system from 1993–2009, using a dataset drawn from the OECD's Banking Statistics – Financial Statements of Banks database.[1]

The empirical literature on banking performance and efficiency is typically based on cross-sectional and time-series samples of individual bank organizations. In this study, we investigate performance and efficiency at the banking system level during a relatively long sampling period, aiming at mitigating problems due to the comparability of data.[2]

During the past few decades, banking markets and institutions worldwide have faced a dynamic, demanding, and increasingly globally competitive environment, which was the catalyst for substantial transformation in their structure, nature, and behavior, fueled by powerful forces of market, regulatory, financial innovation, and technological change.[3] The Portuguese banking system was not immune to the significant and fast-paced transformations experienced by economies and markets across the world in the last few decades.[4] Joining the European Economic Community (EEC) was a major trigger for the Portuguese economy in general, and its financial and banking systems in particular, to experience a major structural readjustment.

At the macroeconomic level, Portugal faced the effects of the increasing integration of economies and markets, the global deregulatory trend, and restructuring pressures dictated by its admission to the EEC in 1986. Joining the third phase of Economic and Monetary Union (EMU) induced another major economic adjustment.

At the banking system level, Portugal might well have been one of the European countries that experienced more substantial pressure to readjust its competitive and operating banking model. However, the Portuguese banks seem to have been quite responsive in terms of accommodating increasingly open, integrated, and competitive banking markets. The privatization of formerly nationalized banks, the trends to financial system deregulation of the 1980s and 1990s, and the challenges of the European single market for financial services were among the major hurdles faced during this liberalization process.[5] These factors may well be at the very heart of the Portuguese banking system restructuring process, from regulatory and supervisory regimes, ownership and governance structures, corporate strategies, operating models, and balance sheet structures. Furthermore, during this period the Portuguese banking system also experienced a very active and dynamic market for corporate control, including privatizations, hostile takeovers, mergers and acquisitions, and other forms of corporate restructuring.[6]

At the outset of the 2007–08 financial crisis, the financial depth of the Portuguese banking system, measured by the assets carried on its balance sheets relative to gross domestic product (GDP), was 125.3%, indicating the size of the banking sector relative to the economy (see Table 6.1).[7]

Between 2007 and 2009 Portugal exhibited relatively stable financial depth, which was below the averages of the world, the European Union, and the euro area. In 2011, when Portugal entered an IMF/European Central Bank/European Commission financial assistance program, the size of the country's banking system relative to GDP rose by 116%, stabilizing well above those benchmarks.

From 1993 to 2009 the Portuguese banking sector grew in terms of both number of institutions and branches (see Table 6.2).

Overall, one may conclude that the Portuguese banking system during this period grew both by the acquisition of external growth and organically. In fact, the average number of branches per institution grew steadily, from 83.9 in 1993 to 136.3 in 2009.

The remainder of the chapter is organized as follows. The next section discusses the theoretical and empirical background of banking performance measurement. There is then a description of the empirical

Table 6.1 Bank assets as percentage of gross domestic product

	2007	2009	2011	2013
World	174.6	160.7	157.9	161.2
European Union	307.9	271.3	256.7	275.5
Euro area	287.2	233.0	223.4	251.6
Portugal	125.3	130.3	281.5	289.1

Source: International Monetary Fund (IMF) Global Financial Stability Reports.

Table 6.2 Structure of the Portuguese banking system

	Institutions	Branches
	Number	
1993	35	2936
1994	37	3155
1995	37	3447
1996	39	3766
1997	44	4121
1998	43	4307
1999	45	4735
2000	42	4895
2001	42	4804
2002	45	4714
2003	46	4754
2004	40	4606
2005	39	4736
2006	39	4896
2007	40	5279
2008	41	5565
2009	41	5588

Source: OECD Banking Statistics.

implementation used in this chapter, followed by an examination of the Portuguese banking system's profitability, risk, and operating performance.

Banking performance measurement: Theoretical and empirical background

The assessment of bank performance is a widespread practice among academics, the banking community, supervisors, regulators, deposit insurers, rating agencies, and financial analysts.[8] This research has generated a large body of theoretical and empirical academic and practitioner literature, devoted to the analysis of banking performance and efficiency.[9]

The theoretical and empirical literature on Portuguese banking performance and efficiency is relatively limited. In a succinct review of those prior research efforts we include:

- Martins and Ribeiro's estimation of a stochastic frontier model, using non-consolidated panel data for 22 banks operating in Portugal between 1995 and 2001.[10]

- Cabrita and Bontis using partial least squares structural equation modeling to investigate "the inter-relationships and interactions among intellectual capital components and business performance in the Portuguese banking industry."[11]
- Portela and Thanassoulis using data envelopment analysis (DEA) to document "positive links between operational and profit efficiency and also between transactional and operational efficiency. Service quality is positively related with operational and profit efficiency."[12]
- Barreto and Baden-Fuller investigating "Portuguese bank branching decisions between 1988 and 1996."[13]
- Mendes and Rebelo's empirical examination of "the structure–performance relationship in the Portuguese banking industry during the nineties."[14]
- Canhoto and Dermine's test of the hypothesis that "*de novo*" banks are likely to experience higher levels of operating efficiency than "established" banks, on a sample of 20 banks of the Portuguese domestic banking market, over the 1990–95 sampling period.[15]
- Results documenting that "new (*de novo*) domestic banks are more efficient than old (established) banks."[16]
- Pinho, who "uses accounting data to provide estimates of productive efficiency in Portuguese banking."[17]
- Mendes' consideration of the scale and scope economies in Portuguese commercial banking.[18]
- Alpalhão and Pinho's use of a dataset including financial statements data for a sample of Portuguese banks to conduct a ratio analysis spanning the 1980–89 period.[19]

Examples of recent research on banking performance and efficiency outside the Portuguese banking market include the following, among many others:

- Ferretti et al. analyzed a set of performance indicators using accounting data for a sample of Italian banks over the 1999–2010 period. Their analysis focused on earnings, efficiency, credit risk, capital adequacy, and stock market performance.[20]
- Dietrich and Wanzenried investigated the profitability of a panel dataset on 372 commercial Swiss banks over the period 1999–2009, finding that "profitability is, for the most part, explained by five factors: operational efficiency, the growth of total loans, funding costs, the business model, and the effective tax rate."[21]

- Albertazzi and Gambacorta used a dataset drawn from the OECD banking statistics database, over the 1981–2003 period, and including yearly balance sheet and income statement data for Austria, Belgium, France, Germany, Italy, the Netherlands, Portugal, Spain, the United Kingdom, and the United States, examining "how banks' activity is affected by the corporate income tax."[22]
- Albertazzi and Gambacorta also investigated the link between banking profitability and macroeconomic and financial shocks associated with the business cycle, using the same dataset drawn from the OECD banking statistics database, covering 1981–2003.[23]
- Bikker and Bos used a panel dataset for 46 countries, including European Union (EU), OECD, Eastern and Central European countries drawn from the BankScope database, to conduct an empirical examination of banking performance and efficiency during the 1996–2005 period, using different methodological approaches.[24]
- Loukoianova employed DEA to analyze the efficiency and profitability of Japanese banks during the 2000–06 period. Findings document that the overall performance of Japanese banks has been improving since 2001, despite differences within the banking sector; and that profitability is low relative to other advanced countries.[25]
- Goddard et al. examined "determinants of profitability in six major European banking sectors: Denmark, France, Germany, Italy, Spain and the UK, for the period 1992–98. Although there are some significant size–profit relationships in some of the estimations, overall the evidence for any consistent or systematic size–profitability relationship is unconvincing."[26]
- Santos conducted a principal components analysis of a sample of 54 Portuguese banks, using financial statement data published by the Portuguese Banks' Association (Associação Portuguesa de Bancos, APB) for a set of 21 banking performance indicators. Findings indicate that new (orthogonal) variables explained 80.1% of the variance in the dataset; the first principal component was associated with bank asset structure; the second with bank capital; the third with income tax; the fourth with profitability; and the fifth with credit risk.[27]
- Fries et al. examined the performance of a sample of 515 banks in Belarus, Bulgaria, Croatia, Czech Republic, Estonia, Macedonia, Hungary, Kazakhstan, Latvia, Lithuania, Poland, Romania, Russia, Slovak Republic, Slovenia, and Ukraine, using a dataset drawn from the BankScope database for the 1994–99 period.[28]

- Lozano-Vivas et al. used DEA to investigate bank performance and technical efficiency at the EU level, using both banking and environmental variables.[29]
- The findings of Resti's econometric and linear programming investigation into a panel of 270 Italian banks suggest that using those two methodological approaches does not yield significantly different results.[30]
- Molyneux and Forbes tested both the structure–conduct–performance (SCP) and the efficiency hypotheses using pooled and annual datafrom the European banking industry over the 1986–89 period. Their findings are consistent with SCP in explaining "the market behavior of European banks."[31]

Empirical implementation

Despite the availability of cross-sectional data on national banking systems, systematic cross-country comparative examination of banking systems performance and efficiency seems to have been somewhat under-researched, when compared to the body of research that has analyzed cross-sectional and time-series samples of individual banks.

In fact, the mainstream empirical literature on banking performance and efficiency mostly uses individual bank data, often drawn from Fitch IBCA's BankScope database. However, when the object of analysis is a banking system as a whole, using data on individual national banks does not seem a sound basis for making meaningful comparisons across national banking systems. Furthermore, differences in national accounting principles and practices, consolidation rules, reporting methods, tax codes, regulatory regimes, and statistical definitions make it difficult to compare banking statistics provided by national central banks. Therefore, the analysis of national banking system data may be problematic, and the interpretation of its results may be potentially misleading.

To conduct the empirical comparative analysis on the Portuguese banking system's performance and efficiency, we use a dataset drawn from the banking statistics published by the Organization for Economic Cooperation and Development (OECD).[32] These publications provide yearly financial statements data for the aggregated national banking sectors of member countries, harmonized to alleviate the problems typically associated with national differences in accounting, statistical definitions, and other sources of methodological concern.[33]

The criteria for the inclusion in the sample were being a European country and the availability of data on OECD bank statistics for most of the sampling period. The sample includes the following countries: Austria, Belgium, Denmark, Finland, France, Germany, Greece, Ireland, Italy, Luxembourg, the Netherlands, Norway, Poland, Portugal, Spain, Sweden, Switzerland, Turkey, and the United Kingdom. The sampling period was defined starting in 1993 and ending in 2009, the last year of data availability in the OECD banking statistics database.[34]

For Portugal, the coverage of the OECD's Bank Profitability statistics refers "to financial statements of all (universal) banks with their head-offices in national territory, and to some resident bank-like institutions. Subsidiaries of foreign banks are included. Excluded from these statistics are savings banks, mutual agricultural credit banks, branches of foreign banks and money market funds. Excluded are also data on non-monetary financial institutions: other financial intermediaries, financial auxiliaries, insurance companies and pension funds."[35]

Banking system profitability, risk, and operating performance analysis

Organizational performance measurement – particularly accounting performance measurement – has been for decades the object of an intense and ongoing debate in the academic and practitioner literatures.[36] Naturally, "a plethora of performance measurement frameworks and methodologies" has been developed and applied.[37]

Business performance measurement attempts to analyze how an organization is performing in terms of "the efficiency and effectiveness of past (business) action(s)."[38] Despite the fact that the approach has well-known caveats, in practice many organizations use accounting-based performance measures to "quantify the efficiency and/or effectiveness of past action(s),"meaning that accounting-based performance indicators are backward looking.[39]

Despite its scope and methodological implementation, an accounting-based banking system performance analysis should be conducted in a risk–return framework. Therefore, in this study we estimate accounting-based performance measures in terms of profitability, risk, and operating efficiency.[40]

Banking performance and efficiency research can be conducted at two levels: at the individual bank or groups of banks level; and at the banking system level. Because the object of this empirical performance examination is a banking system as a whole, understanding its relative performance compared to its cohorts tends to be more useful than the analysis of individual banks' financial statements. Consequently, we use a dataset drawn from the aggregated national banking sector financial statements of OECD member countries.

Portuguese banking system (comparative) profitability analysis

Following the mainstream accounting-based banking performance measurement literature, we use Return on Assets (ROA) and Return on Equity (ROE) as indicators to gauge banking system profitability. ROA is defined as Net Income divided by Total Assets, and provides an accounting measure of overall banking asset base profitability. ROE is defined as the quotient between Net Income and Equity, gauging the accounting profitability of the equity capital base (see Table 6.3).

Using the standard Du Pont decomposition analysis, ROA and ROE are computed as follows (see also Table 6.4):[41]

$$ROA = \frac{Net\ Income}{Total\ Assets} = \frac{Net\ Income}{Operating\ Income} \times \frac{Operating\ Income}{Total\ Assets}$$

ROE can be decomposed in terms of the product of ROA and the so-called leverage multiplier, which is the inverse of the capital ratio:

$$ROE = \frac{Net\ Income}{Equity} = \frac{Net\ Income}{Operating\ Income} \times \frac{Operating\ Income}{Total\ Assets} \times \frac{Total\ Assets}{Equity}.$$

To gauge the profitability performance condition of the banking systems included in our sample, we classified a banking system as "over performing" whenever its profitability/performance indicator was higher than the sample's banking system mean. We classified as "under leveraged" those banking systems whose Leverage Multiplier mean was lower than the sample's, and "over leveraged" when it was higher than the sample's.

On average, the profitability of the Portuguese banking system measured by ROA is below both the means of the countries included in the sample, which indicates that it is underperforming (see Figure 6.1).

Table 6.3 Profitability analysis indicators

Description	Definition
Profit margin	Net income/Operating income
Asset utilization	Operating income/Total assets
Leverage multiplier	Total assets/Equity capital
Return on assets (ROA)	Profit margin × Asset utilization
Return on equity (ROE)	Return on assets × Leverage multiplier

Table 6.4 Portuguese banking system ROA and ROE Du Pont analysis

	Profit margin	Asset utilization	Return on assets	Leverage multiplier	Return on equity
1993	0.064	0.107	0.007	10.549	0.073
1994	0.057	0.092	0.005	11.097	0.058
1995	0.056	0.090	0.005	12.156	0.061
1996	0.063	0.088	0.006	10.923	0.061
1997	0.084	0.078	0.006	11.152	0.072
1998	0.088	0.071	0.006	9.677	0.061
1999	0.106	0.060	0.006	9.315	0.059
2000	0.128	0.069	0.009	8.851	0.078
2001	0.093	0.069	0.006	8.459	0.054
2002	0.098	0.059	0.006	8.152	0.047
2003	0.106	0.056	0.006	8.195	0.049
2004	0.103	0.053	0.006	8.242	0.045
2005	0.094	0.060	0.006	9.354	0.053
2006	0.105	0.067	0.007	9.071	0.064
2007	0.093	0.074	0.007	9.573	0.066
2008	0.026	0.078	0.002	10.738	0.022
2009	0.051	0.057	0.003	10.213	0.030
Mean	0.083	0.072	0.006	9.748	0.056

Source: OECD Banking Statistics.

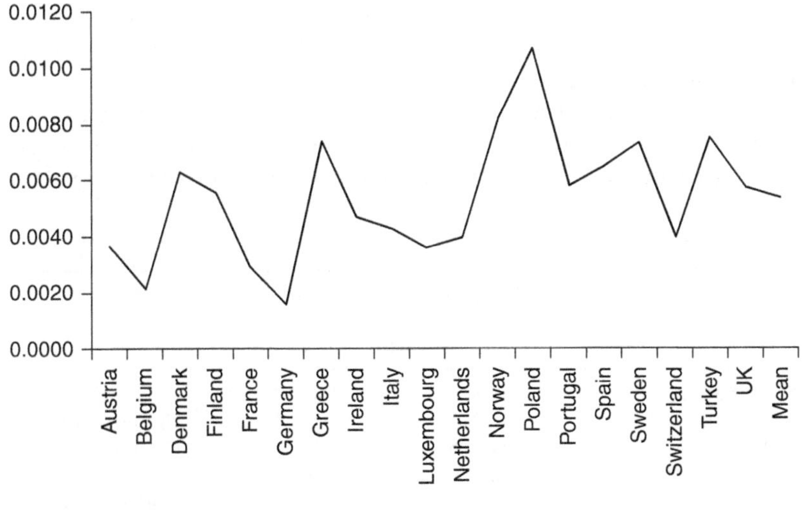

Figure 6.1 Return on assets (ROA)

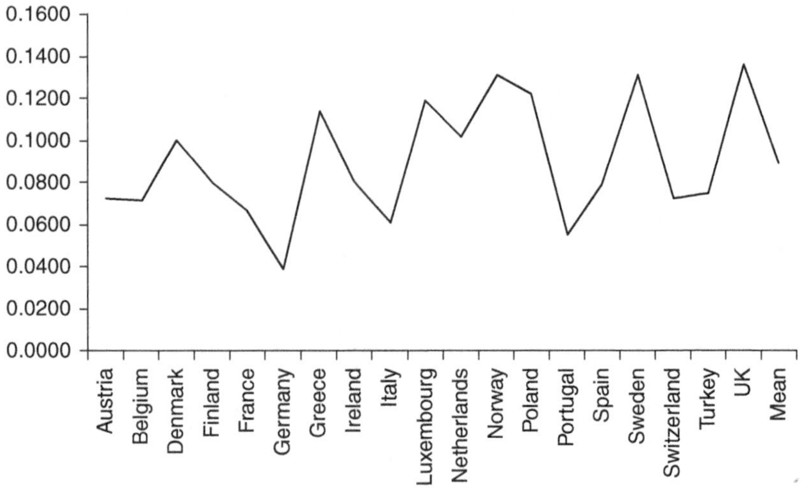

Figure 6.2 Return on equity (ROE)

When we decompose ROA as the product of Profit Margin and Asset Utilization, we find that the Portuguese banking system is also underperforming in terms of ROE because it is significantly less leveraged.

On average, the profitability of the banks in the Portuguese banking system measured by ROE is below the mean of the banking systems included in the sample, suggesting that, on average, they are underperforming relative to those (see Figure 6.2).

As shown in Table 6.5 and Figure 6.3, the ROE decomposition as the product of ROA and the Leverage Multiplier shows that the Portuguese banking system is underperforming in terms of ROE relative to the other

Table 6.5 Banking system profitability performance comparative analysis

	Portugal	Sample	
	(mean)		
Profit margin	0.0832	0.0795	Overperforming
Asset utilization	0.0723	0.0789	Underperforming
ROA	0.0058	0.0065	Underperforming
Leverage multiplier	9.7480	16.3775	Underleveraged
ROE	0.0560	0.1003	Underperforming

Source: OECD Banking Statistics.

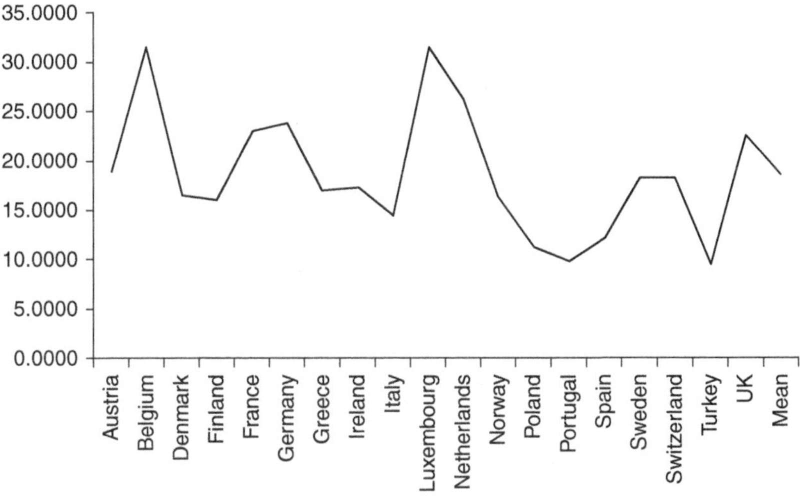

Figure 6.3 Leverage multiplier

banking systems, because it is significantly less leveraged, measured by the Leverage Multiplier, than its peers. Similar conclusions are reached using the median statistic.

In a risk–return framework approach, whenever bank profitability is analyzed using accounting-based metrics, such as ROA and ROE, that analysis should necessarily be contrasted with an accounting-based risk measure.

To measure the overall bank performance risk we resorted to an accounting-based indicator of risk that is known as Hannan and Hanweck's risk index (*RI*):

$$RI = \frac{E\,(ROA) + \frac{E}{A}}{\sigma_{ROA}},$$

where *E* (*ROA*) denotes the mean of return on assets, *E*/*A* is the capital ratio, and σ_{ROA} stands for the standard deviation of the return on assets.[42]

According to Hannan and Hanweck, the *RI* measures, in terms of units of ROA standard deviation, how much the accounting earnings can fall before becoming negative. Therefore, the lower the *RI* score, the riskier the bank (see Table 6.6).

According to our estimates, and based on Hannan and Hanweck's *RI* measure, the Portuguese banking system is the least risky of our sample,

Table 6.6 Hannan and Hanweck's *RI*

Banking system	***RI***
Austria	25.0
Belgium	7.0
Denmark	16.2
Finland	7.7
France	21.1
Germany	23.9
Greece	14.4
Ireland	8.0
Italy	31.8
Luxembourg	21.5
Netherlands	18.2
Norway	28.5
Poland	14.2
Portugal	71.0
Spain	51.9
Sweden	18.4
Switzerland	13.5
Turkey	3.7
UK	13.2
Mean	28.1

Source: OECD Banking Statistics.

Table 6.7 *RI* comparative analysis

	Portugal	**Sample**
E (ROA)	0.0058	0.0065
σ_{ROA}	0.0015	0.0023
E/A	0.1041	0.0588
Risk index	71.0	28.1

Source: OECD Banking Statistics.

exhibiting an *RI* score of 71.0, while the other banking systems sampled yielded an *RI* score of 28.1 (see Figure 6.4 and Table 6.7).

We also use the relative variability of ROA and ROE, measured by their coefficients of variation, to provide a comprehensive proxy of the overall Portuguese banking system risk exposure, since it reflects the effects of the risk portfolio that is embedded in the operating and net income, respectively.

Coefficient of variation estimates included in Table 6.8 show that both the Portuguese banking system's ROA and its ROE were significantly less

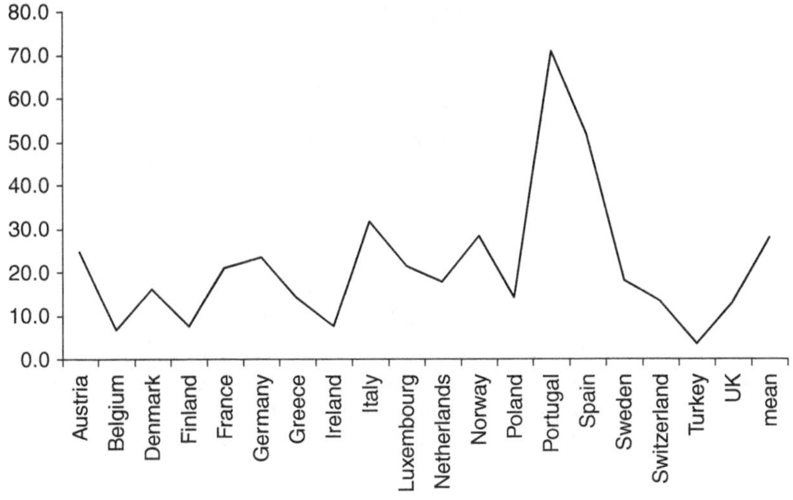

Figure 6.4 Hannan and Hanweck's Risk Index

Table 6.8 ROA and ROE coefficient of variation

	Portugal	Sample
ROA	0.2663	0.4243
ROE	0.2611	0.4797

Source: OECD Banking Statistics.

volatile than the sample's. Consequently, from that standpoint, during the 1993–2009 period the Portuguese banking system was less risky than the other banking systems included in the sample. This result is consistent with Hannan and Hanweck's risk index score, which also indicates that, on average, the riskiness of the Portuguese banking system was substantially lower than the other countries' banking systems.

Banking system risk analysis

In this banking system risk assessment we analyze measures of overall risk, liquidity risk, credit risk, and capital (solvency) risk.

As argued by Nikolaou, an "economic agent would have a preference over liquidity. In that sense, the probability of not being liquid would suggest that there is liquidity risk."[43] From this standpoint, banking liquidity risk can be rationalized as the probability of a bank finding itself

Table 6.9 Liquidity risk indicators

Description	Definition
Liquidity I	(Cash and balance with central bank + Net interbank deposits)/Total assets
Liquidity II	(Cash and balance with central bank + Interbank deposits)/Short-term liabilities

unable to meet the timely repayment of its short-term liabilities, or to refinance the assets it holds on its balance sheet. In other words, liquidity risk is closely associated with the diminished, actual or potential, ability of a bank autonomously to ensure the (re)financing of its assets and in meeting the financial obligations of its liabilities, as they fall due. To analyze the liquidity risk we estimated the measures included in Table 6.9.

According to the BIS definition,"credit risk is most simply defined as the potential that a bank borrower or counter party will fail to meet its obligations in accordance with agreed terms."[44] Thus, credit risk refers to the likelihood that a borrower will default on his or her obligations to pay principal and interest in a timely manner. To measure credit risk we estimated the indicator included in Table 6.10.

To analyze the relative capital (solvency) risk condition of the Portuguese banking system, we computed the ratios in Table 6.11.

Table 6.10 Credit risk indicator

Description	Definition
Credit risk	Provisions on loans/Loans

Table 6.11 Capital risk indicators

Description	Definition
Capital ratio	Equity capital/Total assets
Capital regulatory ratio	Total regulatory capital/Total risk weighted assets
Implicit risk weight	Total regulatory capital/(Total assets × Capital regulatory ratio)
Implicit risk weight variation	(Implicit risk weight$_t$/Implicit risk weight$_{t-1}$) − 1
Tier 1 variation	(Tier 1$_t$/Tier 1$_{t-1}$) − 1

Table 6.12 Portuguese banking system risk analysis

	Liquidity risk I	Liquidity risk II	Credit risk	Capital ratio	Capital regulatory ratio	Implicit risk weight
1993	0.276	0.370	0.027	0.095	0.125	0.449
1994	0.291	0.394	0.019	0.090	0.128	0.434
1995	0.304	0.398	0.013	0.082	0.113	0.442
1996	0.351	0.413	0.013	0.092	0.111	0.500
1997	0.379	0.462	0.011	0.090	0.106	0.512
1998	0.353	0.436	0.012	0.103	0.124	0.525
1999	0.320	0.402	0.009	0.107	0.118	0.560
2000	0.258	0.333	0.008	0.113	0.107	0.630
2001	0.255	0.338	0.005	0.118	0.118	0.630
2002	0.240	0.325	0.005	0.123	0.120	0.644
2003	0.259	0.365	0.010	0.122	0.120	0.637
2004	0.205	0.295	0.009	0.121	0.119	0.677
2005	0.193	0.279	0.009	0.107	0.117	0.669
2006	0.199	0.287	0.008	0.110	0.114	0.658
2007	0.188	0.283	0.007	0.104	0.111	0.696
2008	0.159	0.252	0.013	0.093	0.119	0.593
2009	0.156	0.260	0.012	0.098	0.138	0.567
Mean	0.258	0.347	0.011	0.104	0.118	0.578

Source: OECD Banking Statistics.

Using both proxies of the liquidity risk – [(Cash and balance with Central bank + Interbank deposits)/Total Assets]; and [(Cash and balance with Central bank + Interbank deposits)/Short term liabilities] – the Portuguese banking system, over the 1993–2009 period, was less exposed to the liquidity risk, using the mean statistic, than its sample peers (see Table 6.12).

To assess the exposure to credit risk, we estimated the ratio of Provisions on loans to Loans.

The economic value of the equity capital of a bank is the difference between its assets and liabilities, both valued marked to market. The amount of capital that banks carry on their balance sheets, and the functions that it plays in banking, have been thoroughly debated in the literature.[45] In summary, the economic functions of bank capital include serving as:

- a guarantee of financial independence, and to some extent to allow easier and less costly access to debt financing;
- co-funding of a bank's growth, and therefore its competitive strategy implementation;

- a reassurance to creditors of the value of their claims;
- a buffer for potential losses in particularly adverse conditions, as may be the case in a severe economic cycle downturn.[46]

A bank's risk of capital, also designated solvency risk, translates the potential reduction on the net asset value before the economic value of capital reaches nil. Alternatively, the risk of solvency can be defined by the probability of the bank becoming economically insolvent, meaning exhibiting a negative equity capital.

Just like in any non-financial firm, a bank's risk of capital is closely related to its level of financial leverage.[47] Therefore, we should expect that a bank with a low capital ratio should, *ceteris paribus*, exhibit a high financial risk, and bear a high cost of capital.

Bank capitalization conditions can be evaluated under different approaches: accounting based, market based, and regulatory based. The accounting-based capital ratio – equity capital to total net assets – measures a bank's capacity to absorb unforeseen losses. In abstract, an excessively high capital ratio may indicate that a bank could be overcapitalized in comparison to an appropriate benchmark. Because the cost of equity capital is higher than the cost of debt, that bank would have a higher cost of capital.

There is abundant and compelling empirical evidence documenting that firms' leverage ratio exhibits a mean reverting pattern; and specific industries have an average leverage ratio that tends to be relatively stable over time.[48] Therefore, the mean leverage ratio of an industry is often rationalized as a proxy for an industry preferred/target leverage ratio.

To analyze the capital base condition of the banking systems in our sample, we classified a banking system as "Overcapitalized" when its capital ratio mean was higher than the sample banking system capital ratio mean. We classified as "Undercapitalized" those banking systems whose capital ratio mean was lower than the industry's average capital ratio.

Table 6.13 exhibits the capital ratio for the Portuguese banking system during the sampling period.

Table 6.13 and Figure 6.5 show that, in terms of capital book value, the Portuguese banking system experienced a sustained buildup in its capital ratio between 1995 and 2004. From 2005 to 2007, the capital ratio dropped to approximately the sampling period average. Coinciding with the 2008 financial crisis the ratio dropped even further, to a level not too different from the one registered in 1993.

Table 6.13 Capital ratio of the Portuguese banking system

1993	0.0948
1994	0.0901
1995	0.0823
1996	0.0916
1997	0.0897
1998	0.1033
1999	0.1074
2000	0.1130
2001	0.1182
2002	0.1227
2003	0.1220
2004	0.1213
2005	0.1069
2006	0.1102
2007	0.1045
2008	0.0931
2009	0.0979
Mean	0.1041

Source: OECD Banking Statistics.

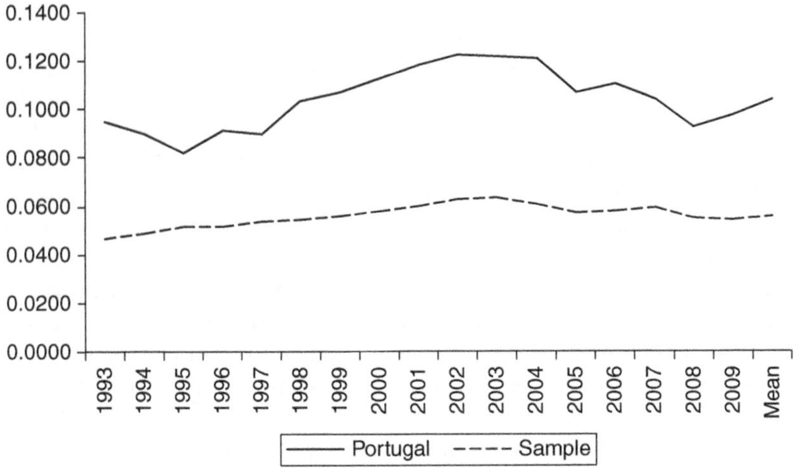

Figure 6.5 Capital ratio

The mean of the capital ratio for the sampled banking systems during the sampling period is 5.6%, and for Portugal it is 10.4%. Using the capital ratio as the yardstick to gauge a banking system's capitalization condition, we found that during the 1993–2009 period, the Portuguese banking system, on average, exhibited a capital ratio 77% above the sample mean. This finding suggests that, on average, the Portuguese banking system was overcapitalized when compared with the sample's mean capital ratio.

Therefore, one might expect a buildup in banks' capital base to comply with the new capital standards (fully enforced by 1992), and consequently a rise in the capital ratio. Additionally, we might also conjecture that we should expect bank capital to pile up in preparation for the governmental privatization program, by that time well underway.

According to our estimate, the average capital ratio peaked in 1991; that is, around the period when capital adequacy standards were imposed following the 1988 Basel Accord. One potential explanation for this phenomenon may be related to Wall and Peterson's hypothesis that the mandatory primary capital requirements enforced by US bank regulators in 1981 influenced changes in large bank holding companies in the three subsequent years.[49]

Capital ratio variability measured by the standard deviation for the Portuguese banking system is higher than the average (see Table 6.14). A plausible explanation for this stylized fact may be related to the fact that a number of *de novo* banks were incorporated in Portugal during the sampling period, whose financial performance is likely to be more volatile than that of their established peers.[50]

It is widely accepted that in a leveraged equity holder limited liability framework, a bank's residual claimants have a call option on the bank's underlying assets.[51] Because the value of a call is positively related to the increases in the volatility of the underlying asset, bank owners have an incentive for morally hazardous opportunistic behavior, taking in excessive and inefficient risk, either in the form of claim dilution or asset substitution.[52]

Governments worldwide guarantee (or insure) banking deposits to protect depositors' claims against banks' excessive risk taking.[53] However, an inefficiently priced deposit insurance premium, meaning one insensitive to banks'asset riskiness, creates an incentive for banks to take in potentially inefficient risk, aiming at maximizing the value of the put-option subsidy on the inefficiently priced deposit insurance.[54]

Because insured depositors can only imperfectly monitor bank owners' actions, these can increase the value of their call option by increasing the riskiness of the bank's underlying assets. A bank's uninsured depositors and other creditors have an incentive to monitor the bank's risk-taking actions, although demanding a higher return on their claims. Thus, *ceteris paribus*, the higher the incentives for equity holders to

Table 6.14 Capital ratio across banking systems

Banking system	Mean	Leverage condition
Austria	0.0477	Undercapitalized
Belgium	0.0329	Undercapitalized
Denmark	0.0609	Overcapitalized
Finland	0.0682	Overcapitalized
France	0.0438	Undercapitalized
Germany	0.0421	Undercapitalized
Greece	0.0629	Overcapitalized
Ireland	0.0473	Undercapitalized
Italy	0.0702	Overcapitalized
Luxembourg	0.0299	Undercapitalized
Netherlands	0.0390	Undercapitalized
Norway	0.0622	Overcapitalized
Poland	0.0901	Overcapitalized
Portugal	0.1041	Overcapitalized
Spain	0.0827	Overcapitalized
Sweden	0.0555	Undercapitalized
Switzerland	0.0557	Undercapitalized
Turkey	0.0812	Overcapitalized
UK	0.0401	Undercapitalized
Mean	0.0588	

Source: OECD Banking Statistics.

transfer wealth for their own benefit, at depositors' and other debt holders' expense, the lower should be the bank's financial leverage, and the higher its capital ratio. Consequently, in banking systems where public deposit insurance is priced insensitively to asset risk, a bank's owners are provided with a distortionary incentive to increase the bank's riskiness.[55] In this case, the banking firm is encouraged to leverage up because of the advantageous cost of deposit funding due to the subsidy granted by public deposit insurers at taxpayers' expense. Instead of using their own financing or risk-sensitive debt financing to fund bank growth, shareholders are very likely to use deposit financing, further enhancing the probability of potentially disruptive and costly insolvency.

Led by the UK and US example in 1981, and under the jurisdiction of the Bank for International Settlements, in 1988 a group of countries, known as the G10, formally adopted the Basel Accord, establishing the first formal banking capital adequacy standard. The regulatory risk-based bank capital adequacy requirements introduced an explicit relationship between bank capital and risk, establishing a mandatory minimum capital regulatory ratio, and making the regulatory capital

Table 6.15 Capital regulatory ratio

Banking system	Mean	Leverage condition
Austria	0.1367	Overcapitalized
Belgium	0.1465	Overcapitalized
Greece	0.1063	Undercapitalized
Ireland	0.1229	Undercapitalized
Italy	0.1363	Overcapitalized
Netherlands	0.1143	Undercapitalized
Norway	0.1249	Overcapitalized
Poland	0.1290	Overcapitalized
Portugal	0.1181	Undercapitalized
Spain	0.0771	Undercapitalized
Sweden	0.1881	Overcapitalized
Switzerland	0.0984	Undercapitalized
Turkey	0.1337	Overcapitalized
UK	0.0962	Undercapitalized
Mean	0.1235	

Source: OECD Banking Statistics.

base (Tier 1 and Tier 2) responsive to changes in banks' portfolio exposure to credit risk.[56]

The capital regulatory ratio was computed as:

$$Capital\ Regulatory\ ratio = \frac{Total\ regulatory\ capital\ (= Tier1 + Tier2)}{Total\ risk\ weighted\ assets}$$

Table 6.15 includes the capital regulatory ratio, computed using the data in our sample.[57]

According to the mean of the capital regulatory ratios included in Table 6.15, over the period 1993–2009 the banking systems of Greece, Ireland, the Netherlands, Portugal, Spain, Switzerland, and the UK evidence mean capital regulatory ratios below the sample's average, and therefore the banking systems of those countries could be considered to be undercapitalized.[58]

To summarize, using the capital regulatory ratio to measure the banking system's average capital adequacy, we found that during the sampling period, the capital regulatory ratio for the Portuguese banking system was for most of the time below the mean of the other sampled banking systems, and consequently, from this standpoint, could be considered as undercapitalized (Figure 6.6). Figure 6.7 compares the capital ratio to the capital regulatory ratio.

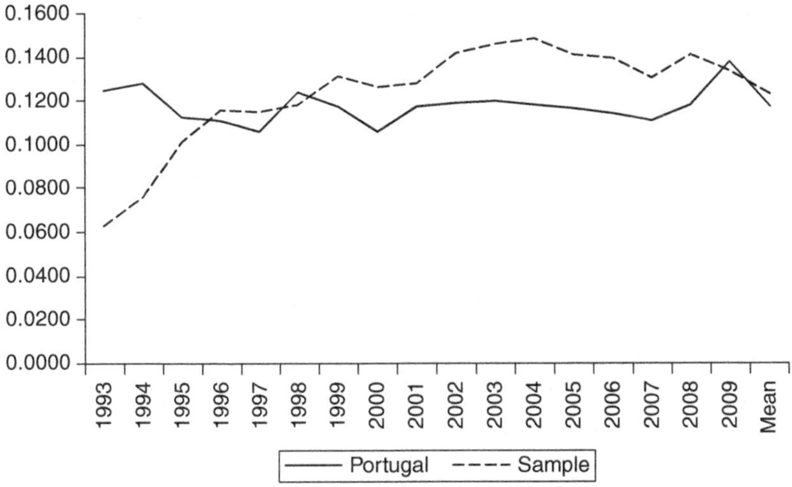

Figure 6.6 Capital regulatory ratio

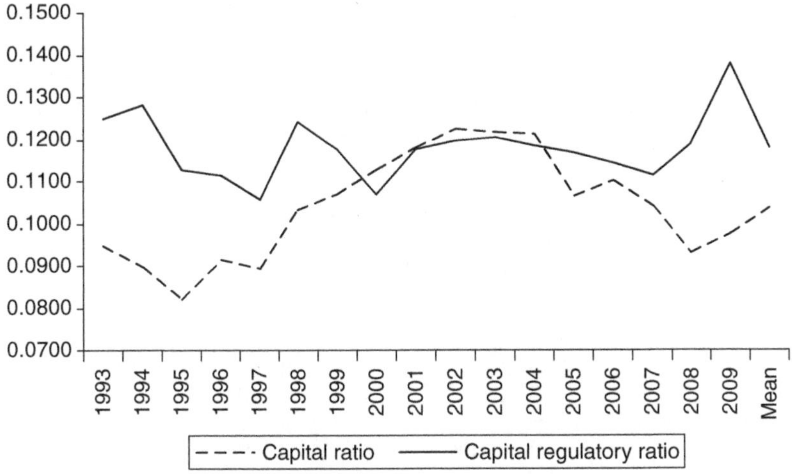

Figure 6.7 Capital ratio vs. capital regulatory ratio

Under a binding capital adequacy standard in the form of a capital regulatory ratio – such as the Basel Capital Accord – a value-maximizing bank has incentives to reduce the riskiness of its overall asset portfolio, to try to avoid issuing additional costly regulatory capital to comply with capital adequacy regulatory requirements.[59] Under binding international risk-based capital requirements, a bank will have an incentive to increase the regulatory capital ratio numerator by issuing new internal and/or external regulatory capital, following a rise in its risk-weighted asset base.

According to this rationale, we should expect a positive correlation between annual changes in regulatory capital and annual changes in the "implicit risk weight," estimated as:

$$\frac{\textit{Total regulatory capital}}{\textit{Total Assets} \times \textit{Capital regulatory ratio}}.$$

Table 6.16 includes the implicit risk weight estimates.

The average implicit risk weight estimated for the banking systems sample is 0.4409, and for Portugal 0.5778.[60]

Table 6.17 includes the average annual percentage change in the riskiness of Portuguese banking system assets, measured by the average implicit risk weight, and the average annual percentage change in regulatory capital. Examination of Figure 6.8 suggests a pattern of weak correlation between changes in the average implicit risk weight and changes in regulatory capital.

The linear association of the two variables, measured by Pearson's correlation, yields a weak correlation coefficient of $r = 0.00194$ and $r = 0.00054$, for contemporaneous and one-year lagged correlations,

Table 6.16 Implicit risk weight

Banking system	Mean
Austria	0.3938
Belgium	0.2605
Greece	0.4698
Ireland	0.4103
Italy	0.5702
Netherlands	0.4608
Norway	0.6277
Poland	0.5483
Portugal	0.5778
Spain	0.4607
Sweden	0.4002
Switzerland	0.3953
Turkey	0.5016
UK	0.0962
Mean	0.4409

Source: OECD Banking Statistics.

Table 6.17 Portuguese banking system implicit risk weight

	Implicit risk weight change	Regulatory capital change
1994	−3.19%	12.78%
1995	1.75%	−0.95%
1996	13.12%	16.47%
1997	2.49%	14.35%
1998	2.50%	34.94%
1999	6.68%	15.36%
2000	12.52%	10.61%
2001	−0.02%	19.33%
2002	2.18%	6.18%
2003	−1.12%	6.57%
2004	6.24%	1.00%
2005	−1.17%	5.38%
2006	−1.64%	4.31%
2007	5.84%	14.91%
2008	−14.78%	0.39%
2009	−4.44%	18.27%

Source: OECD Banking Statistics.

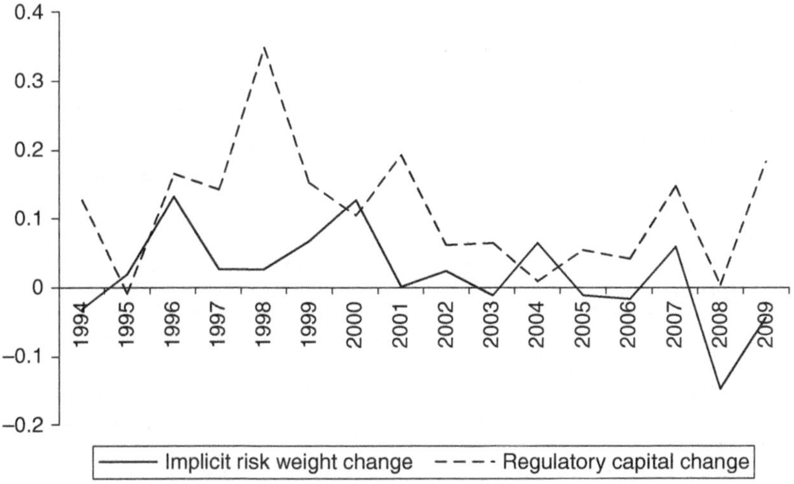

Figure 6.8 Implicit risk weight vs. regulatory capital

respectively.[61] This evidence for the Portuguese banking system is not consistent with the hypothesis that changes in the average implicit risk weight (a proxy of the riskiness of the overall asset base) should be correlated with the average annual percentage change in regulatory capital.

This apparently anomalous finding may be explained by the use of regulatory capital arbitrage techniques, such as that "securitization and other financial innovations have provided unprecedented opportunities for banks to reduce substantially their regulatory capital requirements with little or no corresponding reduction in their overall economic risks."[62]

Banking system operating performance and efficiency analysis

To gauge the accounting-based operating efficiency of the banking systems included in our sample, we estimated the indicators detailed in Table 6.18, with the results shown in Table 6.19.

To compare the efficiency condition of the Portuguese banking system to the peers included in the sample, in relation to each of the estimated indicators, we compared the estimated mean for the Portuguese banking system with the same statistic for the sample. A "more efficient" score was assigned whenever the difference between the means for Portugal and the sample was positive and a "less efficient" score whenever that difference was negative. Table 6.20 documents that the Portuguese banking system, during the 1993–2009 period, was only less efficient than its peers included in the sample in terms of asset–liability management, measured by the Interest Expenses to Total Assets and the Interest Expenses to Total Liabilities indicators.

Corporate income tax liability is an important dimension of banks' performance. Although banks are not prototypical taxpayers, both theoretical and empirical research suggests that they design tax policies and manage their tax liability so as to adjust "their economic balance sheets as their tax-paying status" changes. Other symptoms appear to

Table 6.18 Efficiency indicators

Description	Definition
Operating Income to Total Assets	Operating income/Total assets
Interest Income to Total Assets	Interest income/Total assets
Cost to Income	Operating expenses/Total income
Operating Expenses to Operating Income	Operating expenses/Operating income
Operating Expenses to Total Assets	Operating expenses/Total assets
Interest Expenses to Total Assets	Interest expenses/Total assets
Interest Expenses to Total Liabilities	Interest expenses/Total liabilities
Net Interest Margin	Net interest income/Total assets
Staff Costs to Operating Income	Staff costs/Operating income
Staff Costs to Operating Expenses	Staff costs/Operating expenses

Table 6.19 Portuguese banking system operating efficiency analysis

	Operating income to total assets	Interest income to total assets	Cost to income	Operating expenses to total assets	Interest expenses to total assets	Interest expenses to total liabilities	Staff costs to operating income	Staff costs to operating expenses	Income tax to earnings before taxes
1993	0.107	0.098	0.196	0.021	0.070	0.077	0.110	0.560	0.211
1994	0.092	0.085	0.212	0.019	0.060	0.066	0.118	0.556	0.214
1995	0.090	0.083	0.211	0.019	0.061	0.066	0.117	0.557	0.204
1996	0.088	0.079	0.224	0.020	0.058	0.063	0.122	0.544	0.208
1997	0.078	0.068	0.234	0.018	0.047	0.052	0.128	0.549	0.203
1998	0.071	0.060	0.238	0.017	0.041	0.045	0.123	0.517	0.199
1999	0.060	0.051	0.268	0.016	0.032	0.036	0.136	0.508	0.146
2000	0.069	0.060	0.229	0.016	0.042	0.048	0.117	0.511	0.117
2001	0.069	0.062	0.211	0.015	0.044	0.049	0.101	0.480	0.142
2002	0.059	0.052	0.254	0.015	0.035	0.039	0.120	0.473	0.121
2003	0.056	0.046	0.250	0.014	0.030	0.034	0.120	0.480	0.124
2004	0.053	0.044	0.264	0.014	0.028	0.032	0.122	0.464	0.081
2005	0.060	0.047	0.289	0.017	0.031	0.035	0.131	0.455	0.101
2006	0.067	0.054	0.243	0.016	0.037	0.042	0.122	0.501	0.178
2007	0.074	0.062	0.211	0.016	0.046	0.051	0.102	0.484	0.175
2008	0.078	0.069	0.183	0.014	0.052	0.057	0.087	0.477	0.382
2009	0.057	0.046	0.246	0.014	0.032	0.036	0.115	0.466	0.152
Mean	0.072	0.063	0.233	0.017	0.044	0.049	0.117	0.505	0.174

Source: OECD Banking Statistics.

Table 6.20 Operating efficiency comparative analysis

	Portugal	Sample	Efficiency condition
Operating Income to Total Assets	0.0723	0.0712	More efficient
Interest Income to Total Assets	0.0627	0.0612	More efficient
Cost to Income	0.5809	0.6606	More efficient
Operating Expenses to Operating Income	0.2331	0.2481	More efficient
Operating Expenses to Total Assets	0.2228	0.2367	More efficient
Interest Expenses to Total Assets	0.0438	0.0428	Less efficient
Interest Expenses to Total Liabilities	0.0488	0.0456	Less efficient
Net Interest Margin	0.0189	0.0184	More efficient
Staff Costs to Operating Income	0.1172	0.1274	More efficient
Staff Costs to Operating Expenses	0.5048	0.5119	More efficient

Source: OECD Banking Statistics.

reinforce the notion that banks, either in aggregate or at an individual level, seem to accommodate themselves to modifications in the tax regime.[63]

Osterberg and Thompson examined the impact of regulatory capital standards on leverage ratios for a sample of 232 US bank holding companies in 1986 and 1987, documenting that municipal securities portfolios seemed to be being used to minimize their tax liability.[64] Scholes et al. also report strong evidence showing that banks respond to changes in the tax rules related to the income tax deductibility of interest expense incurred by investing in MUNIs, by adjusting their portfolios of this type of bonds.[65]

More recently, Albertazzi and Gambacorta investigated the relationship between banking profitability and taxation, using a dataset for the banking systems of a sample of countries (including Portugal), drawn from the OECD banking profitability database, over the 1981–2003 period. Their findings indicate that banks' income taxes are strongly related to banking revenues; and that, because of their financial intermediation functions, banks may be able to manage their income tax liability, and therefore "differences in the level of taxation cannot explain the dispersion observed in banks' net profitability across... countries."[66]

To assess the income-tax-paying status of the banking systems included in our sample, we computed the implicit tax rate as the quotient between income tax and earnings before taxes (see Figure 6.9 and Table 6.21).[67]

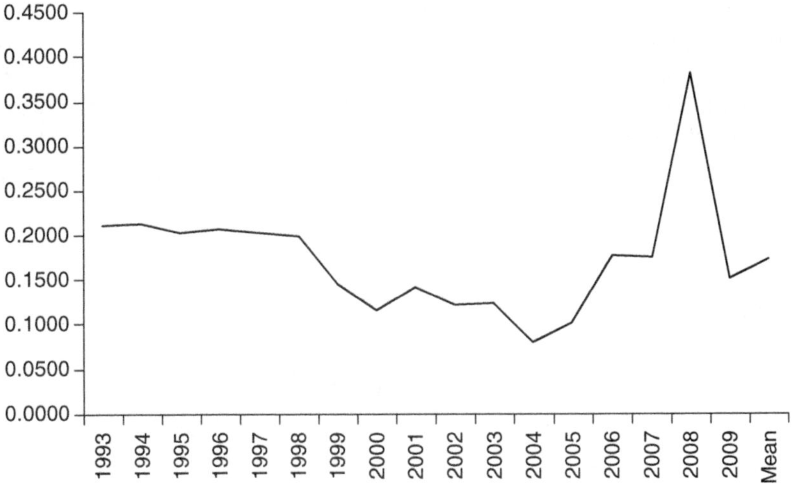

Figure 6.9 Implicit income tax rate, Portugal

Table 6.21 Implicit income tax rate

Banking system	Median	Taxation condition
Austria	0.1174	Undertaxed
Belgium	0.1804	Undertaxed
Denmark	0.1929	Undertaxed
Finland	0.1362	Undertaxed
France	0.1952	Undertaxed
Germany	0.4131	Overtaxed
Greece	0.2855	Overtaxed
Ireland	0.1981	Undertaxed
Italy	0.3790	Overtaxed
Luxembourg	0.2298	Overtaxed
Netherlands	0.2667	Overtaxed
Norway	0.2280	Overtaxed
Poland	0.3097	Overtaxed
Portugal	0.1755	Undertaxed
Spain	0.1924	Undertaxed
Sweden	0.2243	Overtaxed
Switzerland	0.1738	Undertaxed
Turkey	0.1993	Undertaxed
UK	0.3032	Overtaxed
Median	0.1993	

Source: OECD Banking Statistics.

From 1993 to 2009, the median implicit tax rate estimated for the Portuguese banking system is 17.55% (mean 17.40%). This result indicates that Portuguese banks during the sampling period were"undertaxed"relatively to their sample peers, based on the sample's median implicit tax rate (19.93%); sees Figure 6.10 and 6.11. These findings are in line with those of Santos who, using data from the

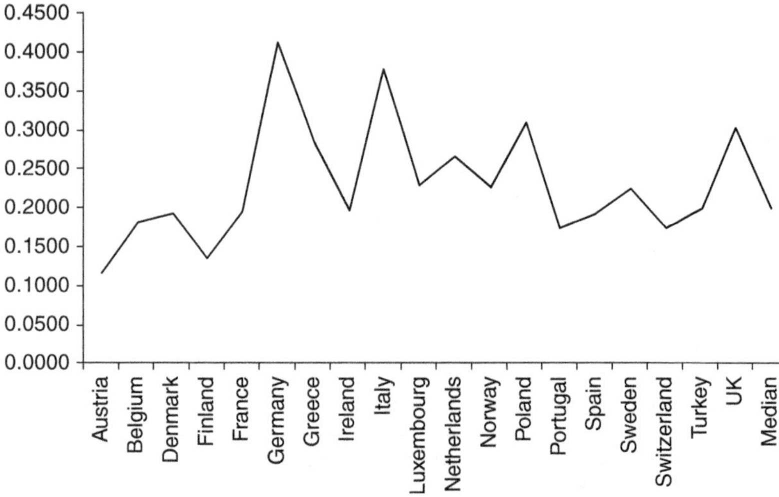

Figure 6.10 Implicit income tax rate, EU countries

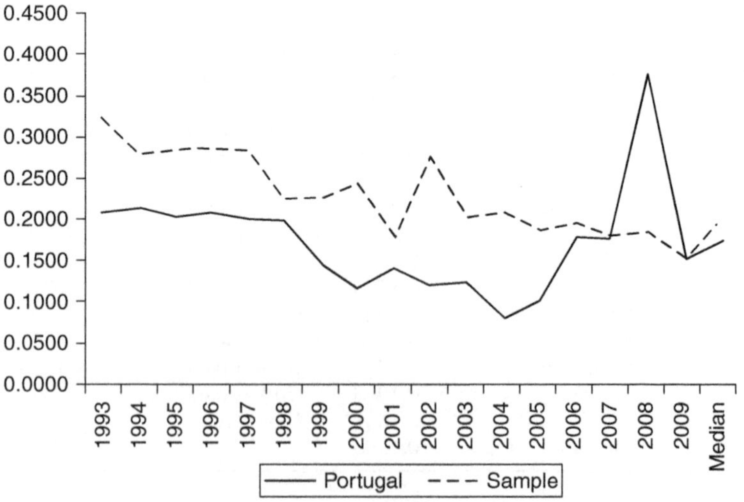

Figure 6.11 Implicit income tax rates compared

Portuguese Banks' Association (APB), estimated an average implicit tax rate of 18.48% (simple average), and 20.4% (net total assets weighted average) over the 1989–98 period.[68]

Acknowledgments

Jorge Mota's helpful research assistance is gratefully acknowledged. Any remaining errors are my own.

Appendix 6.1 Sample scope, data availability, and missing data

Country	Scope	Data availability	Missing data
Austria	All banks	1994–2008	For the capital regulatory ratio, variables in 1993.
Belgium	All banks	1993–2009	
Denmark	All banks	1993–2009	For the capital regulatory ratio, variables from 1993 to 2009.
Finland	All banks		(i) For the capital regulatory ratio, variables from 1993 to 2009; and (ii) from 1993 to 1998 Net provisions was used instead of Provisions on loans.
France	All banks		(i) For the capital regulatory ratio, variables from 1993 to 2009; (ii) for Staff costs and Other operating expenses from 2000 to 2009; and (iii) from 1993 to 2009 Net provisions was used instead of Provisions on loans.
Germany	All banks		For the capital regulatory ratio, variables from 1993 to 2009.
Greece	Commercial banks		For the capital regulatory ratio, variables from 1993 to 1995.
Ireland	All banks	1995–2009	
Italy	All banks		
Luxembourg	All banks	1993–2008	From 1993 to 2009 Net provisions was used instead of Provisions on loans.
Netherlands	All banks		
Norway	All banks		
Poland	All banks		
Portugal	Commercial banks		

Appendix 6.1 (Continued)

Country	Scope	Data availability	Missing data
Spain	All banks		For the capital regulatory ratio, variables from 1993 to 1998.
Sweden	Commercial banks		Net provisions was used instead of Provisions on loans from 1993 to 2009.
Switzerland	All banks		(i) For the Total regulatory capital in 2007; and (ii) Net provisions was used instead of Provisions on loans from 1993 to 2009.
Turkey	Commercial banks	1996–2009	
UK	Large commercial banks	1993–2008	For capital regulatory ratio, variables in 1993 and 1994.

Appendix 6.2 ROA decomposition: Profit margin × Asset utilization

Profit margin

Banking system	Mean	Median	Performance condition	
Austria	0.0669	0.0671	Underperforming	Underperforming
Belgium	0.0216	0.0379	Underperforming	Underperforming
Denmark	0.1107	0.1282	Overperforming	Overperforming
Finland	0.1296	0.1587	Overperforming	Overperforming
France	0.0515	0.0602	Underperforming	Underperforming
Germany	0.0261	0.0363	Underperforming	Underperforming
Greece	0.0859	0.0684	Overperforming	Underperforming
Ireland	0.0674	0.1238	Underperforming	Overperforming
Italy	0.0812	0.0906	Underperforming	Underperforming
Luxembourg	0.0531	0.0507	Underperforming	Underperforming
Netherlands	0.0609	0.0678	Underperforming	Underperforming
Norway	0.1238	0.1281	Overperforming	Overperforming
Poland	0.1053	0.1083	Overperforming	Overperforming
Portugal	0.0832	0.0925	Overperforming	Underperforming
Spain	0.1152	0.1186	Overperforming	Overperforming
Sweden	0.1355	0.1195	Overperforming	Overperforming
Switzerland	0.0764	0.0891	Underperforming	Underperforming
Turkey	0.0614	0.0949	Underperforming	Overperforming
UK	0.0937	0.1157	Overperforming	Overperforming
Mean	0.0816			
Median		0.0925		

Asset utilization

Banking system	Mean	Median	Performance condition	
Austria	0.0542	0.0551	Underperforming	Underperforming
Belgium	0.0773	0.0823	Overperforming	Overperforming
Denmark	0.0592	0.0584	Underperforming	Underperforming
Finland	0.0553	0.0515	Underperforming	Underperforming
France	0.0647	0.0657	Underperforming	Overperforming
Germany	0.0569	0.0567	Underperforming	Underperforming
Greece	0.0873	0.0716	Overperforming	Overperforming
Ireland	0.0480	0.0456	Underperforming	Underperforming
Italy	0.0611	0.0552	Underperforming	Underperforming
Luxembourg	0.0662	0.0704	Underperforming	Overperforming
Netherlands	0.0659	0.0683	Underperforming	Overperforming
Norway	0.0691	0.0730	Underperforming	Overperforming
Poland	0.1183	0.1239	Overperforming	Overperforming
Portugal	0.0723	0.0692	Overperforming	Overperforming
Spain	0.0630	0.0570	Underperforming	Underperforming
Sweden	0.0619	0.0598	Underperforming	Underperforming
Switzerland	0.0526	0.0513	Underperforming	Underperforming
Turkey	0.1664	0.1398	Overperforming	Overperforming
UK	0.0534	0.0582	Underperforming	Underperforming
Mean	0.0712			
Median		0.0598		

Appendix 6.3 Liquidity risk indicators

Liquidity risk I

Banking system	Mean	Median
Austria	0.2863	0.3024
Belgium	0.2669	0.2622
Denmark	0.2083	0.2171
Finland	0.1479	0.0855
France	0.3318	0.3193
Germany	0.2365	0.2368
Greece	0.2177	0.2161
Ireland	0.1457	0.1609
Italy	0.1119	0.1135
Luxembourg	0.5009	0.5232
Netherlands	0.1469	0.1375
Norway	0.0678	0.0630
Poland	0.1981	0.2093
Portugal	0.2580	0.2576
Spain	0.1663	0.1637

Appendix 6.3 (Continued)

Liquidity risk I

Banking system	Mean	Median
Sweden	0.2203	0.2090
Switzerland	0.2528	0.2569
Turkey	0.1013	0.0989
UK	0.0967	0.0966
Mean	0.2085	
Median		0.2093

Liquidity risk II

Banking system	Mean	Median
Austria	0.4190	0.4326
Belgium	0.3621	0.3397
Denmark	0.3093	0.3053
Finland	0.2888	0.1657
France	0.5212	0.5002
Germany	0.3286	0.3274
Greece	0.2774	0.3005
Ireland	0.2378	0.2482
Italy	0.2896	0.2751
Luxembourg	0.6205	0.6542
Netherlands	0.2203	0.2122
Norway	0.1038	0.0955
Poland	0.2817	0.2915
Portugal	0.3465	0.3383
Spain	0.2320	0.2195
Sweden	0.3490	0.3129
Switzerland	0.3620	0.3730
Turkey	0.1302	0.1345
UK	0.1600	0.1612
Mean	0.3074	
Median		0.3005

Appendix 6.4 Credit risk

Banking system	Mean	Median
Austria	0.0072	0.0075
Belgium	0.0030	0.0029
Denmark	0.0084	0.0048
Finland	0.0010	0.0014
France	0.0070	0.0056

Germany	0.0067	0.0060
Greece	0.0120	0.0108
Ireland	0.0035	0.0018
Italy	0.0090	0.0088
Luxembourg	0.0073	0.0056
Netherlands	0.0029	0.0028
Norway	0.0024	0.0013
Poland	0.0176	0.0162
Portugal	0.0112	0.0101
Spain	0.0067	0.0049
Sweden	−0.0025	−0.0021
Switzerland	0.0119	0.0116
Turkey	0.0379	0.0149
UK	0.0053	0.0045
Mean	0.0083	
Median		0.0056

Appendix 6.5 ROA and ROE comparative analysis

ROA comparative analysis

Banking system	Mean	Median	Performance condition	
Austria	0.0037	0.0037	Underperforming	Underperforming
Belgium	0.0021	0.0030	Underperforming	Underperforming
Denmark	0.0063	0.0077	Overperforming	Overperforming
Finland	0.0056	0.0072	Overperforming	Overperforming
France	0.0030	0.0034	Underperforming	Underperforming
Germany	0.0016	0.0022	Underperforming	Underperforming
Greece	0.0074	0.0073	Overperforming	Overperforming
Ireland	0.0047	0.0066	Underperforming	Overperforming
Italy	0.0043	0.0047	Underperforming	Underperforming
Luxembourg	0.0036	0.0039	Underperforming	Underperforming
Netherlands	0.0040	0.0048	Underperforming	Underperforming
Norway	0.0082	0.0084	Overperforming	Overperforming
Poland	0.0107	0.0098	Overperforming	Overperforming
Portugal	0.0058	0.0059	Overperforming	Underperforming
Spain	0.0065	0.0066	Overperforming	Underperforming
Sweden	0.0074	0.0073	Overperforming	Overperforming
Switzerland	0.0040	0.0051	Underperforming	Underperforming
Turkey	0.0075	0.0176	Overperforming	Overperforming
UK	0.0057	0.0069	Overperforming	Overperforming
Mean	0.0054			
Median		0.0066		

Appendix 6.5 (Continued)

ROE comparative analysis

Banking system	Mean	Median	Performance condition	
Austria	0.0733	0.0763	Underperforming	Underperforming
Belgium	0.0724	0.0997	Underperforming	Underperforming
Denmark	0.1006	0.1230	Overperforming	Overperforming
Finland	0.0802	0.0873	Underperforming	Underperforming
France	0.0671	0.0828	Underperforming	Underperforming
Germany	0.0396	0.0533	Underperforming	Underperforming
Greece	0.1150	0.1215	Overperforming	Overperforming
Ireland	0.0813	0.1326	Underperforming	Overperforming
Italy	0.0614	0.0698	Underperforming	Underperforming
Luxembourg	0.1197	0.1327	Overperforming	Overperforming
Netherlands	0.1021	0.1173	Overperforming	Underperforming
Norway	0.1316	0.1376	Overperforming	Overperforming
Poland	0.1232	0.1177	Overperforming	Overperforming
Portugal	0.0560	0.0590	Underperforming	Underperforming
Spain	0.0793	0.0815	Underperforming	Underperforming
Sweden	0.1315	0.1322	Overperforming	Overperforming
Switzerland	0.0729	0.0806	Underperforming	Underperforming
Turkey	0.0756	0.1508	Underperforming	Overperforming
UK	0.1367	0.1682	Overperforming	Underperforming
Mean	0.0905			
Median		0.1173		

Appendix 6.6 Leverage multiplier comparative analysis

Banking system	Mean	Median
Austria	18.8249	19.9743
Belgium	31.4028	30.9428
Denmark	16.5362	16.4650
Finland	16.0070	17.1660
France	22.9668	22.6087
Germany	23.8166	24.2229
Greece	16.8683	16.7231
Ireland	17.1834	17.4993
Italy	14.3193	14.6655
Luxembourg	31.3842	36.7951
Netherlands	26.1076	25.2281
Norway	16.3524	15.9120
Poland	11.2050	11.3404
Portugal	9.7480	9.5732
Spain	12.1534	11.8029
Sweden	18.1483	18.2587
Switzerland	18.2238	17.2799
Turkey	9.4682	9.0262
UK	22.4565	24.0926
Mean	18.5880	
Median		17.2799

Notes

1. As stated in OECD(2011a), the database was developed "based on financial statements of banks in each Member country... presented in the standard OECD framework." Without loss of generality, hereafter we use interchangeably "banking system," "banking sector," and "banking industry."
2. Despite the methodological notes available in OECD (2011a), to help explain "differences across the countries... due to the availability of the data as well as the structural and regulatory features of national banking systems, accounting rules and practices, and reporting methods," the user of the data should "judge how cautiously the figures should be used for comparative purposes."
3. For comprehensive overviews of European banking see Schoenmaker and Peek(2014); Goddard et al.(2007); Dermine(2003); Murphy(2000).
4. See Borges (1993) for an analysis of the Portuguese banking system's integration into the European Single Market. Valério (2010) provides a comprehensive overview of the "political, economic and monetary framework governing the evolution of the Portuguese banking system."
5. The speech of Charlie McCreevy, European Commissioner for Internal Market and Financial Services, on June 14, 2007, "Creating a Single Market for Financial Services," can be found at http://www.euinjapan.jp/en/media/speech/speech2007/20070614/010000/, accessed July 28, 2015.
6. SeeBraz (1999) for further details. For a summary of the most prominent steps in the Portuguese banking system restructuring process, see Appendix 5.1.
7. Financial depth is a comprehensive measure of the size of a banking sector. See, e.g., Čiháket al. (2012).
8. Regulators and deposit insurers are, most probably, among the entities that more regularly and closely conduct assessments of bank performance, because of the practical incidences of the regulatory capital adequacy requirements and the deposit insurance regulations.
9. See, among others, Bikker(2010); Fiordelisi et al. (2010); Fethi and Pasiouras (2010); Sinkey (2002); Altunbaset al. (2001); Berger and Humphrey (1997); Molyneuxet al. (1996); Ernst & Young (1995); Berger et al. (1993); Fraser and Fraser (1990).
10. Martins and Ribeiro(2013).
11. Cabrita and Bontis (2008).
12. Portela and Thanassoulis(2007).
13. Barreto and Baden-Fuller (2006).
14. Mendes and Rebelo (2003).
15. See, among others, DeYoung and Hasan (1998).
16. Canhoto and Dermine (2003).
17. Pinho (2001).
18. Mendes (1991).
19. Alpalhão and Pinho (1990).
20. Ferretiet al. (2012).
21. Dietrich and Wanzenried (2011).
22. See Albertazzi and Gambacorta (2010).
23. Albertazzi and Gambacorta (2009).

24. See Bikker and Bos (2008) for more details.
25. Loukoianova (2008).
26. Goddard et al. (2004).
27. See Santos (2003) for further details.
28. Fries et al. (2002).
29. Lozano-Vivas et al. (2001).
30. See Resti (1997).
31. Molyneux and Forbes (1995).
32. The data set for this empirical examination was drawn from OECD (2001, 2003, 2005, 2008, 2011b, 2012). These publications provide "statistics on financial statements of banks in OECD countries. National Statistics are re-classified and presented according to a standard framework." See also the methodological notes prepared by OECD (2011a) to improve the comparability and "facilitate the comprehension and the interpretation of the data."
33. The dataset used in this study refers to entire banking systems except for Greece, Portugal, Sweden, and Turkey, for which only commercial banks are included in the sample. For the United Kingdom only large commercial banks are considered.
34. See Appendix 6.1 for sample scope, data availability, and missing data.
35. See OECD (2011b), p. 462.
36. See, e.g., Eccles (1991).
37. See Neely et al. (2007).
38. See Neely et al. (2002).
39. Among other problems, this methodological approach ignores the cost of equity capital, and is based on accounting data that is collected and processed under non-universal (changing) accounting principles and practices, and that nevertheless is prone to manipulation.
40. According to Ernst & Young(1995),"performance measures ... are a quantitative assessment of progress toward achieving a particular goal or objective, be it financial or qualitative," and "profitability measures assess only the relationships among different components of an institution's profitability statements, and provide a common basis for evaluating financial performance across the business."
41. The DuPont ROE decomposition model was named after the DuPont Corporation, which started using this method in the 1920s. It is often applied by analysts in order to improve the understanding of the ROA and ROE return processes.
42. Hannan and Hanweck (1988).
43. See, e.g., Nikolaou (2009).
44. Basel Committee on Banking Supervision (2000).
45. Berger et al. (1995).
46. See Saunders and Cornett (2007), p. 586, for a textbook discussion of the functions of bank capital.
47. It is relatively murky to measure a bank's degree of financial leverage because, among other factors, debt financing plays a different role than in non-banking firms.
48. See, among others, Harris and Raviv(1991), Table III, p. 334, for a summary of findings.

49. Wall and Peterson (1996).
50. See Canhoto and Dermine (2003).
51. The idea to view debt and equity as options was pioneered in Merton (1974).
52. See, e.g., John et al. (1991) and Kim and Santomero (1988).
53. As argued in John et al. (1991), even with risk-adjusted deposit insurance premia, incentives for risk shifting will still be present. Therefore, the propensity for excessive risk taking cannot be exclusively attributed to risk-insensitive deposit insurance pricing.
54. Merton (1977) shows that the government deposit guarantee can be viewed as a put option for banks on the government. According to Barth and Brumbaugh(1994), p. 76, "insured depositors are indifferent to the risk of the assets that are acquired with their funds. Protected against losses by deposit insurance, they have no incentive to impose discipline upon the owners and managers of their depositaries." The insensitivity of the deposit insurance premium to bank asset riskiness is related to assets' informational opacity, which prevents outsider investors from accurately assessing asset risk and pricing it at its actuarially fair value.
55. Milney and Whalley(2001)show that "incentives for risk taking depend upon this buffer of capital in excess of the regulatory minimum, not the total level"; and "the regulatory capital requirement has no long run effect on bank risk-taking."
56. See, among others, Milney and Whalley (2001); Basel Committee on Banking Supervision (1999); Calem and Rafael (1999); Wall and Peterson (1996); and Furlong and Keeley (1989).
57. As mentioned in Appendix 6.1, there is missing data in the OECD Banking Statistics database for computing the capital regulatory ratio for Denmark, Finland, France, Germany, and Luxembourg.
58. Greece, Ireland, Spain, and Portugal, in the aftermath of the 2008 financial crisis, were under IMF/EC/ECB financial assistance.
59. See Blum (1999) and references therein.
60. The Basel Capital Accord assigned 0%, 10%, 20%, 50%, and 100% risk weights to different categories of on-balance-sheet assets and off-balance-sheet exposures. See International Convergence of Capital Measurement and Capital Standards (July 1988, updated to April 1998), available athttp://www.bis.org/publ/bcbsc111.pdf, accessed July 28, 2015.
61. At the 5% significance level, the null hypothesis of no correlation in the population ($r = 0$) cannot be rejected for either correlation coefficient.
62. See, e.g., Jones(2000) for an insightful review of the "principal techniques used to undertake capital arbitrage."
63. See Scholes et al.(1990).
64. See Osterberg and Thomson(1996).
65. See Scholes et al. (1990).
66. See Albertazzi and Gambacorta (2010).
67. Because of potential outliers involving data for Denmark (1994), France (1994), Germany (2003), and Greece (2009), for which we were unable to find any satisfactory explanation in OECD (2011a), we used the median as a measure of location.
68. Santos (2003).

Bibliography

Albertazzi, Ugo, and Gambacorta, Leonardo(2009) "Bank Profitability and the Business Cycle," *Journal of Financial Stability*, 5(4): 393–409.

Albertazzi, Ugo, and Gambacorta, Leonardo(2010) "Bank Profitability and Taxation," *Journal of Banking and Finance*, 34(11): 2801–2810.

Alpalhão, Rui, and Pinho, Paulo(1990)*Análise Financeira das Instituições de Crédito Portuguesas, 1980–89: Rentabilidade e Risco*, Lisbon: Sociedade Financeira Portuguesa.

Altunbas, Y., Gardener, E., Molyneux, P., and Moore, B. (2001) "Efficiency in European Banking," *European Economic Review*, 45(10): 1931–1955.

Barata, José M. (1995) "O Sector Bancário em Portugal: Evolução e Análise Estratégica (1986–1992)," *Revista da Banca*, 33:17–60.

Barltrop, Chris, and McNaughton, Diana(1992)*Banking Institutions in Developing Markets Volume 2: Interpreting Financial Statements*, Washington, DC: World Bank.

Barreto, Ilídio, and Baden-Fuller, Charles(2006) "To Conform or to Perform? Mimetic Behaviour, Legitimacy-Based Groups and Performance Consequences," *Journal of Management Studies*, 43(7): 1559–1581.

Barros, Pedro, and Pinho, Paulo(1995)*Estudos Sobre o Sistema Bancário Português*, Lisbon: Banco Mello.

Barth, James, and Brumbaugh, R. Dan(1994) "Moral-Hazard and Agency Problems: Understanding Depository Institution Failure Costs," in G. Kaufmann (ed.)*Research in Financial Services*, Vol. 6,. Greenwich, CT: JAI Press, 61–102.

Barth, James R., Caprio, Gerard, Jr., and Levine, Ross (2001) "Banking Systems around the Globe: Do Regulation and Ownership Affect Performance and Stability?" in F. Mishkin (ed.) *Prudential Supervision: What Works and What Doesn't*, Chicago, IL: University of Chicago Press, 31–96.

Barth, James, Nolle, Daniel, Phumiwasana, Triphon, and Yago, Glenn(2003) "A Cross-Country Analysis of the Bank Supervisory Framework and Bank Performance," *Financial Markets, Institutions & Instruments*,12(2): 67–120.

Basel Committee on Banking Supervision (1999) "Capital Requirements and Bank Behaviour: The Impact of the Basel Accord," Basel Committee on Banking Supervision Working Paper No. 1, Basel: Bank for International Settlements.

Basel Committee on Banking Supervision (2000)*Principles for the Management of Credit Risk*, Basel: Bank of International Settlements.

Berger, Allen, and Humphrey, David(1997) "Efficiency of Financial Institutions: International Survey and Directions for Future Research," *European Journal of Operational Research*, 98(2): 175–212.

Berger, Allen, Herring, Richard, and Szegö, Giorgio(1995) "The Role of Capital in Financial Institutions," *Journal of Banking and Finance*, 19(3–4): 393–430.

Berger, Allen, Hunter, William, and Timme, Stephen(1993) "The Efficiency of Financial Institutions: A Review and Preview of Research Past, Present and Future," *Journal of Banking and Finance*, 17(2–3): 221–249.

Bikker, Jacob (2010) "Measuring Performance of Banks: An Assessment," *Journal of Applied Business and Economics*, 11(4): 141–159.

Bikker, Jacob, and Bos, Jaap(2008)*Bank Performance*, New York: Routledge.

Bonin, John, Hasan, Iftekhar, and Wachtel, Paul(2005) "Bank Performance, Efficiency and Ownership in Transition Countries," *Journal of Banking and Finance*, 29(1): 31–53.

Borges, António(1993) "Portuguese Banking in the Single European Market," in J. Dermine(ed.)*European Banking in the 1990s*, Oxford: Blackwell, 325–343.

Braz, José (1999) "Bank (Re)privatizations in Portugal," working paper presented at the Federal Reserve Bank of Dallas/World Bank Conference on Banking Privatization, Washington, DC, March.

Blum, Jürg (1999) "Do Capital Adequacy Requirements Reduce Risks in Banking?" *Journal of Banking and Finance*, 23(5): 755–771.

Cabrita, Maria, and Bontis, Nick(2008) "Intellectual Capital and Business Performance in the Portuguese Banking Industry," *International Journal of Technology Management*, 43(1–3): 212–237.

Calem, Paul, and Rob, Rafael (1999) "The Impact of Capital-Based Regulation on Bank Risk Taking," *Journal of Financial Intermediation*, 8(4): 317–352.

Canhoto, Ana, and Dermine, Jean(2003) "A Note on Banking Efficiency in Portugal, New vs. Old Banks," *Journal of Banking and Finance*, 27(11): 2087–2098.

Chen, Long, and Zhao, Xinlei(2007) "Mechanical Mean Reversion of Leverage Ratios," *Economics Letters*, 95(2): 223–229.

Čihák, Martin, Demirgüç-Kunt, Aslı, Feyen, Erik, and Levine, Ross(2012) "Benchmarking Financial Systems around the World," World Bank Policy Research Working Paper No. 6175, Washington, DC: World Bank.

Dermine, Jean (2003) "Banking in Europe: Past, Present, and Future," in V. Gaspar, P. Hartmann, and O. Sleijpen (eds.)*The Transformation of the European Financial System*, Frankfurt: European Central Bank.

DeYoung, Robert, and Hasan, Iftekhar (1998) "The Performance of de Novo Commercial Banks: A Profit Efficiency Approach," *Journal of Banking and Finance*, 22(5): 565–587.

Dietrich, Andreas, and Wanzenried, Gabrielle(2011) "Determinants of Bank Profitability before and during the Crisis: Evidence from Switzerland," *Journal of International Financial Markets, Institutions and Money*, 21(3): 307–327.

Eccles, Robert (1991) "The Performance Measurement Manifesto," *Harvard Business Review*, 69(1): 1–8.

Ernst & Young (1995)*Performance Measurement for Financial Institutions*, rev. edn., Chicago, IL: Irwin.

Ferreti, Riccardo, Torresetti, Marzia, and Vezzani, Paola(2012) "Performance and Efficiency of the Italian Banking System Italian Banking System," in S. Cosma and E. Gualandri (eds.)*The Italian Banking System: Impact of the Crisis and Future Perspectives*, Houndmills: Palgrave Macmillan, 67–96.

Fethi, Meryem, and Pasiouras, Fotios(2010) "Assessing Bank Efficiency and Performance with Operational Research and Artificial Intelligence Techniques: A Survey," *European Journal of Operational Research*, 204(2): 189–198.

Fiordelisi, Franco, Marques-Ibanez, David, and Molyneux, Phil(2010) "Efficiency and Risk in European Banking," European Central Bank working paper series No. 1211, Frankfurt: European Central Bank.

Fraser, Donald, and Fraser, Lyn(1990)*Evaluating Commercial Bank Performance*, Rolling Meadows, IL: Bankers Publishing.

Fries, Steven, Neven, Damien, and Seabright, Paul(2002) "Bank Performance in Transition Economies," University of Michigan William Davidson Working Paper No. 505, Ann Arbor, MI: University of Michigan.

Furlong, Frederick, and Keeley, Michael(1989) "Capital Regulation and Bank Risk-Taking: A Note," *Journal of Banking and Finance*, 13(6): 883–891.

Goddard, John, Molyneux, Phil, and Wilson, John(2004) "The Profitability of European Banks: A Cross-Sectional and Dynamic Panel Analysis," *The Manchester School*,72(3): 363–381.

Goddard, John, Molyneux, Phil, Wilson, John, and Tavakoli, Manouche(2007) "European Banking: An Overview," *Journal of Banking and Finance*, 31(7): 1911–1935.

Hannan, Timothy, and Hanweck, Gerald(1988) "Bank Insolvency Risk and the Market for Large Certificates of Deposit," *Journal of Money, Credit and Banking*, 20(2): 203–211.

Harris, Milton, and Raviv, Arthur(1991) "The Theory of Capital Structure," *Journal of Finance*, 46(1): 297–355.

John, Kose, John, Teresa, and Senbet, Lemma(1991) "Risk-Shifting Incentives of Depository Institutions: A New Perspective on Federal Deposit Insurance Reform," *Journal of Banking and Finance*, 15(4–5): 895–915.

Jones, David (2000) "Emerging Problems with the Basel Capital Accord: Regulatory Capital Arbitrage and Related Issues," *Journal of Banking and Finance*, 24(1–2): 35–58.

Kim, Daesik, and Santomero, Anthony(1988) "Risk in Banking and Capital Regulation," *Journal of Finance*, 43(5): 1219–1233.

Kwan, Simon, and Eisenbeis, Robert(1997) "Bank Risk, Capitalization, and Operating Efficiency," *Journal of Financial Services Research*, 12(2–3): 117–131.

Loukoianova, Elena(2008) "Analysis of the Efficiency and Profitability of the Japanese Banking System," IMF Working Paper No. WP/08/63, Washington, DC: International Monetary Fund.

Lozano-Vivas, Ana, Pastor, Jesús, and Hasan, Iftekhar(2001) "European Bank Performance beyond Country Borders: What Really Matters?" *European Finance Review*, 5(1–2): 141–165.

Martins, Francisco, and Ribeiro, Maria(2013) "A Análise da Eficiência no Setor Bancário: Modelo de Fronteira Estocástica com Dados em Painel para a Banca Portuguesa," *Nova Economia*, 23(3): 555–577.

Mendes, Victor (1991) "Scale and Scope Economies in Portuguese Commercial Banking: The Years 1965–88," *Economia*, 15(3): 453–490.

Mendes, Victor, and Rebelo, João(2003) "Structure and Performance in the Portuguese Banking Industry in the Nineties," *Portuguese Economic Journal*, 2(1): 53–68.

Merton, Robert (1974) "On the Pricing of Corporate Debt: The Risk Structure of Interest Rates," *Journal of Finance*, 29(2): 449–470.

Merton, Robert (1977) "An Analytic Derivation of the Cost of Deposit Insurance and Loan Guarantees," *Journal of Banking and Finance*, 1: 3–11.

Milney, Alistair, and Whalley, A. Elizabeth(2001) "Bank Capital Regulation and Incentives for Risk-Taking," research paper, London: Cass Business School.

Molyneux, Phil, and Forbes, William(1995) "Market Structure and Performance in European Banking," *Applied Economics*, 27(2): 155–159.

Molyneux, Philip, and Thornton, John(1992) "Determinants of European Bank Profitability: A Note," *Journal of Banking and Finance*, 16(6): 1173–1178.

Molyneux, Philip, Altunbas, Yener, and Gardener, Edward(1996)*Efficiency in European Banking*, Chichester: John Wiley & Sons.

Murphy, Neil (2000) "European Union Financial Developments: The Single Market, the Single Currency, and Banking," *FDICBanking Review*, 13(1): 1–18.

Neely, Andy, Adams, Chris, and Kennerley, Mike(2002)*The Performance Prism*, London: Prentice Hall.

Neely, Andy, Kennerley, Mike, and Adams, Chris(2007) "Performance Measurement Frameworks: A Review," in A. Neely(ed.)*Business Performance Measurement: Unifying Theories and Integrating Practice*, 2ndedn., Cambridge: Cambridge University Press, 143–162.

Nikolaou, Kleopatra(2009) "Liquidity (Risk) Concepts Definitions and Interactions," European Central Bank working paper series No. 1008, Frankfurt: European Central Bank.

OECD (2001)*Bank Profitability: Financial Statements of Banks*, OECD Banking Statistics, Paris: OECD Publishing.

OECD (2003)*Bank Profitability: Financial Statements of Banks*, OECD Banking Statistics, Paris: OECD Publishing.

OECD (2005)*Bank Profitability: Financial Statements of Banks*, OECD Banking Statistics, Paris: OECD Publishing.

OECD (2008)*Bank Profitability: Financial Statements of Banks*, OECD Banking Statistics, Paris: OECD Publishing.

OECD (2011a)*OECD Banking Statistics: Methodological Country Notes*, Paris: OECD Publishing.

OECD (2011b) *Bank Profitability: Financial Statements of Banks*, OECD Banking Statistics, Paris: OECD Publishing.

OECD (2012)*OECD Banking Statistics: Financial Statements of Banks*, OECD Banking Statistics, Paris: OECD Publishing.

Osterberg, William, and Thomson, James (1996) "Optimal Financial Structure and Bank Capital Requirements: An Empirical Investigation," *Journal of Financial Services Research*, 10(4): 315–332.

Pasiouras, Fotios, and Kosmidou, Kyriaki(2007) "Factors Influencing the Profitability of Domestic and Foreign Commercial Banks in the European Union," *Research in International Business and Finance*, 21(2): 222–237.

Pinho, Paulo (2001) "Using Accounting Data to Measure Efficiency in Banking: An Application to Portugal," *Applied Financial Economics*, 11(5): 527–538.

Portela, Maria, and Thanassoulis, Emmanuel(2007) "Comparative Efficiency Analysis of Portuguese Bank Branches," *European Journal of Operational Research*, 177(2): 1275–1288.

Putnam, Barron (1983) "Early Warning Systems and Financial Analysis in Bank Monitoring: Concepts of Financial Monitoring," *Federal Reserve Bank of AtlantaEconomic Review*, November: 6–13.

Resti, Andrea(1997) "Evaluating the Cost-Efficiency of the Italian Banking System: What Can Be Learned from the Joint Application of Parametric and Non-parametric Techniques," *Journal of Banking and Finance*, 21(2): 221–250.

Rezvanian, Rasoul, and Mehdian, Seyed(2002) "An Examination of Cost Structure and Production Performance of Commercial Banks in Singapore," *Journal of Banking and Finance*, 26(1): 79–98.

Rime, Bertrand (2001) "Capital Requirements and Bank Behaviour: Empirical Evidence for Switzerland," *Journal of Banking and Finance*, 25(4): 789–805.
Rime, Bertrand, and Stiroh, Kevin(2003) "The Performance of Universal Banks: Evidence from Switzerland," *Journal of Banking and Finance*, 27(11): 2121–2215.
Santos, Mário C. (2003) "Firm's Capital Structure Decisions: Theory and Empirical Evidence from Portuguese Banks," PhD thesis, University of Aveiro, Portugal.
Saunders, Anthony, and Cornett, Marcia (2007) *Financial Institutions Management*, 6thedn., New York: McGraw-Hill.
Schoenmaker, Dirk, and Peek, Toon(2014) "The State of the Banking Sector in Europe," OECD Economics Department Working Paper No. 1102, Paris: OECD.
Scholes, Myron, Wilson, Peter, and Wolfson, Mark (1990) "Tax Planning, Regulatory Capital Planning, and Financial Reporting Strategy for Commercial Banks," *Review of Financial Studies*, 3(4): 625–650.
Sinkey, Joseph (2002)*Commercial Bank Financial Management*, 6thedn., Upper Saddle River, NJ: Prentice Hall.
Valério, Nuno(ed.)(2010)*History of the Portuguese Banking System: From the Bank of Portugal's Role as a Central Bank to the European Monetary Union – 1831–1998*, Vol. II, Lisbon: Banco de Portugal.
Wall, Larry, and Peterson, Pamela(1996) "Banks' Responses to Binding Regulatory Capital Requirements," *Federal Reserve Bank of AtlantaEconomic Review*, March/April: 1–17.

7
Retail Banking for Households in Portugal

João Gil Pedreira

In the last 25 years, retail banking for households in Portugal has seen relevant and decisive changes, and its size in relation to GDP has grown significantly. This chapter aims to capture and analyze these changes and this growth from two different perspectives: the main players, their strategies, and their evolution; and the main impacts on the overall financial intermediation figures at a national level and in an international euro area comparison.

Although this is a period in which retail banks and specialized consumer credit institutions assumed a significant role in the lives of Portuguese households, it must be divided into two different subperiods, where the first – which may be called "the rise of the empire" – will lead us through the 1990s and almost the entire first decade of the new millennium, until the outbreak of the financial crisis; and the second – which may be called "the fall of the empire" – will tell us the unfinished story from the outbreak of the financial crisis to the present day.

In this chapter the analysis will be focused on the main endogenous variables of retail banking for the household market, characterizing the development of an unsustainable economy, based on the triangulation between retail banks, construction and real estate companies, and mortgage credit, with the obvious subsequent impacts on financial, economic, and social realities. It will also be focused on exogenous variables, like unemployment and divorce among others, which definitely have to be analyzed together in a systemic and integrated perspective, as they are totally correlated.

Finally, there is a need to stress that to fully understand the economic and social reality of the twentieth century's last decade and the first decade of the new millennium; what led Portugal to request financial assistance from the European Union, the euro area member states, and the International Monetary Fund (IMF) on April 7, 2011; and the crisis of the last three years, there is an absolute requirement to have a broader comprehension of the leverage figures behind the over indebtedness of both families and companies, expressed by one of the highest loan-to-deposit ratios among euro area countries, side by side with Ireland and Spain.

Main retail bank operations and their evolution (1990s and 2000s)

With highly sophisticated and computerized branches (to the usual 1990s standards) and with a strong and differentiated commercial approach, Banco Comercial Português (BCP) and its leading retail banking network (NovaRede) showed the way to a deep sector revolution in Portugal, at the same time as several commercial models were being tested in the group:

- Expresso Atlântico: small retail banking branches in big commercial areas (e.g., supermarkets, shopping malls), usually made operational with no more than two people, and with a very distinctive and differentiated push sales model.
- Lojas Atlântico: ex-BPA branches, totally renewed, with specific and totally separated automatic transaction areas – where customers could perform cash withdrawals, money transfers, payments, etc. – and specific sales areas within the branch, specializing in mortgage credit, consumer credit and credit cards, and mutual funds, among others.
- Cidade BCP: the first universal online banking platform, launched in 2000, with a systematic and integrated approach to household commercial products and transactional services, and with an initial aim to capture more than 800,000 new customers. Although it has never been a successful commercial platform, it has pioneered the online banking approach, and afterward the main retail banking operations in Portugal could easily understand the dos and don'ts of internet online retail banking value propositions.

During the 1990s and 2000s in Portugal there were two main evolutionary trends for retail banking operations: *mergers and acquisitions* (*M&A*) and *endogenous growth*. BCP also led the M&A movement, when in 1995 it bought its parent company Banco Português do Atlântico (BPA), which was incorporated in 2000, at the same time as the recently acquired Banco Pinto e Sotto Mayor (BPSM) and Banco Mello (formerly UBP, União de Bancos Portugueses).

M&A was also the path followed by the investment bank Banco Português de Investimento (BPI), which bought and incorporated Banco Fonsecas & Burnay (BFB) in 1991, Banco Fomento Exterior (BFE) and Banco Borges & Irmão (BBI) in 1996; and by Santander Totta, a group that was created in December 2004 and is the result of the corporate reorganization of three commercial banks: Banco Totta & Açores (BTA), Crédito Predial Português (CPP), and Santander. They have become the fourth and fifth largest retail group banks in Portugal, in terms of market share of client loans (see Table 7.1).

The evolutionary trend of championing endogenous growth was followed by Banco Espírito Santo (BES), a financial and economic family-based group that kept growing throughout the 1990s and 2000s, increasing not only its balance sheet but also the number of its branches, not from acquiring other financial institutions' networks, but by building up from scratch its own branch network.

While the 1990s were the years of discovery of multispecialist models and of specialist strategies, depending on the size of the operation, the 2000s were the consolidation of the multichannel systemic and integrated approach and branch capillarity.

Multichannel approach and branch capillarity

The multichannel systemic and integrated approach was one of the most important focus points of the *free-market model* implemented during the 1990s, in the most significant Portuguese retail banking operations. The first of its objectives was to achieve total separation between the sales and the servicing or transactional models, as this was the strategic approach to get 100% sales focus among direct and automatic sales channels and sales forces. By migrating a full range of transactions, such as cash withdrawals, balance inquiries, money transfers, payments, and others, to automatic servicing channels, such as automated teller machines (ATMs), call centers, or from the late 1990s the internet, retail banking operations could focus themselves on the four main star products of the last decade of the twentieth century: *mortgage credit, consumer credit, credit cards*, and *mutual funds*.

Then, the second main objective of this multichannel systemic and integrated approach was to potentiate and maximize all sales channels capabilities in commercial activities, from branch tellers and sellers to telemarketing and call centers. New specialized branches were appearing in major towns, mainly focused on mortgage credit and other related products, such as an additional overdraft account (arranged according to the client's income); consumer credit to buy furniture, a car,

Table 7.1 The top five retail banking groups in Portugal

1995			2010	
Banking Institutions	**Client loans Market share***		**Banking Institutions**	**Client loans Market share***
CGD	17.5%		CGD	24.2%
BNU	2.7%	Merger of BNU into CGD, 2000–01		–
BCP	12.3%		BCP	18.4%
BPA	5.7%	Acquired in 1995 and incorporated in 2000		–
BPSM	11.2%	Acquired and incorporated in 2000		–
UBP/MELLO	3.2%	Acquired and incorporated in 2000		–
BES(CL)	7.5%		BES	14.2%
BES(S)I	0.2%	Investment bank	BESI	0.3%
BEST	–	Internet/online bank	BEST	0.03%
BPI	2.6%		BPI	9.8%
BFB	2.5%	Acquired and incorporated in 1991		–
BFE	4.1%	Acquired and incorporated in 1996		–
BBI	1.9%	Acquired and incorporated in 1996		–
BTA	7.9%	Santader Totta was created in December 2004	Santander Totta	8.1%
CPP	3.3%	and is the result of the corporate reorganization		–
SANTANDER	–	of the three commercial banks		–
SANTANDER CONS.	–			–

* Approximate values.
Source: Associação Portuguesa de Bancos.

or for property improvements; life and non-life insurances; and credit cards.

On top of the star product in the market – mortgage credit – banks usually followed a cross-selling strategy, using the third main objective of the multichannel systemic and integrated approach, which was – as the name indicates – to systematize and integrate all the personal and automatic sales channels available at a specific time, in order to maximize their growth. Push over pull campaigns, through telemarketing or mailing, focused on pre-approved consumer credit or credit cards, and were flooding the household market. The essence was to analyze the credit profile of the household mortgage consumer and proactively to suggest another product, such as consumer credit, credit cards, mutual funds, or insurance products, on a *banking and insurance* and *insurance funds* combined approach.

The multichannel systemic and integrated approach was starting to spread among all the relevant retail banking players, not only for transactional support but also to boost their commercial models. This approach resulted in the emergence and rise of call centers, telemarketing, push mail campaigns, online banking, and ATM transactional services diversification – where, for example, Santander Totta led the way with cash and check deposit facilities throughout Portugal and Spain. However, the truth behind the main players' strategy was to build the biggest and most sophisticated brick-and-mortar branch structure. Capillarity was the name of the game, and retail banking networks were seen as an indispensable asset to sell mortgage credit, consumer credit, credit cards, and mutual funds at high speed. So, it should not come as a surprise that Portugal quickly achieved the highest banking capillarity in the whole of Europe, with fewer than 1,700 people per branch (considering the entire Portuguese population).

This trend can be easily observed in Figure 7.1, which illustrates the evolution in the number of branches and its constant growth until 2011, except in 2001 and 2002, when BCP was rationalizing its recently acquired retail network banking operations; namely, BPA, BPSM, and Banco Mello.

However, in Portugal the second half of the 1990s also saw the emergence of several players specializing in consumer credit, with a new direct commercial approach, initially based on call centers and push telemarketing campaigns, and then based on internet sales and communication. In the beginning, specialized credit institutions accounted for a small percentage of the overall market, but they soon established a new strategic approach to households, much more aggressive in terms

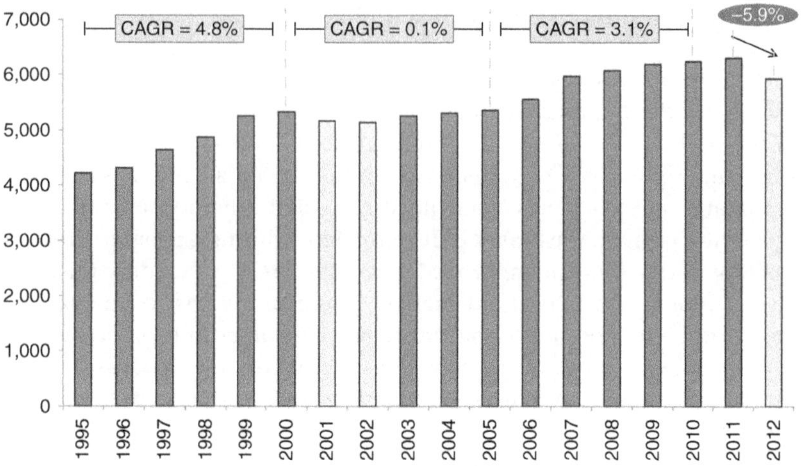

Figure 7.1 Branches of member institutions of APB – Associação Portuguesa de Bancos (Portuguese Banking Association)
Source: Associação Portuguesa de Bancos.

of marketing and client-acquisition strategies, which made them grow very rapidly in the overall consumer credit market.

Relevant players like Cetelem (later integrated in the BNP Paribas operation), Credibom, Santander Consumer, or Oney accounted for very aggressive commercial campaigns and push over pull strategies. They helped to change the banking paradigm from a conservative, risk-averse model to a very liberal and risky one, based on high interest rates, commissions, and penalties.

Portuguese retail banking figures

As seen in the previous section, the growth engine of Portuguese retail banking in the last few decades was definitely mortgage credit. Starting the 1990s at less than €6 billion, mortgage credit grew significantly throughout the following decades, with a compound annual growth rate (CAGR) of 24% during the 1990s, and 8% during the first decade of the new millennium. It reached a peak of more than €114 billion in 2010, nearly 20 times more than in 1990.

Figure 7.2 represents the growth path of mortgage lending in Portugal up to 2010, when it reached its peak, and the decline that followed, resulting endogenously from total market saturation and exogenously from the international financial crisis; namely, subprime lending.

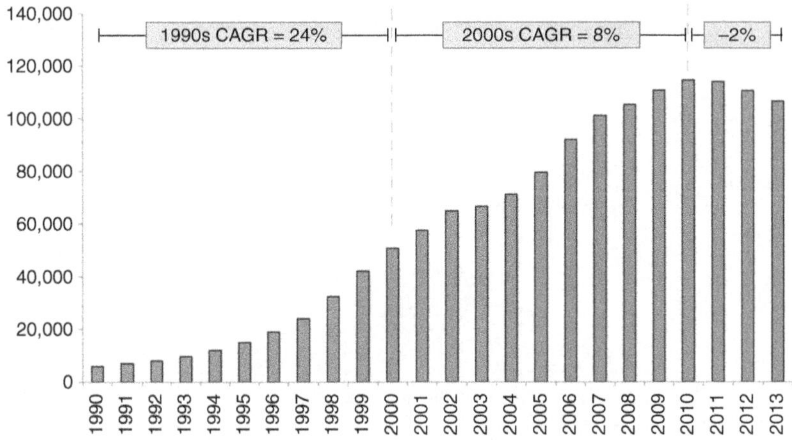

Figure 7.2 Lending for house purchase, million euros and percentage
Source: Bancos de Portugal (1990–2002) and European Central Bank (2003–13).

The path based on specialist and multispecialist strategies, built on the free-market model, which was being spread throughout the main Portuguese banks, elected lending for house purchase as the "anchor product" for retail banking growth. In this context, Portuguese banks significantly expanded the amounts, duration – often 50-year contracts were signed between banks and borrowers – and LTV (loan to value) of their home loans (frequently above 100%). This final point induced the creation and development of a new market, very little known in Portugal until the mid-1990s: credit for consumption, adding consumer loans and credit cards to the mortgage anchor product.

As can be seen in Figure 7.3, credit for consumption and other household lending also experienced significant growth in the 1990s (27% CAGR) and in the following decade (6% CAGR).

When adding lending for house purchase, consumer credit, and other household lending purposes, the number of households with loans was impressive for a country of 10 million people (see Table 7.2).

The overall economic and social impact of this banking strategy can only be fully understood when comparing the growth of lending to households and to non-financial corporations, and observing the progressive growth of the percentage of household lending in total retail banking credits during the 1990s and 2000s. In less than a decade, from a 32% share in 1990, household lending assumed more than 50% of overall retail credit, continuing to grow until the present day (Figure 7.4).

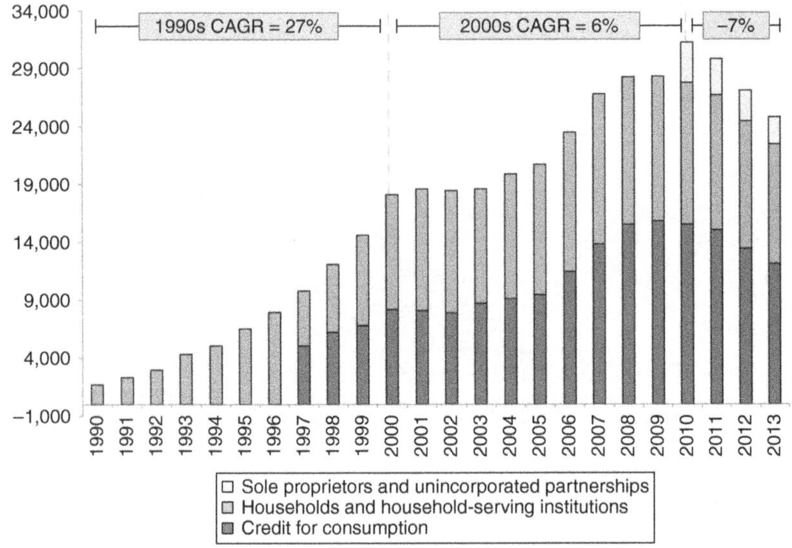

Figure 7.3 Credit for consumption, households and household-serving institutions, sole proprietors, and unincorporated partnerships (SP/UP) – million euros and percentage

Note: Until 1997 "Credit for consumption" and "Household and household-serving institutions" were a single item in Banco de Portugal statistics.

Source: Banco de Portugal (1990–2002) and European Central Bank (2003–13).

Table 7.2 Number of households with loans

	Q4 2012	Q1 2013	Q2 2013	Q3 2013	Q4 2013
Total	4,564,588	4,392,546	4,435,130	4,419,686	4,440,899
Mortgage	2,437,891	2,356,627	2,371,288	2,357,938	2,351,064
Consumption and other purchases	3,739,749	3,570,170	3,604,741	3,596,223	3,624,996
Portuguese population	10,542,398				10,487,289

Source: Banco de Portugal.

When the analysis considers the growth patterns of lending to non-financial companies (Figure 7.5), the picture is finally clear, as construction and real estate activities are the main drivers of this growth. This means that Portuguese retail banks were betting on a fast-growing – but unsustainable – model. This was based on lending to construction,

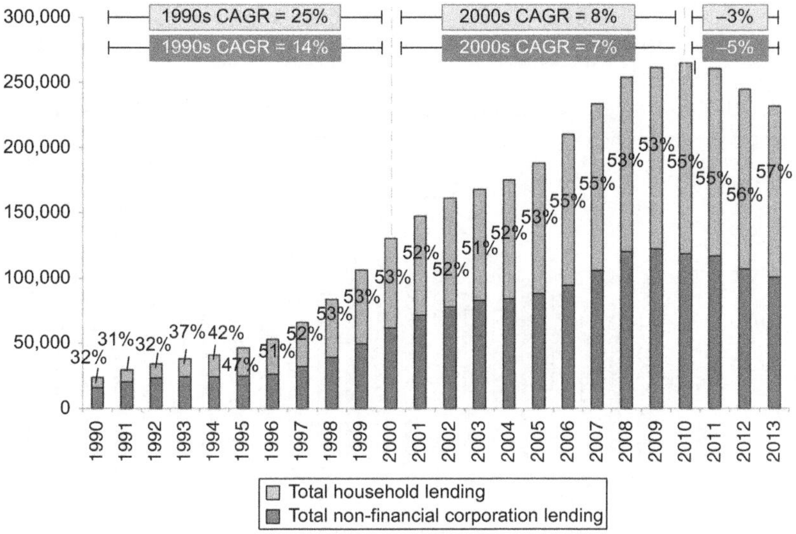

Figure 7.4 Non-financial corporation and total household lending, million euros and percentage
Source: Banco de Portugal (1990–2002) and European Central Bank (2003–13).

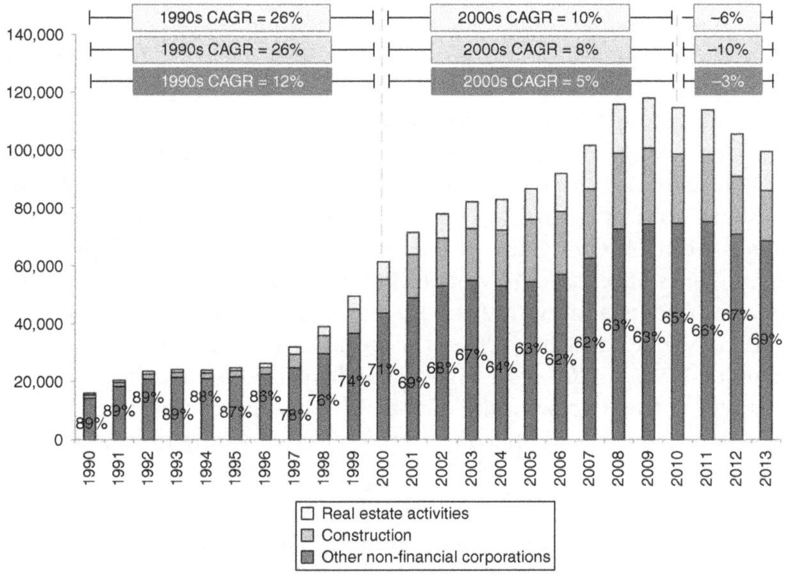

Figure 7.5 Non-financial corporation lending by branch of activity, million euros and percentage
Source: Banco de Portugal.

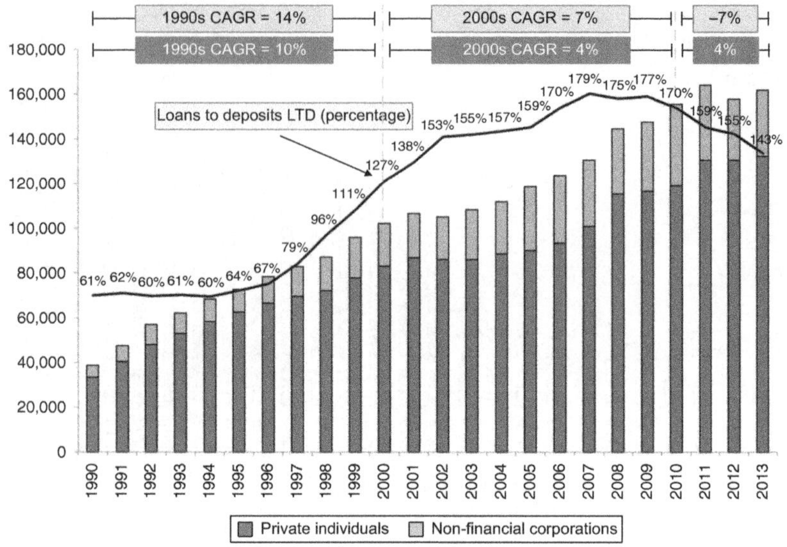

Figure 7.6 Deposits and deposit-like instruments of private individuals and non-financial companies, million euros and percentage
Source: Banco de Portugal.

real estate activities, and their main clients, mortgage borrowers, and afterward accelerating their growth with push over pull campaigns to spread consumer credit and credit cards, as seen in the previous section when describing the free-market model.

When asking how it was possible to sustain such high growth rates in Portuguese retail credit markets, when in fact the country did not present significant growth in GDP over the last few decades, the answer comes from observing the evolution of the deposits and deposit-like instruments of private individuals and non-financial companies. It also requires understanding that the loan-to-deposit ratio has evolved from a conservative level of 61% at the beginning of the 1990s to a peak value of 179% in 2007 (see Figure 7.6). This means that the incredible Portuguese credit growth rate of the last few decades was based not on residents' deposits, but on loans from foreign banks and from securitized operations.

Portuguese retail banking euro area comparison

The fast-moving path described in the last section contributed in a decisive way to the over indebtedness of Portuguese households. When related to GDP, lending for house purchase, consumer credit, and

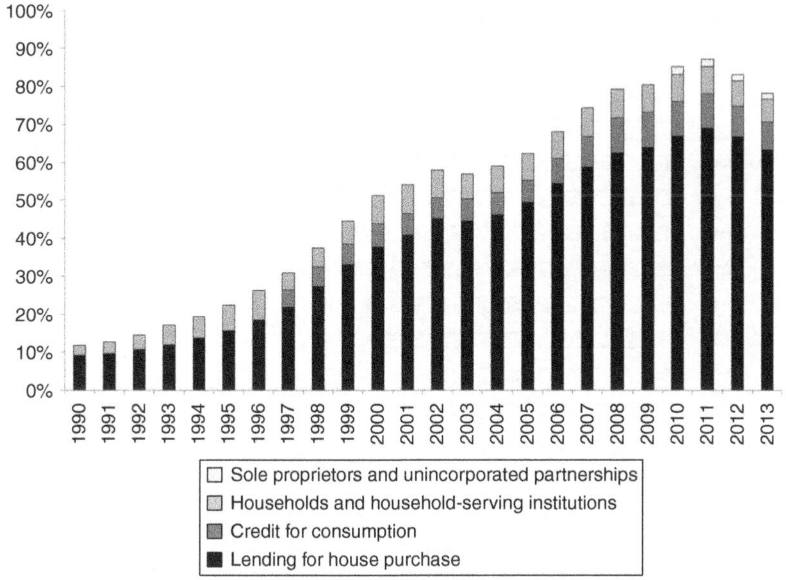

Figure 7.7 Household lending as a percentage of GDP
Source: Banco de Portugal (1990–2002) and European Central Bank (2003–13).

other personal loans has grown to a very significant percentage (see Figure 7.7).

When compared with the remaining euro area countries (Figures 7.8–7.10), Portugal assumes one of the leading roles regarding lending for house purchase and credit for consumption, which for a country with one of the lowest GDPs per capita in the area is effectively buying a rich country's problem for what is in fact a quite poor region by European standards.

Recalling the 57% household lending assumed in 2013, when compared with overall retail banking credit in Portugal, and comparing this number with the remaining euro area countries (Figure 7.11), it can easily be observed that despite Portugal having entered the rich countries' club in what is possibly the wrong way, the truth is that the majority of euro area countries made a enormous bet on household lending, as they had more than 50% exposure to household lending compared to total retail banking credit in 2013.

In terms of international euro area comparisons, the final point that should be stressed is that countries like Ireland, Spain, and Portugal leveraged their banking operations on private external loans much more than did the remaining euro area countries, basing their incredible credit

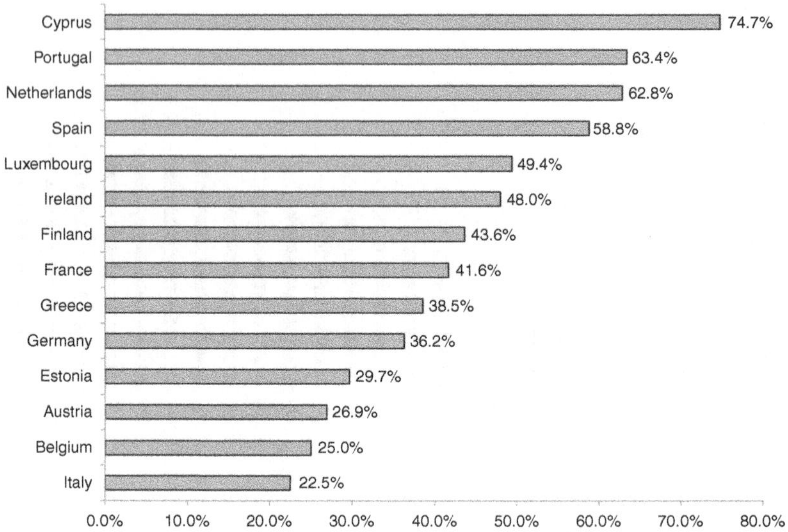

Figure 7.8 Lending for house purchase, euro area comparison (percentage to GDP)
Source: European Central Bank.

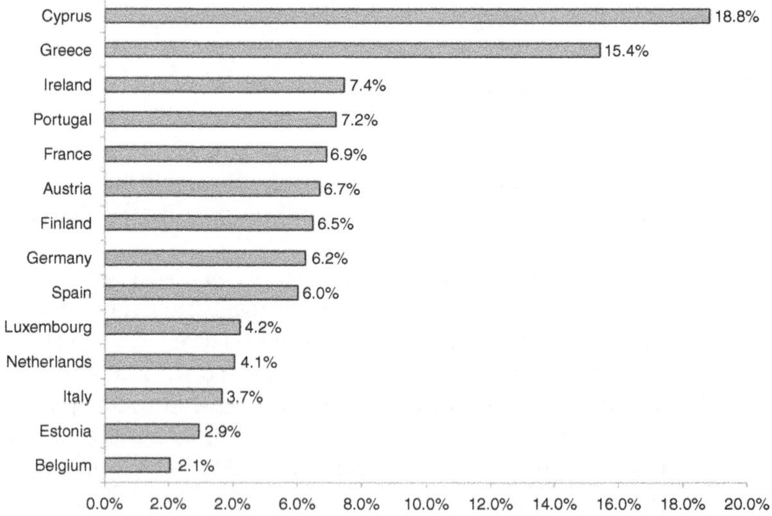

Figure 7.9a Credit for consumption, euro area comparison (percentage to GDP)
Source: European Central Bank.

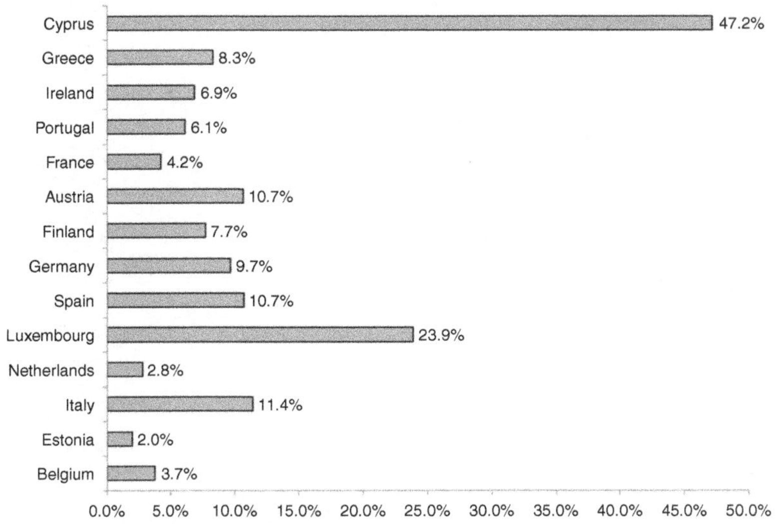

Figure 7.9b Households and non-profit institutions serving households, euro area comparison (percentage to GDP)
Source: European Central Bank.

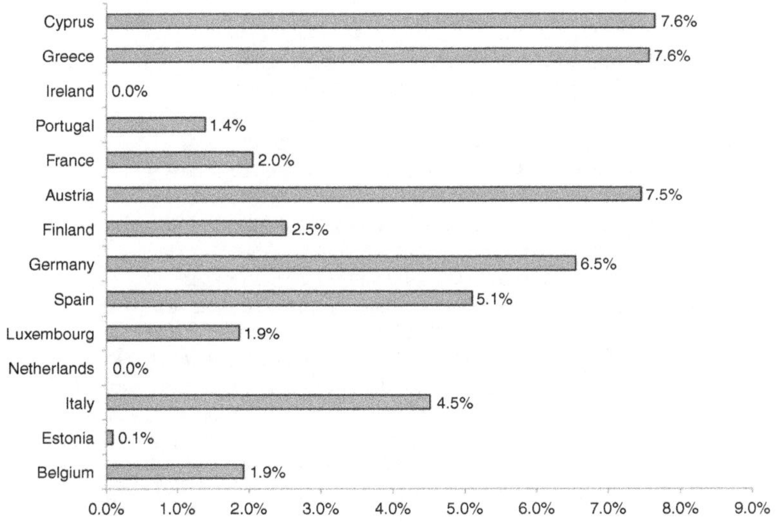

Figure 7.9c Sole proprietors and unincorporated partnerships, euro area comparison (percentage to GDP)
Source: European Central Bank.

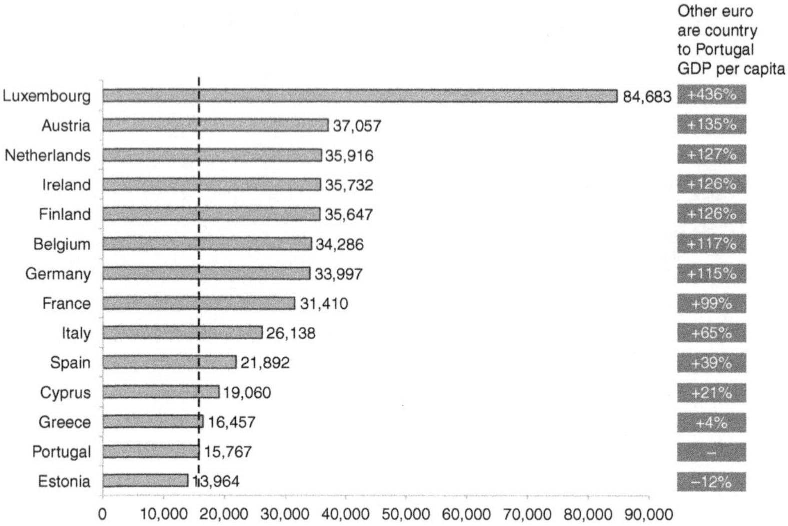

Figure 7.10 GDP per capita, euro area comparison (euros and percentage)
Source: European Central Bank; Eurostat.

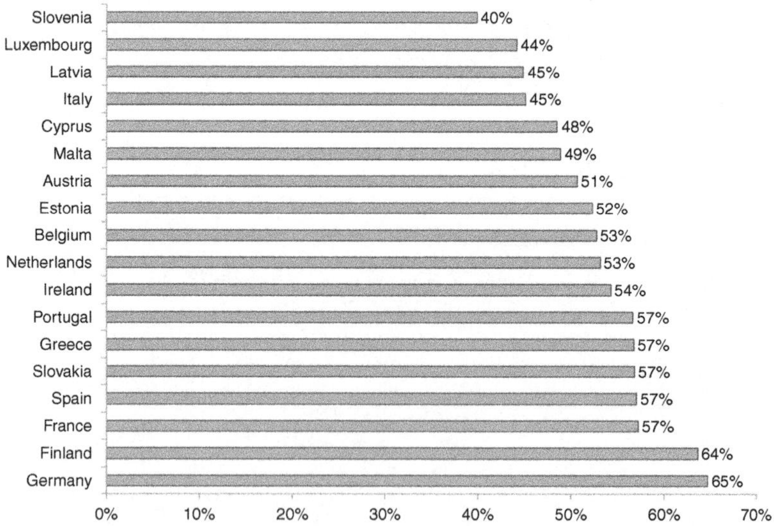

Figure 7.11 Lending to households as a percentage of total lending, euro area comparison
Source: European Central Bank.

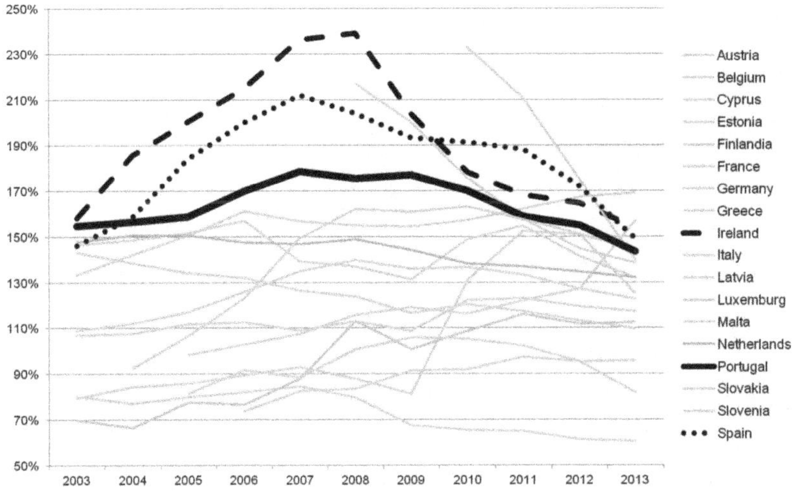

Figure 7.12 Loans to deposits evolution, euro area comparison (percentage)
Source: European Central Bank.

growth rate of the last few decades not on residents' deposits but on foreign bank and securitized loans (Figure 7.12). In fact, this could be the main difference between the rationale of the bailout programs of countries like Ireland, Spain, and Portugal and countries like Greece, which had a completely different debt problem, mainly focused on sovereign debt unsustainability.

Facts and figures after the financial crisis

After peaking at the end of the 2000s, the household credit market started to decline in the period following the financial crisis. The path was essentially settled by three main drivers: a sharp reduction in credit production (new credit underwriting); the duration of initial loans, meaning that household mortgage lending, with its long term, presented a rather less intense decrease than consumer credit; and strong growth in default levels, which resulted in recent years in strong efforts toward provisioning and write-offs among the main retail banking operations in Portugal.

The retail credit market triangle based on banks, construction loans, and mortgage credit has reached the peak of its unsustainability and started its fall. Real estate prices followed this path, as can be seen in Figure 7.13. This means that suddenly a big (but non-statistically

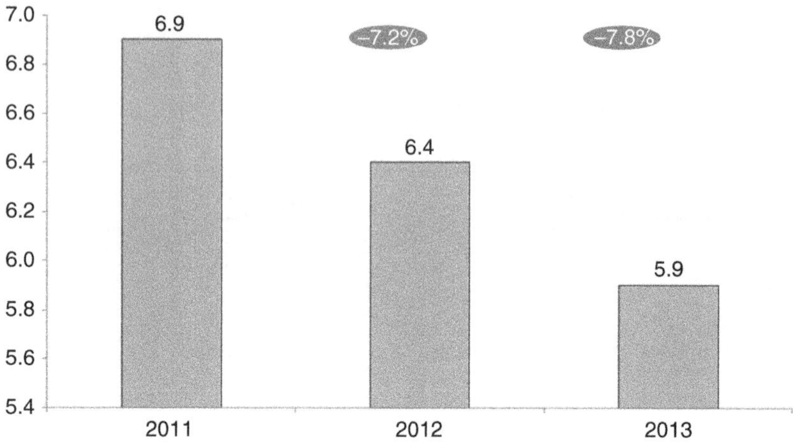

Figure 7.13 Average value of houses for sale and for rent (euros/m^2)
Source: Confidencial Imobiliário.

determined) percentage of households were now starting to be in "negative equity," with the value of their debts – namely, mortgage debt – much higher than the real commercial value of their belongings – namely, their properties.

As construction and real estate activities had been playing a relevant and decisive role in Portugal's employment and gross domestic product in the previous two decades, the country experienced a significant impact from unemployment after the financial crisis ripped through the western world. As can be seen in Figure 7.14, the unemployment rate grew very rapidly, more than doubling in the last five years.

One needs to add to this systemic analysis the fact that the divorce rate in Portugal doubled in the first decade of the twenty-first century, beginning with an average of 30 divorces per 100 marriages, and ending with an average of 64.8 divorces per 100 marriages. This had an intense impact on default levels among the main products of the retail credit market, namely mortgage credit, consumer credit, and loans for other purposes, as can be seen in Figure 7.15, since unemployment and the divorce rate play a major role in the level of non-performing loans.

However, in Portugal another trend was emerging in the years after the financial crisis. While more conservative banks strongly reduced the quantities of new consumer credit granted, contributing decisively to the reduction in amounts outstanding on the market, the ten biggest specialized credit institutions continued to grant significant volumes

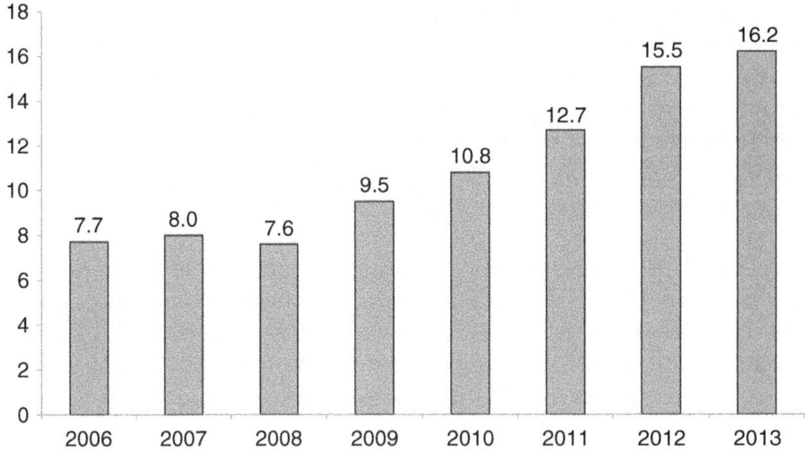

Figure 7.14 Unemployment rate in Portugal (percentage)
Source: Instituto Nacional de Estatísticas.

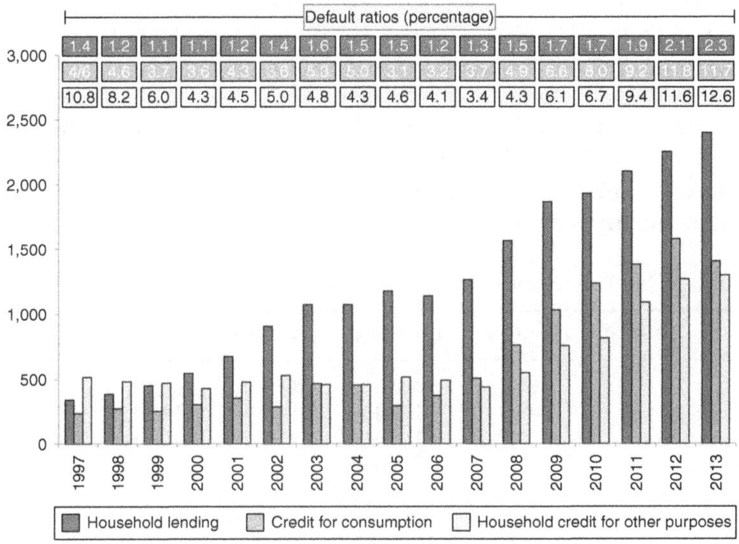

Figure 7.15 Households' non-performing loans and default ratios (million euros and percentage)
Source: Banco de Portugal.

of credit. For example, the amount of outstanding credit increased by more than 7% in the first quarter of 2010, while overall consumer credit was already decreasing. The growth of specialized credit institutions, in relation to more conservative credit institutions, meant that households were substituting less costly consumer credit with much more expensive lending, as these credit institutions usually propose higher risk premiums, expressed in higher interest rates, commissions, and penalties.

With all these macro-economic exogenous drivers and banking sector endogenous factors, default levels continued to grow throughout the last few years (and in fact through the first months of 2014). This meant that in mid-2014 Portugal had not seen the end of the household over indebtedness crisis, which was directly affecting more than 661,000 households (number of people with non-performing loans) at the end of 2014 (Table 7.3).

Nevertheless, the extent of this specific crisis cannot only be viewed in the levels of default, as many families are in fact living with the economic and social consequences of serious over indebtedness, without having any credit in arrears (Table 7.4). That is what Euro found analyzed and reported in its 2012 working paper, the executive summary of which stresses: "Many EU citizens are struggling to service their mortgages or consumer credit, and to pay their rent and utility bills. In 2010, more than one in four persons reported that they felt at risk of becoming over-indebted, while 11.6% were in arrears with payments related to such debts or bills (up from 9.9% in 2007)."

Although there are not enough statistics to express the complete magnitude and intensity of Portuguese families' over indebtedness, those

Table 7.3 Number of households with defaulted loans

	Q4 2012	Q1 2013	Q2 2013	Q3 2013	Q4 2013
Total	689,253	680,845	687,445	662,953	661,694
Mortagage	148,711	146,111	147,020	146,192	145,766
Consumption and other purposes	632,018	621,210	630,830	600,569	596,973
Portuguese population with loans	4,564,588	4,392,546	4,435,130	4,419,130	4,440,899
Portuguese population	10,542,398				10,487,289

Source: Banco de Portugal.

Table 7.4 Household lending, in millions of euros

	Lending for house purchase	Lending for consumption and other household lending				Total household lending
		Credit for consumption	Households and household-serving institutions	Sole proprietors and unincorporated partnerships	Total lending for consumption and other household lending	
1990	5,812			1,718	1,718	7,530
1991	6,853			2,270	2,270	9,123
1992	7,933			2,901	2,901	10,835
1993	9,670			4,302	4,302	13,972
1994	12,013			5,031	5,031	17,044
1995	15,006			6,462	6,462	21,468
1996	18,904			7,945	7,945	26,849
1997	24,087		5,013	4,747	9,760	33,847
1998	32,433		6,191	5,866	12,057	44,490
1999	42,180		6,770	7,803	14,573	56,753
2000	50,735		8,177	9,901	18,078	68,813
2001	57,365		8,074	10,511	18,585	75,950
2002	64,838		7,872	10,534	18,406	83,244
2003	66,485		8,720	9,817	18,537	85,022
2004	71,139		9,089	10,806	19,895	91,034
2005	79,488		9,427	11,261	20,688	100,176
2006	91,916		11,416	12,058	23,474	115,390
2007	101,106		13,820	12,969	26,789	127,895
2008	105,222		15,495	12,748	28,243	133,465
2009	110,693		15,779	12,495	28,274	138,967
2010	114,521	3,488	15,524	12,240	31,252	145,773
2011	113,923	3,094	15,022	11,674	29,790	143,713
2012	110,525	2,612	13,401	11,057	27,070	137,595
2013	106,592	2,344	12,106	10,341	24,791	131,383

Note: Until 1997 "Credit for consumption" and "Household and household-serving institutions" were a single item in Banco de Portugal statistics.
Source: Banco de Portugal (1990–2002) and European Central Bank (2003–13).

that exist and have been expressed in this chapter are more than enough to understand that, rather than this being a side effect or an economic externality from the financial crisis, the retail household credit market continues to play a significant and decisive role in the overall social and economic situation in Portugal. Urgent solutions need to be put in place in order to prevent even bigger consequences for this western European country.

Bibliography

Associação Portuguesa de Bancos (Portuguese Banking Association) (various dates) *Activity Reports*, Lisbon: APB.

Banco de Portugal (various dates) *Statistical Bulletins,* Lisbon: Banco de Portugal.

Confidencial Imobiliário (various dates) *Indexes and Publications,* Lisbon: Confidencial Imobiliário.

Eurofound (2012) "Household Debt Advisory Services in the European Union," working paper, Dublin: Eurofound.

European Central Bank (various dates) Eurosystem, various statistics, www.ecb.int.

Instituto Nacional de Estatística (various dates) *Unemployement Statistics,* Lisbon: INE.

PORDATA (various dates) Banco de Dados Portugal Contemporâneo, www.pordata.pt.

8
Corporate and Investment Banking in Portugal

Pedro Gouveia Alves

Corporate banking in Portugal in the mid-1980s was related to the regular commercial banking needs of small and medium enterprises (SME), mainly from the manufacturing and services sectors. The offer portfolio was mainly composed of products and services for short-term financial loans (based on working capital needs, such as overdrafts or hot money for very short-term loans) and commercial loans (based on trade financing needs, such as factoring and confirming, or similar instruments). The main players in the Portuguese market were banks with a wide tradition in short-term loans such as Banco Espírito Santo and Banco Português do Atlântico (later merged with Millennium bcp), Banco do Fomento Exterior (acquired by BPI, Banco Português de Investimentos) as a main specialist in industrial promotion based on mid- and long-term loans for capacity increases, and Banco Nacional Ultramarino (later merged with Caixa Geral de Depósitos) with a huge tradition in trade finance loan instruments due to the trade of goods between Portugal and overseas territories during colonial times.

Until the end of the 1980s, there were several restrictions on housing loans. Only three financial institutions were allowed to offer housing loans: one mutual institution (Montepio Geral), one public saving bank (Caixa Geral de Depósitos), and one institution specializing in promoting construction loans (Crédito Predial Português).

In the early 1990s, the Portuguese financial market was liberalized, with the end of the privatization phase of banks that were nationalized following the 1974 revolution. The model, based on market mechanisms, encouraged banks to enlarge their offers to housing loans and construction on a large scale. The scarcity of housing in Portugal, together with very restrictive house letting laws, opened the door to a period of rallying in real estate leverage. In 2012, Portugal had 74.5%

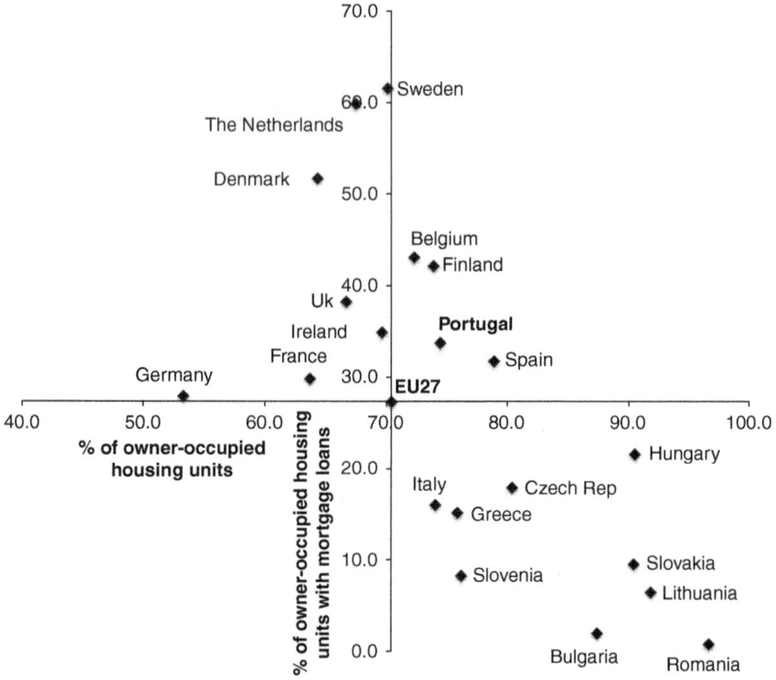

Figure 8.1 Home ownership rate in EU countries

owner-occupied housing units, above the European Union 27 countries (EU27) average (70.4%), of which 33.8% were with mortgage loans, compared to the EU27 average of 27.3% (Figure 8.1).

After the market liberalization in the late 1980s, Banco Comercial Português (Millennium bcp) surged as a disruptive player, proposing a new distribution model based on segments for corporates (small businesses, SMEs, and large corporates). Thus, the first account managers appeared dedicated to dealing with corporate customers. This model was widely adopted by the Portuguese banking system up to the end of the 1990s, although with some particularities: a dedicated account manager in the universal branches or offices dedicated to corporates (mainly small businesses and SMEs) with mid-office facilities or with centralized backoffices.

During the mid-1990s, the bank loans market became more dynamic and attractive due to the expansionist budget and monetary policies of the western economies. Large companies, mainly related to public investments and large-scale private investments in facilities and infrastructure, demanded more specialized services, such as structured loans adjusted to a project's characteristics, offering financing solutions with longer maturities requiring new structures of funding (not only classic loans, but structured high-grade debt and raising funds in capital markets). This was the arrival of corporate and investment banking in Portugal, close to what we know today.

Lending to companies

During the last few decades, Portuguese companies have maintained a preference for bank loans as a way to obtain funding for their activities. The domestic stock market is still very narrow and is mainly for small businesses and lower-profile companies, whose size seems to be an obstacle to obtaining funding abroad. For this reason, banks play the role of getting funding not only in the domestic market, but also mainly in international markets recording historically lower interest rates.

The Portuguese business structure continues to be based on SMEs, often family based, whose governance is simple and, in most cases, centered on its owner (an individual or a few family members). Although the stock market is weak, the cultural matrix of Portuguese business tends to be averse to strengthening the capital structure via a consideration for participation (direct or indirect) in management. Thus, bank credit appears to be the simplest way to use funding, particularly in the short term (since it is the practice of banking market demand for stronger guarantees in long-term loans). The debt-to-equity ratio of Portuguese companies is among the highest of the EU countries and has maintained an upward trend, from 0.94 in 1999 to 1.26 in 2013 (Figure 8.2).

Although part of the debt is explained by the ease of access to credit provided by the banking sector, there are other reasons that led to company managers'choices. Recently, the European Commission (EC) has identified the excessive leverage of the private sector as a concern, and this may be related to the corporate tax policy. That is due to the tax shield effect of the cost of bank loans, contrary to what happens to dividends arising from equity.

In 2012, the EC published a report containing a survey of areas with potential imbalances among member countries.[1] It examined debt levels in the private sector and defined an annual procedure to identify at an early stage high private indebtedness in comparison to GDP among member states. With regard to indebtedness in a country's private sector, the EC has set an indicative threshold of 160% of GDP. If the debt ratio

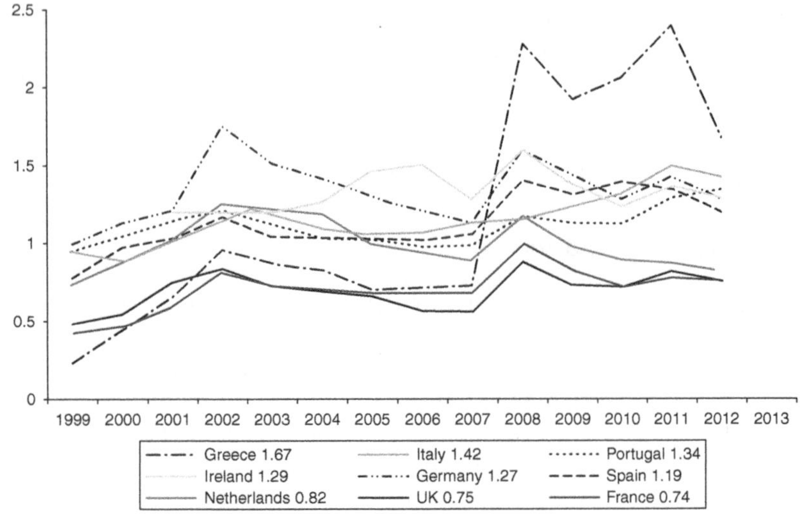

Figure 8.2 EU countries comparison of debt-to-equity ratio for non-financial companies

Source: OECD(2014). Debt is obtained as the sum of the following liability categories, whenever available/applicable in the financial balance sheet of the institutional sector: currency and deposits, securities other than shares, except financial derivatives, loans, insurance technical reserves and other accounts payable.

in a country's private sector exceeds that threshold, the country will be subjected to specific in-depth analysis.

Since the mid-2000s, the debt-to-GDP ratio of non-financial companies has not stopped growing, and is well above the EC threshold of 160% (Figure 8.3).

Table 8.1 shows the dependence of companies' liabilities structure relating to bank loans. It demonstrates 40.1% of obtained funding, almost 2.5 times the weight of debt securities. The structure of companies' balance sheets even shows the decrease in the weight of equity, from 42.3% to 36% in only six years.

Evolution of companies' bank loans

Bank loans to companies registered remarkable growth in the last two decades. In 1995, the Portuguese banking system had a total outstanding of €24,653 million (Figure 8.4), reaching a maximum of €117,807 million in 2009. (It should be noted that the published data do not include securitized credit or loans written off. For that reason, these figures do

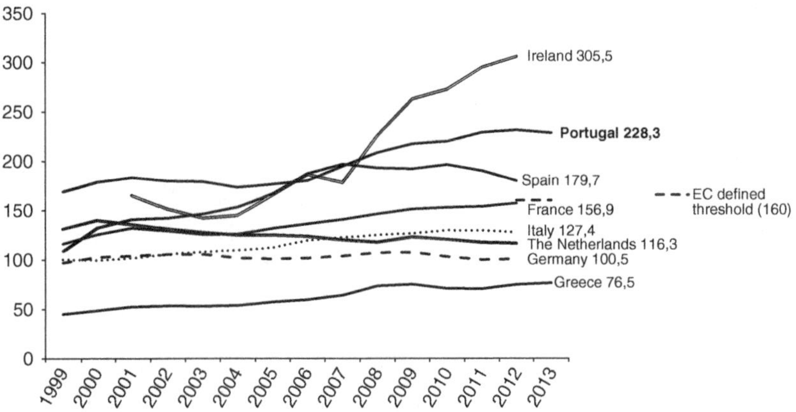

Figure 8.3 EU countries comparison of debt of non-financial companies as % of GDP

Source: OECD (2014). Debt is obtained as the sum of the following liability categories, whenever available/applicable in the financial balance sheet of the institutional sector: currency and deposits, securities other than shares, except financial derivatives, loans, insurance technical reserves and other accounts payable.

Table 8.1 Financing of Portuguese non-financial companies

Year	Total Balance Sheet						Equity
	Total Liabilities	Trade Creditors	Other Liabilities	Obtained Funding	(of which Bank Loans)	(of which Debt Securities)	
2006	336,788	56,101	99,069	181,618	90,623	23,995	256,354
2007	385,434	60,250	118,613	206,571	100,163	29,592	273,406
2008	419,095	58,281	127,200	233,614	113,989	35,153	272,630
2009	431,618	57,988	129,874	243,757	115,885	36,740	278,533
2010	444,823	61,857	127,333	255,632	112,590	38,735	299,204
2011	442,740	60,922	122,674	259,143	111,767	41,114	252,773
2012	429,203	55,058	116,137	258,008	103,459	42,475	241,806

Year	As % of Liabilities			As % of Obtained Funding		Equity/ (Equity + Liabilities)
	Trade Creditors	Other Liabilities	Obtained Funding	Bank Loans	Debt Securities	
2006	16.7%	29.4%	53.9%	49.9%	13.2%	43.2%
2007	15.6%	30.8%	53.6%	48.5%	14.3%	41.5%
2008	13.9%	30.4%	55.7%	48.8%	15.0%	39.4%
2009	13.4%	30.1%	56.5%	47.5%	15.1%	39.2%
2010	13.9%	28.6%	57.5%	44.0%	15.2%	40.2%
2011	13.8%	27.7%	58.5%	43.1%	15.9%	36.3%
2012	12.8%	27.1%	60.1%	40.1%	16.5%	36.0%

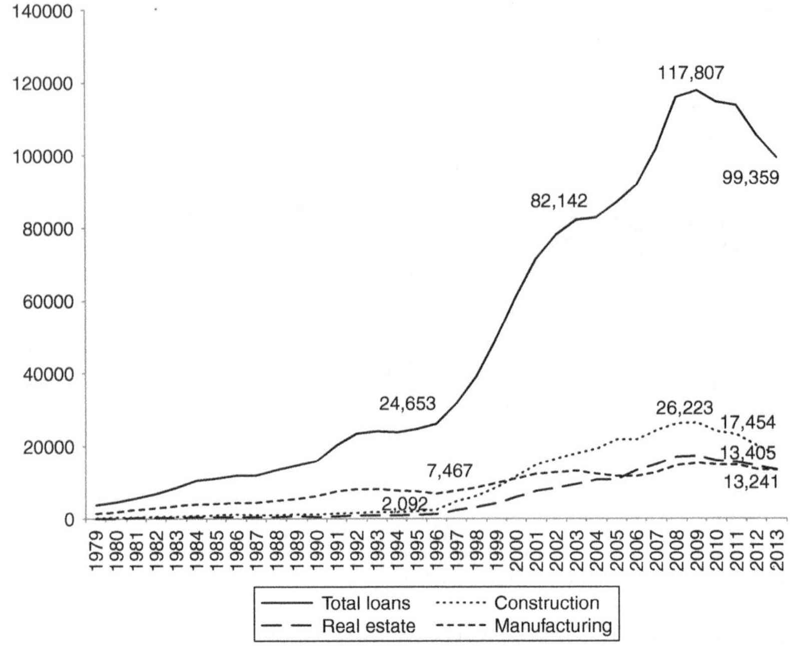

Figure 8.4 Non-financial banking loans to companies in Portugal (10^3 million €)

not reflect the whole reality of credit outstanding.) Growth occurred in two major periods:

- Between 1995 and 2002, credit more than tripled, coinciding with a period of significant decline in interest on international markets and strong expansionary public budget policies in the late 1990s.
- Between 2003 and 2009, there was a period of remarkable public investment in infrastructure based on public–private partnerships (see later in this chapter), interrupted by the outbreak of the international financial crisis in 2008 and the consequent widening of spreads in debt markets.

Figure 8.5 is instructive as to the choice of economic growth model followed in Portugal. The allocation of resources to the production of non-tradable goods is quite clear, instead of allocation to larger export enhancers. The weight of the manufacturing sector in total bank loans falls from 43.9% in the early 1980s to 30.3% in 1995 and 13.3% in 2013. Rather, there was a jump in construction from an 8.5% weight of total

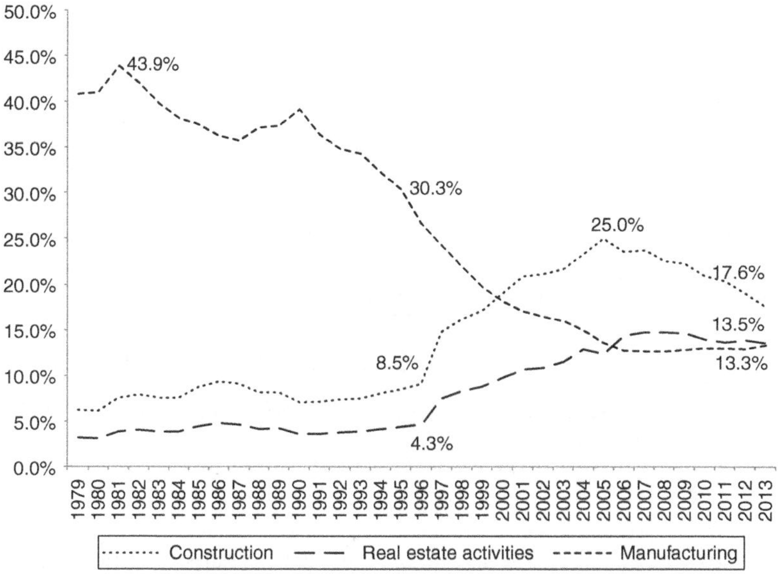

Figure 8.5 Non-financial banking loans to companies in Portugal (percentage)

bank loans in 1995 to a maximum of 25% in 2005, growth stopped by the reduction of economic activity in Portugal and the funding shortfall caused by the international liquidity crisis. Currently, the weight of construction (17.6%) is still significantly above the manufacturing sector (13.3%).

Deleverage of the Portuguese banking system

Following the recent Portuguese financial bailout, the Financial Assistance Programme agreed by the Portuguese government and the Troika – International Monetary Fund (IMF), EC, and European Central Bank (ECB) – for the period 2011–14 fixed new targets for deleveraging and increasing capital and liquidity in the financial system in general and the banking sector in particular. In order to achieve these targets, the largest banking groups were required to draw up a Funding and Capital Plan to put in place until 2015. This fixed goals of reducing the leverage ratio to 120% and increasing the Core Tier I solvency rate to a minimum of 9% by the end of 2012 and 10% by December 2013.

Considering the deleveraging commitment, the Portuguese banking system recorded a reduction in credit to households when analyzed in comparison with GDP (Figure 8.6), from 103.5% in the first quarter

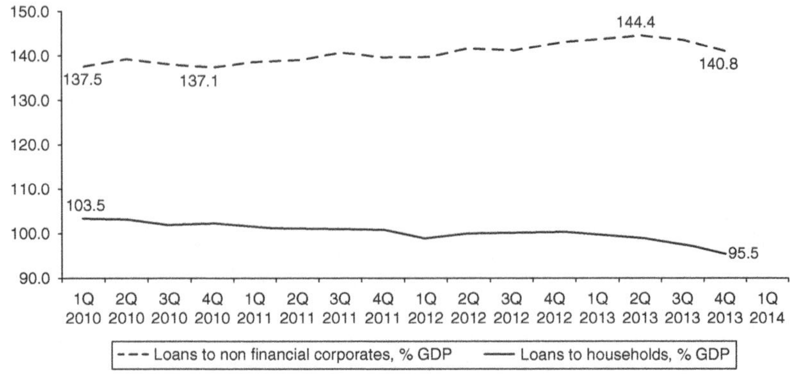

Figure 8.6 Deleverage of the Portuguese banking system as a percentage of GDP for 2010–14 period per quarter
Source: Bank of Portugal, "Portuguese Banking System – Recent Developments" (available data to June 9, 2014).

of 2010 to 95.5% in the last quarter of 2013. Loans to non-financial companies only declined from the second quarter of 2013 (up to 144.4%).

The effort of deleveraging threatened to become a crowding-out phenomenon, with as light increase in the weight of other debt instruments (including sovereign debt obtained by banks). This was avoided by the fact that the Financial Assistance Programme loan parcels were released to the public treasury based on the liquidity needs of the Portuguese state (expected up to a total of €78billion). A weight reduction in loans to customers is clearly visible in the total banking system balance sheet (67.9% in the first quarter of 2010 to 64% in the first quarter of 2014). That corresponds to less than €61billion euro in just four years (Figure 8.7).

With the Portuguese bailout, the banking system suffered severe credit rating downgrades, closing access to international debt markets. For that reason, on the liabilities side, the banking system changed its funding portfolio, competing for a further stake in domestic deposits. The weight of customers' deposits rose from 41.7% to 54.6% in four years. On the other hand, outstanding issued bonds (mainly in international markets) experienced an extensive drop, from 23.2% to 9.3% in the same period (Figure 8.8).

Thus, the Portuguese financial system was able to fulfill the goal of a 120% leverage ratio ahead of schedule, reaching 117.2% in the first quarter of 2014 (Figure 8.9).

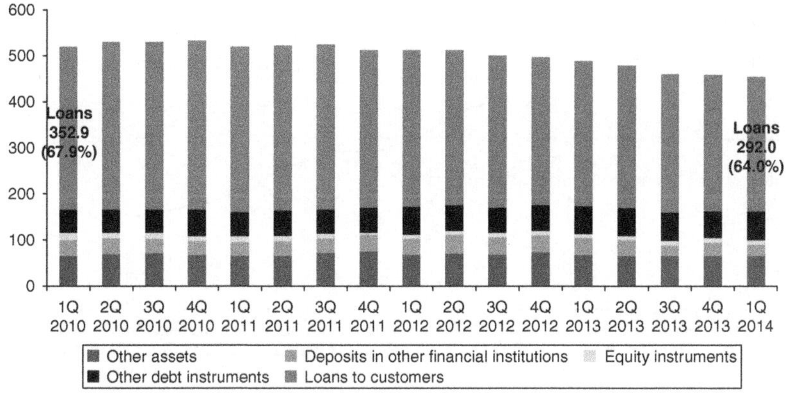

Figure 8.7 Deleverage of the Portuguese banking system as a percentage of total banking system assets for the 2010–14 period per quarter
Source: Bank of Portugal, "Portuguese Banking System – Recent Developments" (available data to June 9, 2014). Author's analysis.

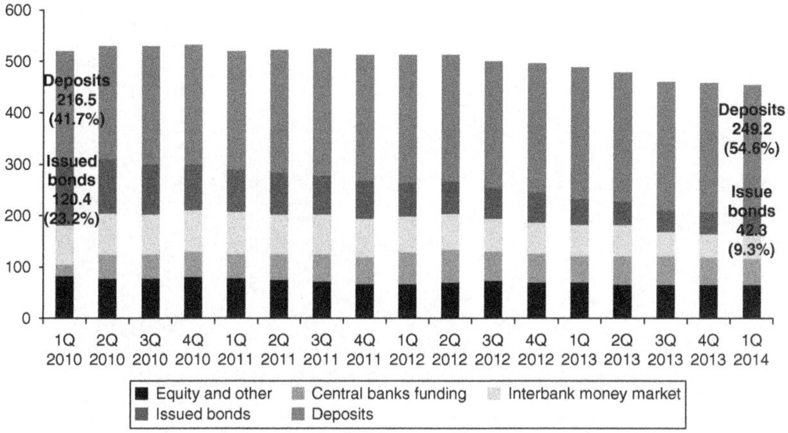

Figure 8.8 Deleverage of the Portuguese banking system – customers' deposits as a percentage of total liabilities plus equity for the 2010–14 period per quarter
Source: Bank of Portugal, "Portuguese Banking System – Recent Developments" (available data to June 9, 2014). Author's analysis.

On the assets side, the bailout measures had an impact both on new loans for households and on non-financial corporate loans, mainly regarding short-term credit limits due to the ability to easily cancel overdrafts and other contracts for working capital loans. In 2013, up to one-year loans reached the minimum weight ever registered

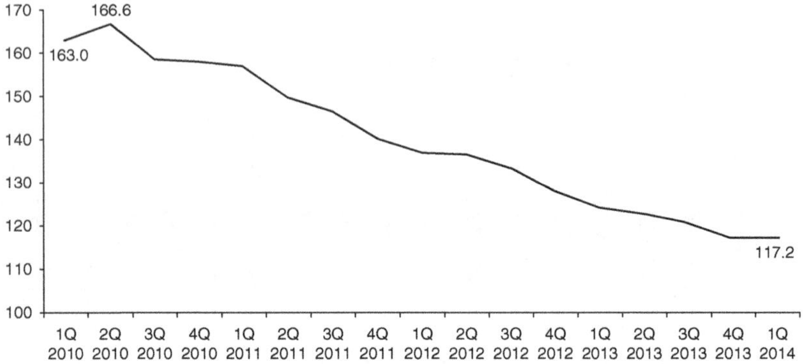

Figure 8.9 Leverage ratio of the Portuguese banking system – loans to customer deposits for the 2010–14 period per quarter

Source: Bank of Portugal, "Portuguese Banking System – Recent Developments" (available data to June 9, 2014). Author's analysis.

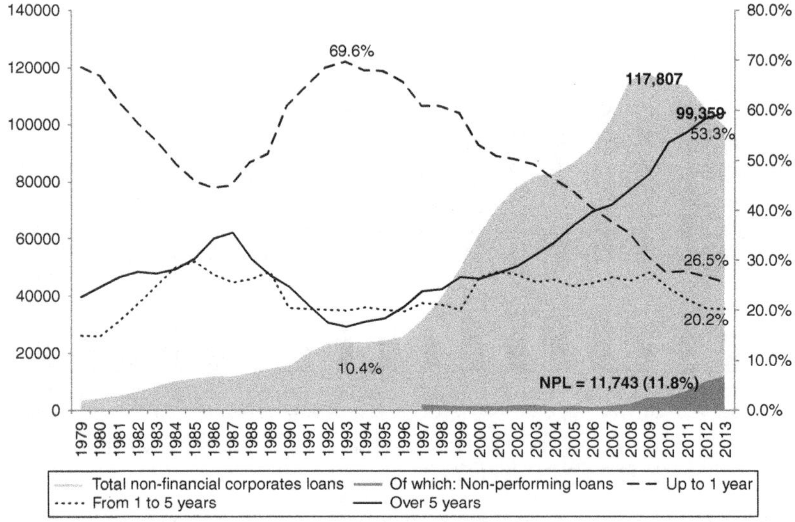

Figure 8.10 Non-financial corporate loans of the Portuguese banking system

(26.5%). On the other hand, loans with a longer maturity rose to 53.3% (Figure 8.10).

Effects of the 2011–14 bailout on banking loans to construction

The weakness shown in the balance sheet structure of companies has immediately suffered from the implemented measures, on the one hand

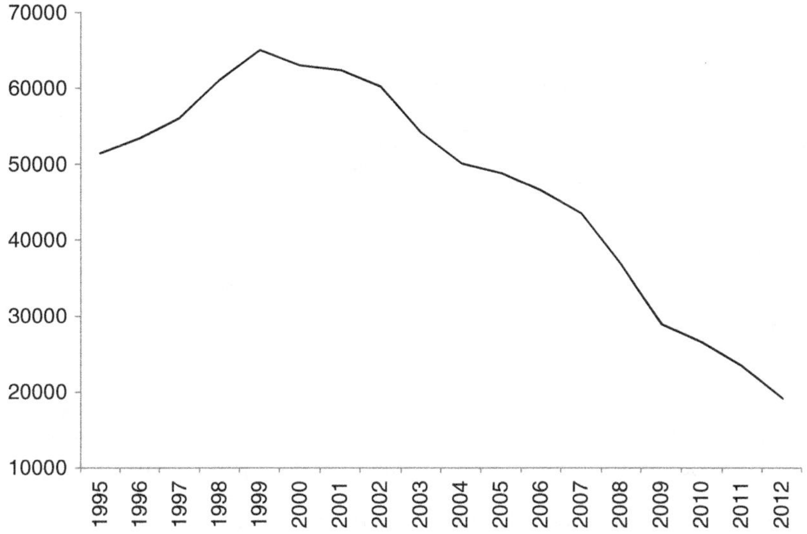

Figure 8.11 Number of licensed buildings per year in Portugal

from weak capitalization to withstand longer periods of stock flow, and secondly from the dependence on the necessary working capital that led to a drop in credit quality. That mainly happened in construction due to the scarcity of new public investments and also due to the shrinking home loan market.

In fact, building construction activity had already shown signs of slowing since early 2000 (Figure 8.11). In 2012, the number of building licenses represented less than a third that of 1999. With the Portuguese financial bailout, public investment declined significantly. In 2013, engineering works (mainly represented by public works) represented less than half the number reported in 2005 (Figure 8.12).

The result of the agreement with the Troika on the conditions of the Portugal bailout had a severe and sudden impact on Portuguese economic activity, as the model followed hitherto was heavily dependent on construction activity. The restrictive conditions for the granting of new mortgage loans caused a significant downturn in real estate transactions.

These events led to an interruption in the flow of housing stock, leading to a significant growth in breach of the payment obligations of loans in the construction sector. The weight of non-performing loans in total loans jumped from 7.5% in 2009 to a maximum of 23.78% in 2013 (Figure 8.13).

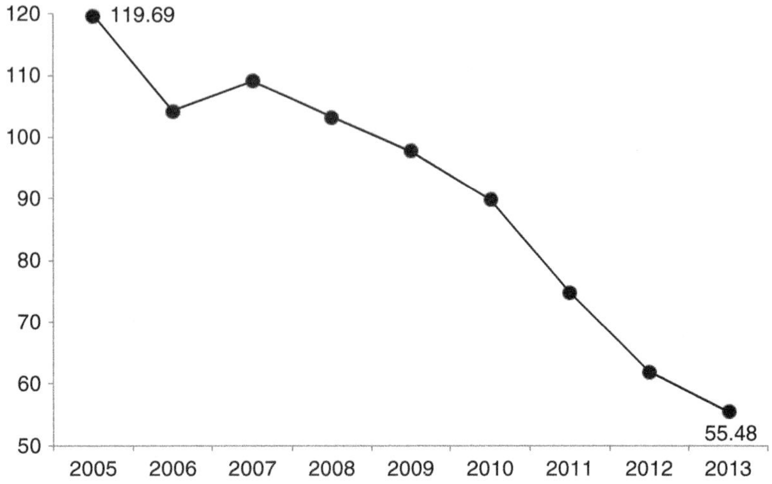

Figure 8.12 Index of production in civil engineering works (base Jan 2010 = 100)

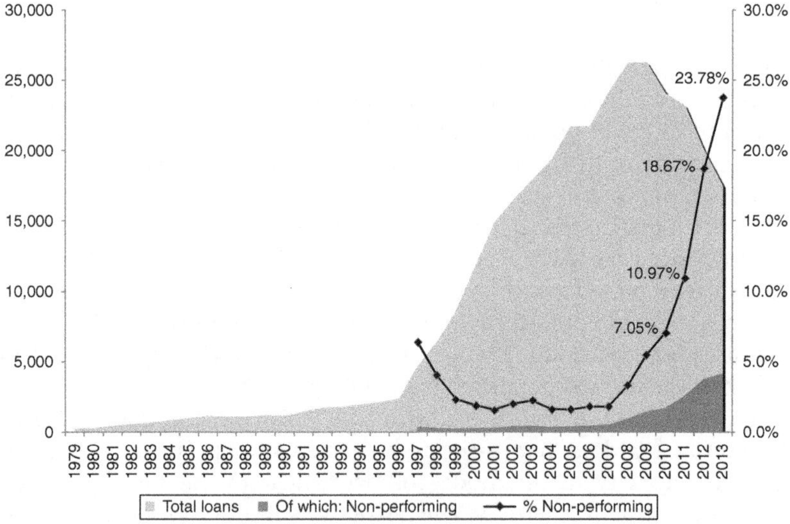

Figure 8.13 Bank loans to construction in the Portuguese banking system

Corporate and investment banking business segments

Generally, Portuguese banks segment their enterprise customers into three major groups (Figure 8.14):

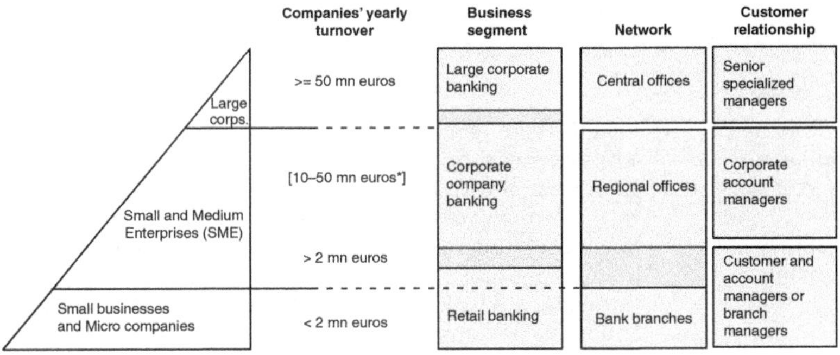

Figure 8.14 Business segmentation for enterprises in the Portuguese banking system

*European Union Commission Recommendation 2003/361 for SME definition by yearly turnover.

- Small businesses and micro companies, which include very small firms (including sole proprietors) with an annual turnover of less than €2 million. These companies are followed by account managers or branch managers, who have relationships with a pool of customers at the branch.
- Small and medium enterprises (SMEs), with an annual turnover exceeding €2 million (there are banks that subdivide this into companies with a turnover of between €10 and €50 million). Usually regional centers deal with these companies, which are part of a pool looked after by corporate account managers.
- Large corporates, with an annual turnover exceeding €50 million. Central offices monitor these companies through specialized senior managers.

Banking services to companies have been increasing their degree of sophistication and go far beyond traditional financing needs. Today, the main Portuguese banks have a set of extended services, and organize themselves internally in specific technical and commercial areas, including expertise in investment banking project finance, corporate finance, brokerage, investments, and management research.

Table 8.2 highlights the services that the four largest Portuguese banks perform for companies and the areas they cover. It can be seen that some banks include investment banking services within the structure of a retail and commercial bank. Nevertheless, there are other banks (such as Caixa Geral de Depósitos and Banco Espirito Santo) that have specialized investment banks in each financial group.

Table 8.2 Corporate and investment banking segments, Portuguese banking system – four largest banks (assets > €30 billion)*

Banco BPI	
Corporate banking, project finance and institutional banking	Includes commercial operations with companies with a turnover of more than €2 million and operates in coordination with the retail banking segment for companies with a turnover of up to €5 million. Also includes project finance services and relationship with public-sector entities, foundations and associations. This segment operates through a network of business centers, institutional centers, and home banking services adapted to business needs.
Investment banking	Brokerage – includes brokerage (purchase and sales of securities) on account of customers.
	Private banking – is responsible for implementing strategies and investment proposals presented to customers and managing all or part of their financial assets under management mandates given to the bank. In addition, private banking provides asset management, tax information, and business consulting services.
	Corporate finance – includes rendering consultancy services relating to the analysis of investment projects and decisions, market privatization operations, and the structuring of merger and acquisition processes.
Equity investments and others	Includes essentially financial investments and private equity activities. The BPI Group private equity area invests in unlisted companies with the following objectives: the development of new products and technologies, financing of investments in working capital, acquisitions, and the strengthening of financial autonomy.
Millennium bcp	
Companies	The companies in Portugal segment includes: the companies network, which covers the financial needs of companies with an annual turnover between €2.5 million and €50 million, and focuses on innovation, offering a wide range of traditional banking traditional banking products complemented by specialized financing; specialized recovery division; the activity of the real estate division; and interfundos (restructuring operations for real estate markets).
Corporate and investment banking	The corporate and investment banking segment includes: the corporate network in Portugal, targeting corporate and institutional customers with an annual turnover in excess of €50 million, providing a complete range of vale-added products and services; specialized nonitoring division; investment banking unit; and the activity of the bank's international division.

Banco Espírito Santo (BES)	
Corporate banking and institutional clients	Corporate banking and institutional clients are divided into four sub-segments so as to better address their specific needs: medium-sized companies with a turnover of between €2.5 million and €50 million; large corporations, national companies with a turnover of over €50 million; international corporate (multinational companies present in Portugal); and municipalities and institutional customers.
Investment banking	Investment banking offers BES Group's clients a wide range of specialized products and services, including advisory services in mergers and acquisitions, access to transactions in the capital markets (equities and debt), brokerage and portfolio management services, leveraged finance, project finance, and private equity. Espirito Santo Investment Bank manages BES's investment banking offer.
Caixa Geral de Depósitos (CGD)	
Commercial banking	Includes lending operations and resource-taking from major enterprises and SMEs. This segment also includes loans, current accounts, investment project finance, bill discounting operations, venture capital, factoring, equipment and property leasing, syndicated loans underwriting, and loans to the public sector.
Corporate finance	Includes activities related to acquisitions, mergers, restructuring operations, privatizations, subscriptions for and placements of securities in primary market, securitizations, preparation and organization of syndicated loans (merchant banking – loan placements), investment management, market and corporate financial analysis, and advisory services. Caixa Investment Bank runs the main operations.
Trading and sales	Includes banking activity related to management of the own securities portfolio, management of issued debt instruments, money and foreign exchange market operations, repo-type operations, securities lending operations, and wholesale brokerage. Investment in and claims on other credit institutions and derivatives are also included in this segment. Caixa Investment Bank runs the main operations.

*Portuguese banks that have taken part in the Single Supervisory Mechanism (SSM) of the ECB since November 2014. It is expected that the ECB will directly supervise around 130 credit institutions, representing almost 85% of total banking assets in the euro area.
Source: Banks' annual reports, 2006 and 2013. Author's analysis.

Investment banking is characterized by a specialization in providing financial services to businesses. More than the traditional analysis of credit risk, the activity of investment banking deepens its knowledge concerning projects and the appropriate financial structure, either the company or the sector in which it operates. Thus, it is expected that it will generate more revenue in commission and fees than in interest income.

There are several models in Portugal for running the investment banking business (Table 8.3):

- Investment banks integrated into groups with branches for retail and commercial banks, but with independent management.
- Independent investment banks with no branches (this is also the model adopted by international investment banks with offices in Portugal).
- Investment banking as a business line supported by a department in the retail and commercial bank structure.

In either model, we find structures that include services in the following areas:

- Project finance of which the main functions are to take part in non-recourse and limited-recourse operations, related to investment projects that involve, among other contractual models, service concessions and public–private partnerships; and to deliver to customers high-quality services and technical innovation in advisory matters as well as arranging and lending, providing access to the best financing structures in the best market conditions.
- M&A (mergers and acquisitions): services based on companies' need to run acquisition operations. Usually, the client company mandates the bank (purchase or sale mandate) through a service contract. The M&A team's role is to assist the client in the following transactions: valuation of the company, drafting an information memo, searching for potential buyers, conducting negotiations, and setting up the deal, in which legal and taxation aspects can also be addressed. These services include operations of privatizations and issuing fairness opinions.
- Brokerage: usually, the mission of this segment is the development of trading and sales activities in organized stocks and other securitiesmarkets.
- Debt issuing and management: trading operations to clients in public debt, foreign debt, other securities and corporate debt products, and placing debt products structured in several distribution networks. This includes sovereign debt and corporate debt book-running and issuing arrangements.
- Risk management: responsible for the study, setting up, and management of new structured products (derivatives), as well as of

Table 8.3 Portuguese banks operating corporate and investment banking services in Portugal

	Bank	Start date	Group	Notes
BIG4	Banco Português de Investimento	1981	BPI	Integrates BPI Group. Is a business line in Banco BPI – Retail Bank
	Espirito Santo Investment Bank	1983	BES	Operates as an independent bank in BES Group
	Caixa Banco de Investimento	1987	CGD	Operates as an independent bank in CGD Group
	Millennium bcp	n.a.	BCP	Investment banking is a business line in Millennium bcp – Retail Bank
OTHER	Banco Finantia	1988		Independent bank with no retail branch network
	Banco Efisa (ex-Soc. Investimento)	1988		Independent bank with no retail branch network
	Banif Investimentos	1992	BANIF	Operates as an independent bank in BANIF Group
	Banco Invest (ex-Banco Alves Ribeiro)	1997		Independent bank with no retail branch network
	Banco Português de Gestão	2001		Independent bank with no retail branch network
	Montepio Investimento (ex-Finibanco)	2013	Montepio	Operates as an independent bank in Montepio Group
	Banco Santander Totta		Santander	Investment banking is a business line in Banco Santander Totta – Retail Bank

hedging products structured to mitigate foreign exchange rate risk and interest rate risk.

- Private equity and venture capital, financial advisory, and research.

From the annual reports and accounts of the four main banks operating in Portugal, we conclude that there is a decline in the weight of operating income generated from the investment banking activity between 2006 and 2013, in Banco BPI from 10.8% to 6.5% of total operating income from operations in Portugal (Table 8.4). In contrast,

Table 8.4 Banco BPI, corporate and investment banking segments – operating income structure (10^3 euros)

	Investment Banking	Equity Investments	Sub-total	Total Domestic Operations	% of Total Domestic Operations
	2013				
Net interest income	2,366	396	2,762	284,450	1.0
Net commission income	33,309	−7	33,302	256,453	13.0
Other	10,389	−1	10,388	174,801	5.9
Operating income from banking activity	46,064	388	46,452	715,704	**6.5**
	2006				
Net interest income	7,876	−1,012	6,864	494,814	1.4
Net commission income	31,812	984	32,796	269,093	12.2
Other	24,993	29,760	54,753	111,440	49.1
Operating income from banking activity	64,681	29,732	94,413	875,347	**10.8**
	2006	**2013**			
Corporate loans	9,965.20	4,865.50			
Project finance	1,739.10	1,897.90			
Public-sector loans	2,033.20	1,979.10			
Total loans in Corporate and IB	13,737.60	8,742.60			

Table 8.5 Banco Espírito Santo, corporate and investment banking segments – operating income structure (10^3 euros)

	Investment Banking	Total Operations	% of Total Operations
		2013	
Net interest income	82,073	1,034,308	7.9
Net commission income	101,777	665,637	15.3
Other	62,797	200,994	31.2
Operating income from banking activity	246,647	1,900,939	**13.0**
		2006	
Net interest income	25,647	724,476	3.5
Net commission income	21,970	371,566	5.9
Other	49,915	392,595	12.7
Operating income from banking activity	97,532	1,488,637	**6.6**

Source: Banco Espírito Santo, annual reports 2006 and 2013, segments reporting. Author's analysis.

Banco Espírito Santo reflects a growing percentage of this activity in total operating income, from 6.6% to 13.0%in the same period (Table 8.5). Millennium bcp also recorded an increase in the weight of the activities of corporate and investment banking (Table 8.6), growing from 28.7% to 35.4%, but this is mainly due to the significant reduction in total domestic operating income (from €2,084 million to €932 million), mainly as a result of the diversification of its business in international markets (with a significant weight in markets such as Poland, Angola, and Mozambique). With regard to Caixa Geral de Depósitos, the weight of the activities of corporate and investment banking remained stable (Table 8.7), but also in a context of a severe global reduction of total operating income.

Considering only Portuguese investment banks operating in the Portuguese market (excluding banks with investment banking activities included in their structure), their weight in asset size remained stable at between 1.8% and 2.0% (Table 8.8). However, investment banking activity shows significance in the formation of operating income, with a higher weight, of about 3% (Table 8.9). There is, however, a progressive decline in total operating income in Portuguese investment banks (from €342.3 million to €292.7 million, which corresponds to a CAGR of -3.84%). This is related to the decrease in the number of corporate finance and debt issuance market transactions that occurred during this

Table 8.6 Millennium bcp, corporate and investment banking segments – operating income structure (10^3 euros)

	2013		
	Corporate and Investment Banking	Total Domestic Operations	% of Total Domestic Operations
Net interest income	217,387	385,002	56.5
Net commission income	112,463	388,779	28.9
Other	0	158,110	0.0
Operating income from banking activity	329,850	931,891	35.4

	2006					
	Corporate Banking	Investment Banking	Subtotal	Total Domestic Operations	% Investment Book of Total Domestic Operations	% of Total Domestic Operations
Net interest income	323,682	−23,350	300,332	1,090,553	n.d.	27.5
Net commission income	132,398	46,183	178,581	703,880	6.6	25.4
Other	0	120,160	120,160	290,434	41.4	41.4
Operating income from banking activity	456,080	142,993	599,073	2,084,867	6.9	28.7

	2006	2013
Company loans	16,734	4,809
Corporate loans		7,922
Investment banking loans	702	
Total loans in Corporate and IB segments	17,436	12,731

Source: Millennium bcp, annual reports 2006 and 2013, segments reporting. Author's analysis.

Table 8.7 Caixa Geral de Depósitos, corporate and investment banking segments – operating income structure (10^3 euros)

	Corporate Finance (1)	Trading and Sales (2)	Commercial Banking (3)	Total Operations	% of Total Operations (1)+(2)	% of Total Operations (1)+(2)+(3)
			2013			
Net interest income	124, 223	−212, 920	−27, 191	858, 261	n.d.	n.d.
Net commission income	60, 378	13, 153	111, 746	522, 043	14.1	35.5
Other	−14, 685	267, 913	26, 632	324, 122	78.1	86.3
Operating income from banking activity	169, 916	68, 146	111, 187	1, 704, 426	**14.0**	**20.5**
			2006			
Net interest income	14, 665	159, 585	181, 660	1, 704, 879	10.2	20.9
Net commission income	23, 443	14, 308	59, 349	364, 719	10.4	26.6
Other	−1, 184	237, 626	−11, 822	914, 573	25.9	24.6
Operating income from banking activity	36, 924	411, 519	229, 187	2, 984, 171	**15.0**	**22.7**

Source: Caixa Geral de Depósitos, annual reports 2006 and 2013, segments reporting. Author's analysis.

Table 8.8 Total Assets (in 10^3 euros)

	Investment Banks*	Total System	Weight (%)
2009	9,317,002	479,163,575	1.9
2010	9,712,342	506,185,293	1.9
2011	9,340,097	505,923,453	1.8
2012	9,465,711	471,838,150	2.0

*Only investment banks (excluding investment banking services operated by retail and commercial banks). Banks considered in the analysis: Espirito Santo Investment Bank, Caixa Banco de Investimento, Banif Banco de Investimentos, Banco Finantia, Banco Invest.

Table 8.9 Weight of Portuguese investment banks in income statement structure

	Investment Banks*	Total System	IB weight (%)
		Net Interest Income (in 10^3euros)	
2009	85,457	5,552,990	1.5
2010	87,055	5,179,894	1.7
2011	93,053	5,288,441	1.8
2012	110,196	4,316,698	2.6
		Net Income Fees and Commissions (in 10^3euros)	
2009	171,386	2,262,265	7.6
2010	184,350	2,559,500	7.2
2011	124,115	2,473,549	5.0
2012	105,866	2,393,906	4.4
		Operating Income (in 10^3 euros)	
2009	342,352	10,525,448	3.3
2010	327,709	9,918,732	3.3
2011	221,531	9,500,682	2.3
2012	292,684	9,416,039	3.1

*Only investment banks (excluding investment banking services operated by retail and commercial banks). Banks considered in the analysis: Espirito Santo Investment Bank, Caixa Banco de Investimento, Banif Banco de Investimentos, Banco Finantia, Banco Invest.
Source: APB – Associação Portuguesa de Bancos (Portuguese Banking Association), individual balance sheets, 2014.

period, characterized by a significant decline in public investment. This fall was higher than that which occurred in the overall financial system (CAGR of -2.75% for the same period).

When the structure of net interest income is analyzed, we find that service delivery is important in investment banking. More than mere financial intermediaries, Portuguese investment banks managed to evolve in the provision of financial advisory services, valuing those in the market through advice in various areas. When we compare

Table 8.10 Weight of Portuguese investment banks in income statement structure

	Fees and Commissions/Operating Income	
	Investment Banks*	**Banking System**
2009	50.1%	21.5%
2010	56.3%	25.8%
2011	56.0%	26.0%
2012	36.2%	25.4%

*Only investment banks (excluding investment banking services operated by retail and commercial banks). Banks considered in the analysis: Espirito Santo Investment Bank, Caixa Banco de Investimento, Banif Banco de Investimentos, Banco Finantia, Banco Invest.

Source: APB – Associação Portuguesa de Bancos (Portuguese Banking Association), individual balance sheets, 2014.

the structure of net interest income, it becomes clear that the weight of fees and commissions on operating income is relevant: more than 50% (excluding the year 2012), compared with about 25% of the total structure of the system (Table 8.10). These figures confirm investment banking's importance in Portugal in providing specialized services to corporates.

Trends in companies' loan quality

The beginning of the financial crisis changed significantly the evolution of interest rates for bank loans to companies. By 2008, the spreads of operations against the Euribor index rate remained stable, but from that year the differential worsened, especially in the early period of the bailout (2011). Since then, the financing costs for companies have not changed significantly (Figure 8.15).

The increased prices of financing and the significant reduction in domestic economic activity affected the quality of loan portfolios. The overdue loans ratio peaked at 13.3% in the total system concerning non-financial company loans (Figure 8.16), with sectors heavily dependent on the downturn in domestic demand indicators showing major complications, including construction (25.6%), real estate activities (18.6%), and wholesale and retail (15.8%).

Nevertheless, the way of monitoring loans to companies tends to be different. The demands to improve loan portfolio quality have been changing how companies are monitored. Recently, the governor of the Bank of Portugal advised banks to carry out effective monitoring of

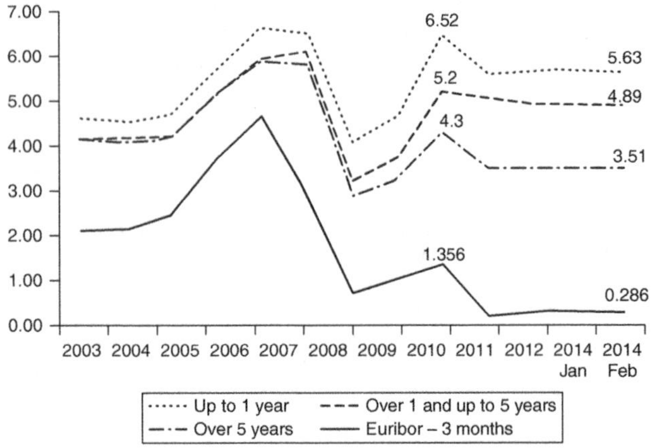

Figure 8.15 Non-financial companies' average interest rate loans by maturity comparing Euribor 3 months

Sources: Bank of Portugal, Financial and Monetary Statistics (2014); Euribor (2014). Author's analysis.

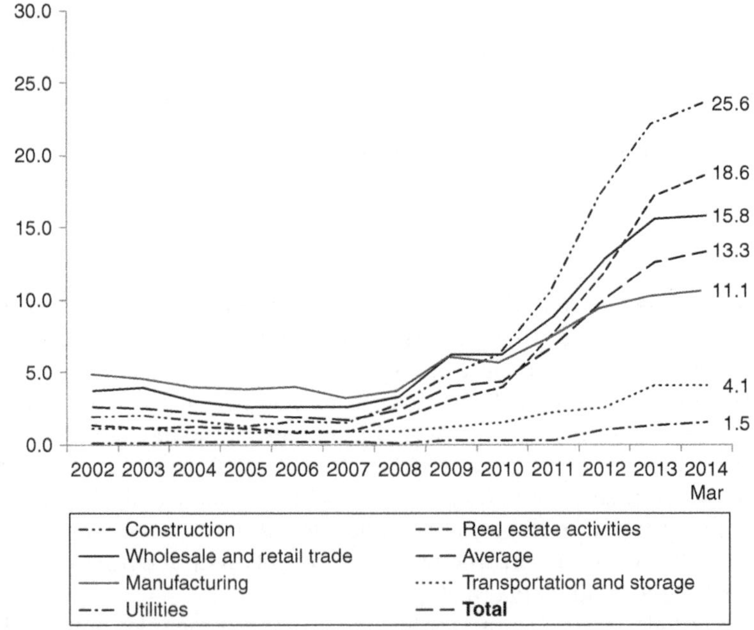

Figure 8.16 Non-financial companies overdue loans as a percentage of total loans

enterprises as a way to avoid default and insolvency:"If we, actors of the financial system, could have anticipated with the necessary measures, we were not only working to safeguard the financial part, we were saving the corresponding jobs. Take the example of private equity funds, which finance companies but assume an important role regarding their management."[2]

The economic cycle and lending portfolio management

The increase of credit risk in the construction and real estate sectors put banks' balance sheets under pressure, mainly regarding the compliance requirements of new capital ratios. With a large number of players in the construction industry near to collapse, the banks had to find solutions quickly in order to convert their exposure to debt instruments with a need to extend maturities, anticipating the long period required to enable recent investments in real estate projects to come to fruition. That gave rise to a new perspective (Figure 8.17): the equity loan (mezzanine debt and turnaround capital).

The majority of Portuguese banks put in place significant changes in structured monitoring of the enterprises they financed by gradually shifting from a perspective of risk analysis based only on track record to a more forward-looking approach. However, for this to be possible

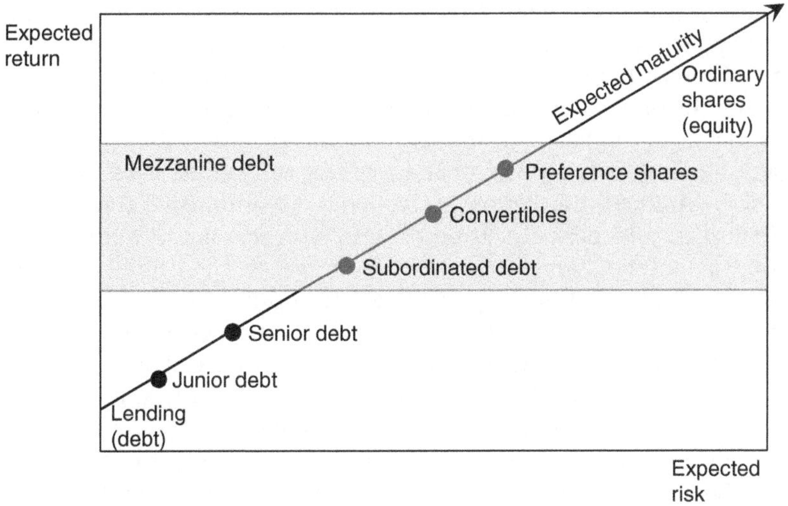

Figure 8.17 From debt (credit risk model) to equity (project risk model)

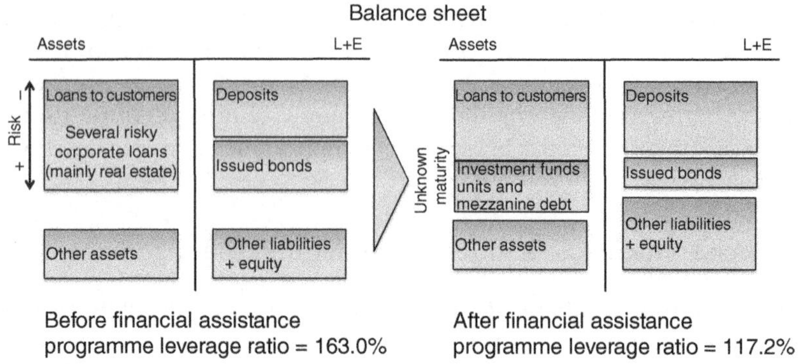

Figure 8.18 Balance sheet management trends in retail banking

without collapsing the structure of companies' financing, banks have come to restructure debt, extending maturities, and, in some sectors such as construction and real estate activities, opting to transform debt into hybrid or equity instruments (Figure 8.18).

Although the solutions put significant pressure on the capital ratios of banks' balance sheets, the prospect of supporting businesses, either directly or indirectly (through specialized investment funds or through private equity companies), may be a route to avoid the destruction of value and thereby keep assets performing.

Real estate investment funds recorded remarkable growth in the Portuguese market (Figure 8.19). Most real estate funds consist of closed-ended funds, the result of investments made by real estate developers and family offices that want better management of their assets, but also are the result of placing in specialized funds the assets that comes into bank ownership as a result of the recovery of overdue loans. In 2008 (Law 64-A/2008), the Portuguese government authorized the creation of Funds for Residential Letting (FIIAH), with the aim of finding solutions to households overindebted with mortgages. These funds allow the transfer of occupied housing in the event of difficulties in payment of installments to the banks. Families in this situation deliver their homes to the Funds for Residential Letting and pay rent instead of loan installments. Funds for Residential Letting reached €1,611.9 million at the end of 2013 (13.1% of total real estate investment funds).

Venture capital funds have grown in importance in Portugal since the early 2000s. The total amount under management rose from €357 million in 2003 to €3,125.9 million in 2012 (Figure 8.20). If at first venture capital funds presented themselves as an alternative to accessing equity from companies (especially SMEs), or even to helping entrepreneurs

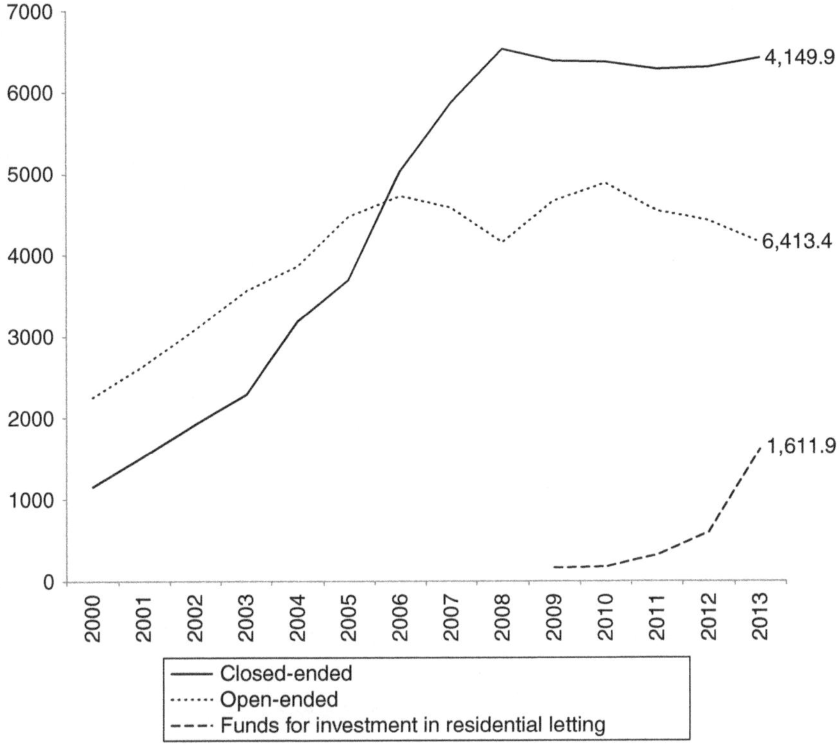

Figure 8.19 Real estate investment funds (total value under management)

develop their projects, today it appears that the total amount of funds under venture capital management is dominated by values assigned to non-financial holdings (Figure 8.21). In Table 8.11, it appears that the market is concentrated in turnaround funds managed by ECS, SCR, and SA (50.9% of market share). Table 8.12 shows that the value assigned to turnaround was €1,155.6 million in 2012.

However, this value appears to be underestimated, because from the analysis of the annual reports (2012 and 2013) of the main Portuguese banks, it can be concluded that at the end of 2012, gross assets transferred from the balance sheets of banks to turnaround funds amounted to €2,610.7 million (Figure 8.22), rising to €3,353.9 million in 2013 (Figure 8.22).

The main assets transferred to turnaround funds are directly or indirectly related credits to construction, real estate activities, and tourism. In Figure 8.23, it appears that the weight of the transferred assets is significant in funds managed by ECS (Tourism Turnaround

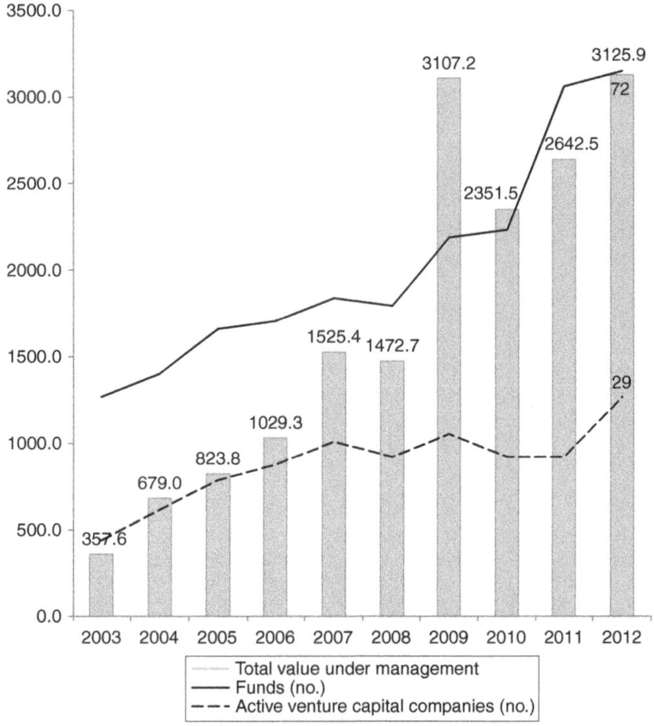

Figure 8.20 Venture capital in Portugal (total value under management)

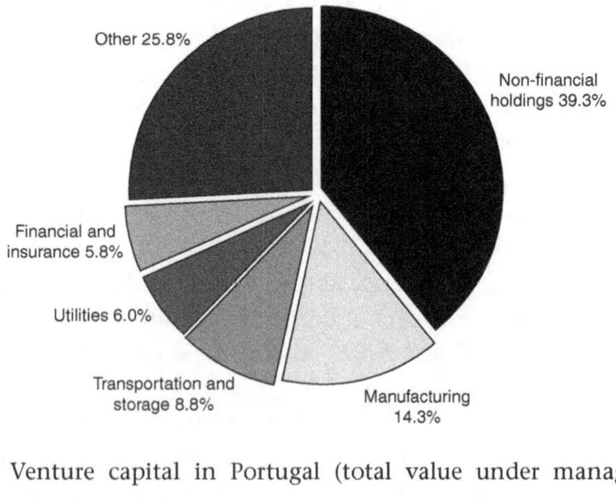

Figure 8.21 Venture capital in Portugal (total value under management per sector)

Table 8.11 Players in the Portuguese venture capital market, 2012

Company	Main Stage	Market Share (%)
ECS, SCR, SA (2)	Turnaround	50.9
Caixa Capital, SCR, SA (4)	Several	15.3
Portugal Capital Ventures, SCR, SA (25)	Several	8.2
ES Ventures, SCR, SA (6)	Venture (Seed, Startup, Early Stage)	6.7
Explorer Investments, SCR, SA (3)	Several	5.8
ES Capital, SCR, SA (3)	Several	4.7
Inter Risco, SCR, SA (2)	Several	2.3
Other	Several	6.1
Oxy Capital, SCR, SA	Turnaround	New player
Vallis Capital Partners, SCR, SA	Turnaround	New player

Source: Comissão do Mercado de Valores Mobiliários (Portuguese Securities Market Commission), Venture Capital Annual Report, 2012. Author's analysis. Number of managed funds in brackets.

Table 8.12 Investment stage of venture capital funds, 2012

Investment Stage of Venture Capital Funds	Type	Values under Management
Seed Capital	Venture	47.5
Startup	Venture	234.9
Early Stage	Venture	57.7
Growth	Private Equity	702.9
Substitution of Shareholders	Private Equity	199.1
Turnaround	Private Equity	1,155.6
MBO	Private Equity	137.2
MBI	Private Equity	51.8
Other	Private Equity	232.0

Source: Comissão do Mercado de Valores Mobiliários (Portuguese Securities Market Commission), Venture Capital Annual Report, 2012. Author's analysis. Values in 10^6euros.

Fund – tourism sector assets; Turnaround Fund –construction and real estate activities; FLIT – construction and real estate activities), by Vallis (Vallis Construction Sector Consolidation Fund); and by Explorer Investments (Discovery Fund – especially hospitality and tourism sectors).

Trends in Portuguese investment banking

Investment banking in Portugal has developed its activity supported by the dynamics of mergers and acquisitions (M&A), debt

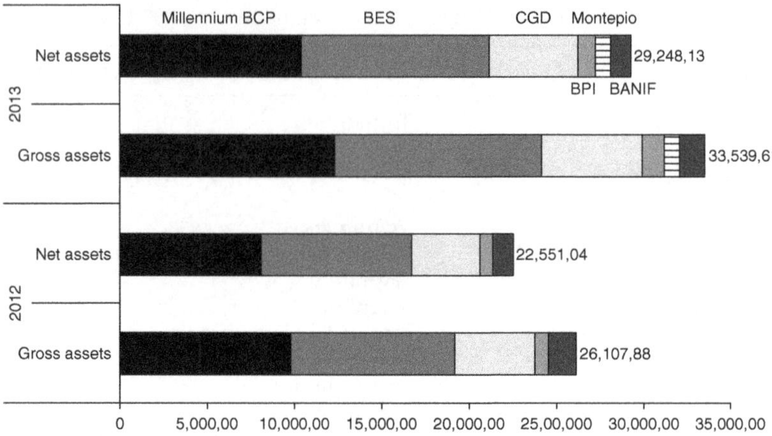

Figure 8.22 Transfers from balance sheet assets to stakes in private equity and turnaround venture capital funds (10^3 euros)

Source: Annual Reports 2012 and 2013 of the six major banks that transferred assets to turnaround private equity and capital funds. Author's analysis.

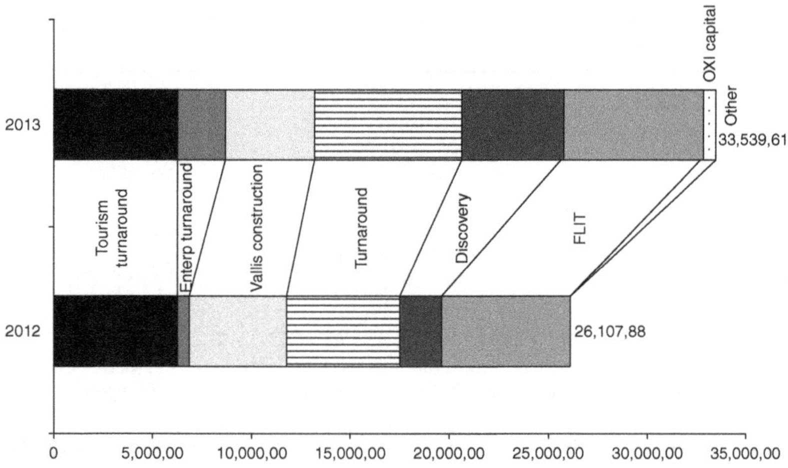

Figure 8.23 Transfers from banks' balance sheet gross assets to stakes in private equity and turnaround venture capital funds (10^3 euros), by turnaround fund

Source: Annual Reports 2012 and 2013 of the six major banks that transferred assets to turnaround private equity and capital funds. Tourism Turnaround, Enterprises Turnaround FLIT and Turnaround Funds are managed by ECS Capital, SCR, SA.; Vallis Construction Sector Consolidation is managed by Vallis Capital Partners, SCR, SA; Discovery is managed by Explorer Investments, SCR, SA.; Oxy Capital is managed by Oxy Capital, SCR, SA. Author's analysis.

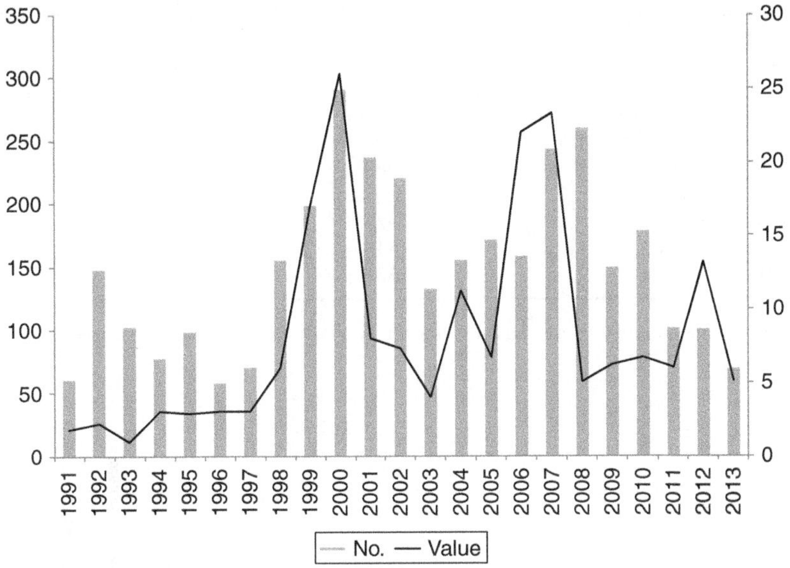

Figure 8.24 Announced mergers and acquisitions in Portugal, 1991–2013

issuance, brokerage, and project finance. When the periods of increased investment banking activity are analyzed, these tend to coincide between 1995 and 2002 and between 2003 and 2008.

Mergers and acquisitions

Figure 8.24 illustrates the mergers and acquisitions activity in Portugal. The activity peak in number and value of announced transactions was reached by 2000. Although the M&A market recovered between 2004 and 2008, it fell significantly at the time ofthe international financial crisis.

Debt issuing

The main Portuguese investment banks (Caixa Banco de Investimento and Espirito Santo Investment Bank) are responsible for most of the debt issues in Portugal. Together they represent more than 20% of the book-running market in 2013 (Table 8.13).

With regard specifically to the public debt market (Figure 8.25), the period up to 2006 is characterized by the issuance of medium- to long-term debt. From the onset of the financial crisis, short-term issues gained weight. From 2011, with the Financial Assistance Programme,

Table 8.13 Main bookrunners in the Portuguese market, 2013 (value in 10^3 mn euros)

Bookrunners	Value	Market Share	Number
Caixa Banco de Investimento	1,420	10.8%	11
Espirito Santo Investment Bank	1,287	9.8%	10
Deutsche Bank	1,168	8.9%	6
Société Générale	924	7.0%	5
Morgan Stanley	813	6.2%	2
Other	7,536		

Sources: Banks' annual reports 2013; Bloomberg. Bonds issued by Portuguese issuers.

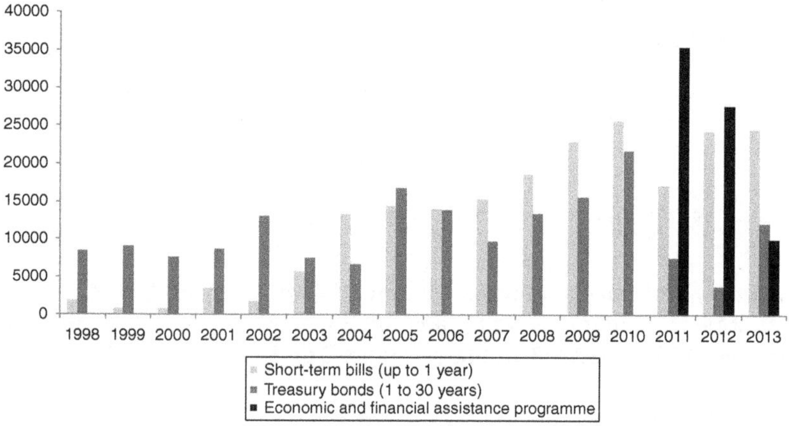

Figure 8.25 Public debt issued by the Portuguese state

the funding needs of the Portuguese state were assured by the entities represented by the Troika, removing the role of market players normally present in long-term issues.

With regard to the securitization market (Figure 8.26), the downward movement recorded from 2009 adversely affected the business of investment banking. A significant part of this activity was affected by the ending of the acquisition of assets-backed securities (ABS) on international markets. This meant that the securitization that was performed was almost exclusively synthetic;that is, to maintain securities on bank balance sheets in order to strengthen collateral via liquidity injection by the European Central Bank (ECB).

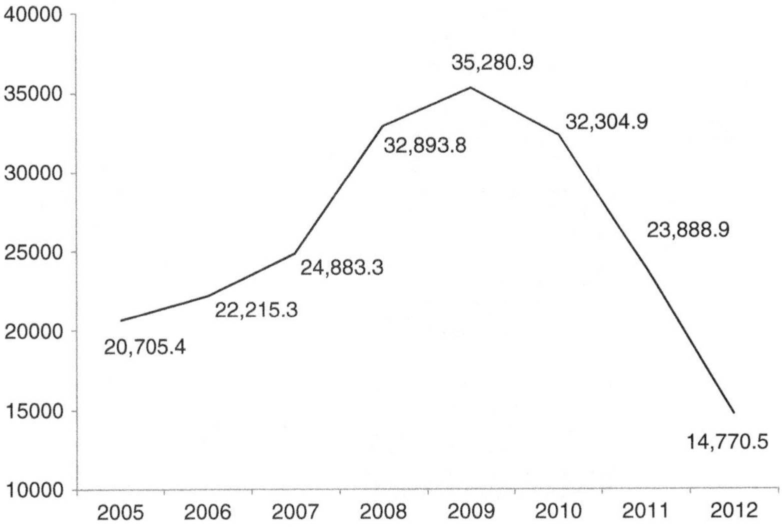

Figure 8.26 Total securitized assets managed by securitization funds

Project finance and public–private partnerships (PPP)

Project finance is based on the financing of long-term infrastructure, industrial projects, or public services based on a limited-recourse financial structure where the project debt and equity used to finance the project are paid back from the cash flow generated by the project (as defined by the International Project Finance Association). This means that classic banking loans usually do not fit investors' needs, even considering long-term loans, due to the risk level concerning cash-flow generation.

For that reason, investment banking is highlighted to provide financial advice for project promoters concerning the most adequate finance structure. Afterward, investment banking teams may be asked to take part in raising funds, as arrangers and book runners for debt issuing.

Figure 8.27 shows typical corporate loans where payment is predetermined and fully independent from cash flows generated. Existing assets or personal guarantees as collateral usually mitigate the credit risk.

Figure 8.28 shows a concept of project finance where there are several counterparties: the promoting company, which owns the special-purpose vehicle (SPV) that concentrates the project risk; the SPV, which is responsible for contracting startup services such as design and engineering, construction, and financial services; and the financial

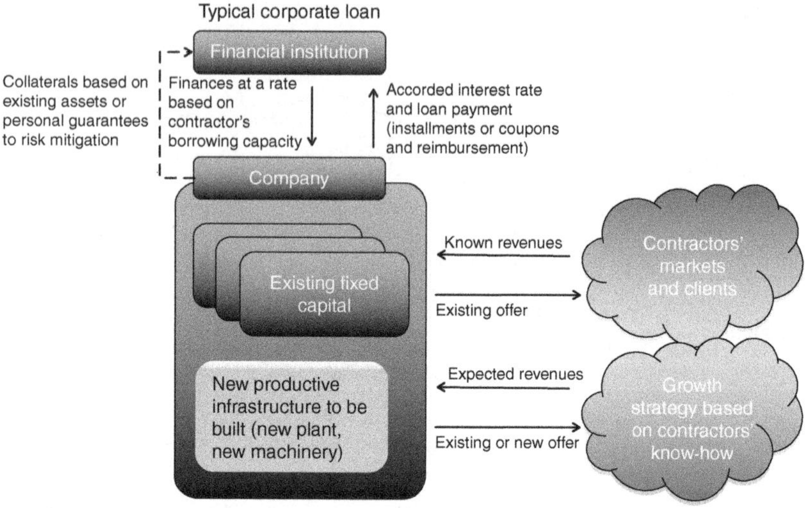

Figure 8.27 A typical corporate bank loan (author's concept)

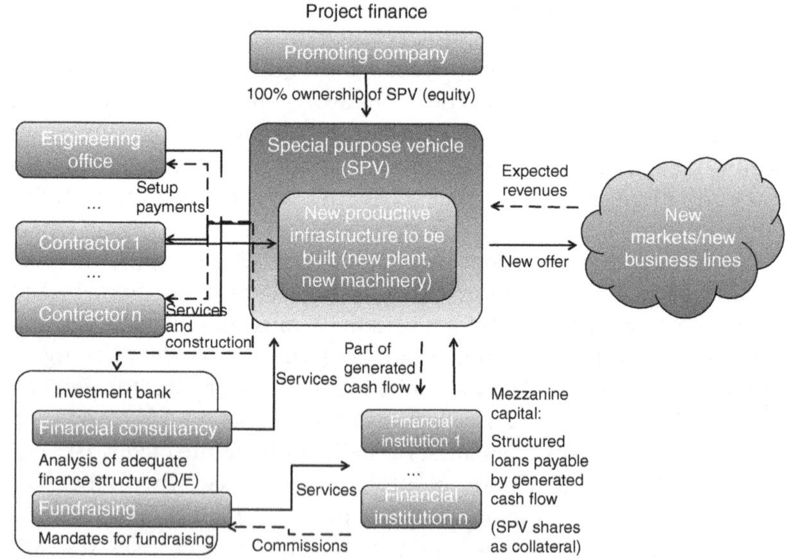

Figure 8.28 Project finance (author's concept)

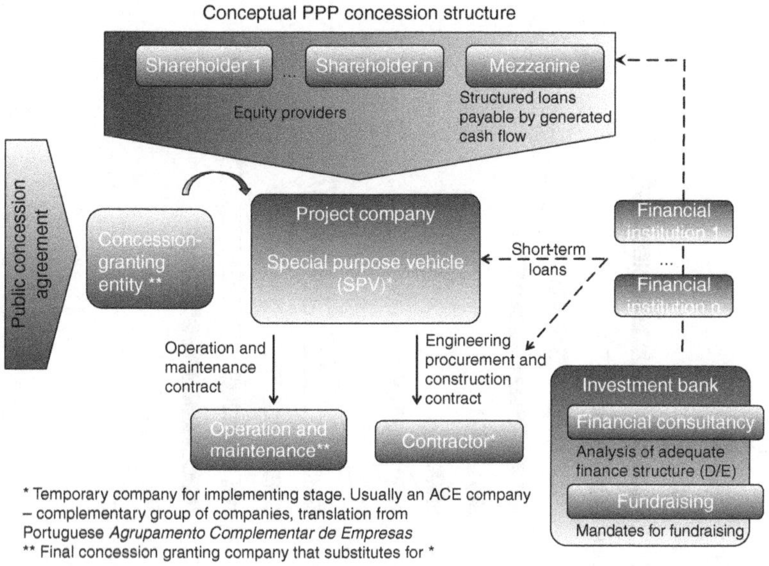

Figure 8.29 Conceptual public-private partnership (author's concept)

consultant (such as an investment bank), which plays the role of raising funds, mainly composed of loans whose payment is guaranteed by the project's expected cash flow. In most cases, SPV shares guarantee these loans.

Since the 1980s, PPPs have become a particular instance of project finance in the Portuguese market (see Figure 8.29). The expansionist budgetary policy of the Portuguese state took place due to infrastructure needs.

Over the last 20 years, there have been two important periods of public–private partnerships:

- Between 1995 and 2002, with the launch of 34 new PPPs, particularly aimed at infrastructure for seaports and highways, corresponding to an investment of over €12.5 billion.
- Between 2006 and 2010, with the launch of 37 new PPPs, with a greater variety of purposes (seaports, highways, health, and energy), corresponding to a total investment of €12 billion.

Figure 8.30 shows only the PPP initiatives of central government that are part of the report prepared by the Ministry of Finance technical

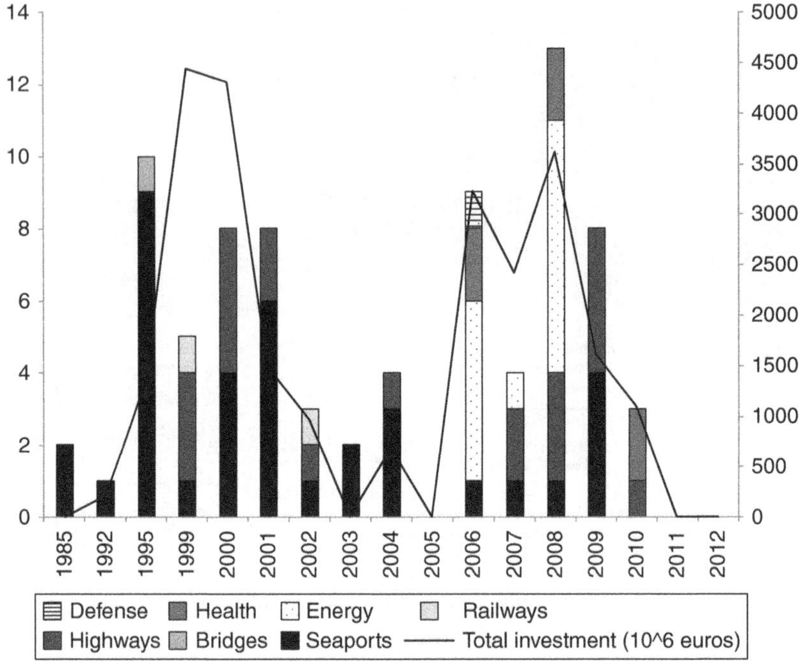

Figure 8.30 Number of and total investment in public-private partnerships in Portugal

services, with the aim of analyzing the charges made and to include the Portuguese state in the analysis of the evolution of public debt.

During the most active periods, the PPP initiatives boosted corporate and investment banking due to the financial advisory services charged to these projects (consulting, assembly operations, and debt issuance mandates). Currently, PPP contracts are being widely criticized because of the risks that are involved, since they tend to save private concessionaires from the externalities related to the evolution of demand (especially in highways).

Notes

Notes about Banco Espírito Santo resolution and transfer of assets and liabilities to Novo Banco: after the closing of this chapter, there were important forward facts impacting the analysis when reading some of the information above. Considering the information issued by the Bank of Portugal, at the end of July 2014, the first half results disclosed of Banco Espírito Santo *"reflected the practice of management acts seriously detrimental to the interests of Banco Espírito Santo, S.A. and non-compliance with the determinations issued by the Banco de Portugal."* The Extraordinay Meeting of the Board of Directors of the Banco of Portugal occurred on Sunday, 3 August 2014, issued a deliberation setting up Novo Banco determining that assets, liabilities, off-balance-sheet items and assets under management by Banco Espírito Santo , S.A., were transferred to Novo Banco, S.A., as listed specifically in that Deliberation.

Nevertheless, information about Espírito Santo Investment Bank (recently acquired by the Chinese Haitong group), keeps valid due to its management independence from Banco Espírito Santo.

1. European Commission (2012) *Alert Mechanism Report,* 14 February, Brussels: EC.
2. Carlos Costa, Governor of the Bank of Portugal, speech at *Current Trends and Prospects Revolution of Regulation and Supervision of the Financial Sector in the EU,* University of Lisbon, June 19, 2014.

9

Portuguese Banks and Their Expansion in Portuguese-Language Countries

Anabela Sérgio

Several Portuguese banks have been established in Portuguese-language countries for a long time, with different strategies and aims. These banks are Banco BIC; Montepio, under the brand of Finibanco Angola; Millennium bcp (Banco Comercial Português); BPI (Banco Português de Investimentos), under the brand of Banco de Fomento Angola (BFA); and CGD (Caixa Geral de Depósitos), the only state-owned bank. These banks are operating in several countries, including Angola, Mozambique, Cape Verde, Guinea-Bissau, Timor, and Brazil, with different levels of strength and geographical coverage. Individual analyses of each bank's performance, strategies, and aims follow.

Banco BIC

Banco BIC focuses its activities abroad in Angola, under the name of Banco BIC AO. It is legally established there as a local bank. Banco BIC has experienced recent and impressive success, which can be demonstrated by looking at Tables 9.1–9.3.

As a result of all the effort and commitment of the professionals working in Banco BIC, through a particular emphasis given to supporting customers, a permanent attitude of full availability, and strict cost controls, Banco BIC closed the 2013 financial year in growth.

In fact, sustainability is the keyword in relation to all its financial highlights. These allow us to conclude that total net assets grew from US$425 million in 2005 to US$7,696 million in 2013 (Table 9.1). During the same eight years, net Income, from the low level of US$5 million at the beginning, reached US$201 million in 2013 (Table 9.2). Moreover, equity (Table 9.3) increased steadily from US$12 million in 2005, reaching the level of US$889 million in 2013.

Table 9.1 Banco BIC total net assets (in US$ million)

Year	Amount
2005	425
2006	1,249
2007	2,327
2008	4,529
2009	4,318
2010	4,868
2011	5,513
2012	6,931
2013	7,696

Source: Financial statements, not audited.

Table 9.2 Banco BIC net income (in US$ million)

Year	Amount
2005	5
2006	33
2007	80
2008	141
2009	149
2010	142
2011	156
2012	168
2013	201

Source: Financial statements, not audited.

Also important to discuss concerning BIC is its business centers, divided into branches, corporate centers, investment centers, and private banking units. Currently, in Angola there are:

- 202 branches, of which 109 are in the capital, Luanda, and 93 distributed throughout the remaining provinces;
- 15 corporate centers;
- 3 investment centers;
- 2 private banking units.

We should emphasize that Banco BIC won the Sirius Award 2013 for the best financial-sector company. This is one of the most prestigious

Table 9.3 Banco BIC equity (in US$ million)

Year	Amount
2005	12
2006	68
2007	153
2008	293
2009	460
2010	565
2011	650
2012	760
2013	889

Source: Financial statements, not audited.

distinctions in the country and it highlights the best management practices in the financial sector in Angola.

On the other hand, Banco BIC is a newly established bank in Portugal. Therefore, it is worth remarking on some landmarks of its performance within the framework of the Portuguese banking system. Using as a criterion net income (by accumulated value), Banco BIC reached break-even by October 2013, and the net profit at the end of that year means that it had made a successful turnaround (after experiencing negative values for net income in all previous months of the year).

In Portugal, Banco BIC is a medium-size bank, covering the following business centers:

- 201 branches around Portugal, from north to south, including the Portuguese islands the Azores and Madeira;
- 15 corporate centers, focused on establishing a diversified and personalized offer to BIC customers;
- 2 private banking units, one in Oporto and another in Lisbon;
- external promoters, a complementary network between retail, corporate, and individual banking.

Furthermore, Banco BIC was the first bank to provide currency exchange services for Kwanzas in Portugal. This service, which began in November 2013, is exclusive to notes issued from October 2012 and is available in 15 branches spread around the country.

Finally, BIC is developing a new strategy of international expansion. Currently, its shareholders are studying markets with a close relation with Angola and Portugal. Banco BIC operates now in Brazil and Cape Verde and it will launch from scratch further operations in Namibia, South Africa, and the Democratic Republic of Congo.

Finibanco Angola

Finibanco Angola is the brand in that country of the mutual Portuguese bank Montepio, which splits its activities between Angola and Mozambique, as will be explained subsequently. Its core business area is retail banking.

For a long time Montepio conducted operations by itself in formerly Portuguese colonies such as Mozambique, Cape Verde, and Guinea-Bissau. These operations did not belong to the bank's core activities or objectives, so they were dropped. This strategy led to the selling of all of Montepio's ventures in these countries between 2005 and 2008, except for one operation in Cape Verde. There was also a branch in Macau, which was sold in 2004.

In 2010, Montepio launched a successful IPO (initial public offering) over Finibanco and adopted the operations of Finibanco Angola (keeping the name). Angola was a flourishing and dynamic economy with great potential for growth, which was one of the reasons that contributed to Montepio's takeover of Finibanco.

In Angola, there were three reasons for Montepio keeping the Finibanco name:

- The Finibanco brand was already well established in the market.
- Another institution, outside the financial sector, already existed with the name Montepio.
- Montepio is a major shareholder in Finibanco Angola, with a participation of 87.67% of the capital (data from Q2 2014); the remaining shares are split between local shareholders.

In Angola, the strategy of Montepio (and Finibanco, therefore) is to grow by organically enlarging its geographical presence.

In September 2014 Finibanco Angola had:

- 15 branches;
- 3 corporate centers.

It expected to open six branches and three corporate centers over the following year. Montepio's overall strategy is to grow in operational strength in Angola, focusing its activities on financial activity in the retail banking sector. A model of traditional commercial banking has been adopted, which goes together with a small/medium scope. This operational model is very important for the bank, which targets its operational strategic growth at aiming to obtain higher levels of profitability.

Mozambique is also an important country for Montepio. Since 2013 it has had a presence there with a shareholding of 44% in Banco Terra, the remaining capital in which belongs to Netherlands and Norwich shareholders. The strategy for Banco Terra is tightly defined: to launch and improve banking activity in the retail field.

Banco Fomento Angola (BFA)

Banco de Fomento Angola became part of BPI (Banco Português de Investimentos) in 1996. From 2002 BFA was legally an Angolan bank, with US$30 million in capital.

BPI held 100% of BFA's capital until November 2008. That is the moment when a new shareholder from Angola, Unitel (from the mobile communications sector), bought 49.9% of BFA's capital. That was an important landmark in the transformation of the shareholder structure, representing a strategic partnership.

BFA is characterized by:

- 1,192,513 customers;
- 175 branches;
- a status as the 2nd private bank in Angola;
- 2,400 employees;
- the first bank in debit card market share;
- 20 years in the Angolan market.

In 2003 the new headquarters of BFA were established in Luanda, representing an investment of US$20 million.

In Angola only 15% of the population holds deposits in the banking system. Therefore, currently the country faces a huge potential for growth in the banking sector.

The strategy for the presence of BFA in Angola is a long-term project, with a lifespan of 20–30 years. Its main objectives are:

- Retail banking development.
- Funding by the population's savings.

- Growth in its client base.
- Risk management equalizing European and Portuguese standards and demanding certain procedures.

A segmentation strategy began in 2004 with the inauguration of the first corporate center, followed by BFA's first investment center in 2006.

Some financial highlights are detailed in Table 9.4.

We may conclude that on the one hand Banco de Fomento Angola has experienced exponential growth over the past few years, and on the other there still is space for further development in its ability to grow even more.

Caixa Geral de Depósitos (CGD)

CGD's aim of internationalization dates from 1876, the year of its foundation. Since then, CGD has expanded its network in several countries, covering both the economic and financial fields as well as the social, cultural, and environmental fields. During the nineteenth century and at the beginning of the twentieth, the path of internationalization was centered on three geographical areas: India (1868), Brazil (1887), and Asia (1902). These are the areas of the most dynamic growth in the world and the greatest potential dynamism, where Portuguese companies center their own businesses and ambitions.

Table 9.4 BFA total assets (in US$ million)

Year	Amount
1996	135
2002	579
2003	806
2004	1,088
2005	1,579
2006	2,309
2007	3,552
2008	6,306
2009	5,897
2010	6,450
2011	7,062
2012	7,930
2013	8,892

Source: Bank's annual reports.

Of significant relevance is the entry to Africa, through what was then called Banco Nacional Ultramarino (BNU), which CGD absorbed in 2001. The group subsequently consolidated its presence on that continent.

Currently, the international expansion of CGD is centered on 23 geographical locations, strategically aimed at developing its own business and continuing to meet the needs of Portuguese companies. This means providing ongoing support to the Portuguese economy and society.

The presence in Portuguese-speaking countries, which are now fully covered by CGD (with the exception of Guinea-Bissau), represents a cornerstone of the group's business strategy.

Table 9.5 presents the various units of CGD's international network covering Portuguese-speaking countries (and some others as well). There follows a short historical review of the steps in the bank's process of internationalization, together with an explanation of its strategic orientations, tools, and objectives within the international framework.

Brazil

CGD's presence in Brazil dates from 1924. At the beginning, CGD received funds from Agência Financial, but in 1972 this agency, which had in the meantime changed its name to Banco Financial Português, was assigned as a commercial bank, therefore operating as a subsidiary of CGD.

After 20 years, within the overall context of the internationalization of the Portuguese banking system, CGD significantly changed its presence and its business model in Brazil, aiming to meet the business needs of Portuguese companies.

In 1994, CGD acquired 8% of the shares in Brazilian bank Banco ITAU, hence obtaining two seats on the administrative board.

In 1997, a new strategy for Brazil was announced. This was characterized by the establishment of CGD in the most important centers for the development of Portuguese interests.

In 1998, Caixa Brasil SGPS emerged, which in May of that year bought 80% of the shares in the financial system Bandeirantes, the owner of Banco Bandeirantes, with a presence in 27 states. At the same time, CGD expanded its activities to the insurance sector. The core business was expanded as well, targeting the segments of individuals and small and medium-size companies.

In 1999, the participation of CGD in Banco Bandeirantes increased to 98.11% of total capital.

Table 9.5 Units of CGD's international network covering Portuguese-speaking countries

Retail banking	
Timor-East: Timor branch	
Spain: Banco Caixa Geral	
France: French branch	
Luxembourg: Luxembourg branch	
South Africa: Banco Mercantile	
Angola: Banco Caixa Geral Totta Angola	
Cape Verde: Banco Comercial Atlântico and Banco Interatlântico	
Mozambique: Banco Comercial e de Investimentos	
São Tomé e Príncipe: Banco Internacional de São Tomé e Príncipe	
Wholesale and investment banking	
Brazil: Banco Caixa Geral Brasil	
USA: New York branch	
Cayman Islands: Cayman Islands branch	
UK: London branch	
Angola: Banco para a Promoção e Desenvolvimento	
Mozambique: Banco Nacional de Investimentos	
Non-residential banking	
Macau: Offshore branch	
Switzerland: CGD representative office	
Germany: CGD representative office	
Belgium: CGD representative office	
Canada: CGD representative office	
Venezuela: CGD and Banco Caixa Geral representative office	
Other international business	
Algeria: business delegation	
México: BCG representative office	
China: Zhuhai branch and Shanghai representative office	
India: Mumbai and Pagim (Goa) representative offices	

In 2000, CGD switched its share holding in Banco Bandeirantes for 12.3% of the share capital of Unibanco. The objective was to enhance its performance in the Brazilian market, going well beyond the links with only Portuguese communities and the bilateral relationship between Portugal and Brazil. With this cross-share participation, CGD became the second biggest shareholder in Unibanco, just behind the Moreira Salles family.

In 2005, CGD reformulated its presence in Brazil, after recognizing that its business model did not cope with the size of the market itself. It decided to end its participation in Unibanco and to dissolve Caixa Brasil. In this way, CGD gave up its model of being a universal bank, instead establishing a small bank that targets companies, and mainly developing the activities of investment banking and corporate finance.

In 2009, Banco Caixa Geral Brasil began operations, its capital fully owned by CGD. It provides services in Brazil, Europe (especially in the Iberian Peninsula), and Africa, regions where the CGD Group already has a sustainable trend of business and prominent results. Banco Caixa Geral Brasil has its headquarters in São Paulo and a branch in Rio de Janeiro. In December 2013, the bank had 73 employees.

Mozambique

In Mozambique, CGD Group's presence began with Banco Nacional Ultramarino (BNU). The latter opened its first subsidiary in 1887 and owned several coal and gold mines.

Today, the CGD Group is present in Mozambique through a reference bank in that country, Banco Comercial e de Investimentos (BCI), whichwas established in January 1996 under the name of AJM-Banco de Investimentos and with an initial capital of MZN30 million, mainly underwritten by local investors. The same year the bank's name changed to Banco Comercial de Investimentos, with its core business as activity in the investment banking field.

One year later, in 1997, the shareholder structure of BCI was modified with the entrance of Caixa Geral de Depósitos. CGD then had 60% of BCI's capital, with the remaining shares belonging to SCI, Sociedade de Controlo e Gestão de Participações SARL (38.63%), and 1.73% of shares distributed among small investors. That year BCI extended its activities to operate as a commercial bank.

In December 2003, BCI consolidated with another company, Banco de Fomento (BF), by integrating all of the assets of BF into BCI and the extinction of BF. Following that integration, the bank adopted the commercial name of BCI Fomento. At that time a new shareholder came on the scene, Group BPI (Banco Português de Investimentos), with 30% of the total shares.

In 2007, the shareholder structure of BCI was once again changed with the exit of Group SCI and the entrance of INSITEC Group, with 18.12% of total shares. The capital participation of CGD went up to 51%, and that of the BPI Group to 29.55%.

BCI is a bank with a Mozambiquan culture and it has a reference position in the country's financial system. Commercial banking is its dominant business field, in terms of both turnover and results.

Agriculture is an important pillar of the social and economic development of Mozambique; hence BCI has been strengthening its support to the sectors of agriculture, agriculture and industrial, and food industries. BCI offers these sectors specific solutions and also direct follow-up by specialized managers.

The activities of BCI in Mozambique, and those of CGD in Portugal, offer financial solutions to companies that carry out operations in both countries.

BCI has developed remarkable improvements in electronic banking, adopting a multichannel approach to clients, individuals, and enterprises, with high levels of access and stimulating results.

Notwithstanding fierce competition in the market, BCI reinforced its presence and performance within the Mozambiquan financial system, displaying in 2013 market shares of 28.37% in volume of assets, 28.20% in deposits, and 28.90% in credit.

BCI has focused on the expansion of its network, which in 2014 had 120 branches, 20 BCI exclusive centers, and 1 corporate center. The policy of network expansion should be maintained in the near future, with the bank reinforcing its presence in geographical areas of strong dynamism.

For the second consecutive year, the Global Banking and Finance Review assigned to BCI two prizes: "Best Retail Bank Mozambique 2014" and "Best Commercial Bank Mozambique 2014."

In December 2014, BCI had 2,243 employees, 1,351 of whom were concentrated in commercial activity. BCI's policy of study grants concessions has contributed to the increase in the number of employees with higher qualifications; in December 2013 these employees represented 30.1% of the total number.

Angola

CGD Group's history in Angola began in the nineteenth century and has assumed different forms over time. Nowadays CGD Group has a presence in the country through its subsidiary Banco Caixa Geral Totta de Angola, with its roots in Banco Totta de Angola, which, in its turn, succeeded Banco Totta & Açores (inaugurated in April 1993 and closed in July 2002). Both assets and liabilities were incorporated into Banco Caixa Geral Totta de Angola, 99.96% owned by Santander Group. On July 2, 2009, the bank adopted the name Banco Caixa Geral Totta de Angola, with the entry of new shareholders. After that, both Caixa Geral de Depósitos and Banco Santander hold 51% of the share capital. The remaining 49% belongs to Angolan shareholders, among which is Sonangol EP with 24%.

Banco Caixa Totta directs its activities mainly to the segment of medium and big enterprises, in particular in the export sector. It does support small and medium companies as well, and it is gradually developing its presence and support in the individuals segment, targeting higher-income individuals.

Since its foundation, Banco Caixa Totta has more than doubled its branch network, now being present in nine Angolan provinces: Luanda, Benguela, Huíla, Cabinda, Lunda Sul, Zaire, Bengo, Huambo, and Namibe.

It undertakes any kind of banking and financial transaction, paying special attention to commercial exchanges and investment operations between Portugal and Angola.

In Angola, the bank operates with 447 employees (in December 2014).

Cape Verde

Caixa Geral de Depósitos also operates in Cape Verde. The origins of its activities were in 1865, when Banco Nacional Ultramarino (BNU) opened its first subsidiary in Cidade da Praia, Ilha de Santiago. In 1975 Banco de Cabo Verde was formed, with the role of money issuer, and this bank replaced BNU.

In 1993, the New Organic Law segregated commercial functions from those of development. The latter were transferred to the newly established Banco Comercial do Atlântico (BCA), together with a distribution network of 12 branches and 3extensions (smaller branches).

In 2002, following the privatization of BCA, which until then had been a state-owned bank, Caixa Geral de Depósitos was chosen as a strategic partner, holding 52.5% of the share capital with Banco Interatlântico (BI). BI had been in augurated in 1999, with 70% of its shares held by CGD.

Today, CGD's presence in Cape Verde is represented by BCA and by Banco Interatlântico (BI) in the banking sector, by Garantia in the insurance sector, and by Promotora, a joint venture company.

BCA has a network of 33 branches, covering all the Cape Verde islands, with 4 branches specializing in the enterprise segment. BI has a network of 9 branches on the islands of Santiago, São Vicente, and Sal.

BCA is the market leader in both credit and deposits, with market shares of 40.3% and 43%, respectively.

In December 2014, BCA had 433 employees and BI 120.

São Tomé and Príncipe

The presence of Caixa Geral de Depósitos on the islands of São Tomé and Príncipe began in 1993, when Banco Internacional de São Tomé e Príncipe (BISTP) was established, the first privately owned commercial bank on the islands.

BISTP is a retail-oriented bank of which CGD owns 27%, the State of S. Tomé 48%, and the Investment African Bank 25% of share capital. It is a leader in the market on both the deposit and credit sides of its balance sheet, with 71% and 47% market shares, respectively.

Until November 2007, BISTP had a distribution network of three branches: headquarters, the market branch, and the Príncipe branch. In December of the same year the bank inaugurated two more branches, in Sé and Miramar. Two more branches followed in 2009 (Giovani and Vila Maria), offering a total network of eight branches aimed at a better coverage of the territory and, at the same time, providing a better service to its clients.

Giving continuity to its expansionary strategy, in May 2012 BISTP opened its ninth branch, located on the Academia Campus of Instituto Superior Politécnico. The same year, the first branch outside the city was opened, the Santana branch in the District of Cantagalo. Other branches followed: Hospital Central (2013), a subsidiary on Príncipe Island, and a branch in Trindade, the twelfth (2014).

This expansionary strategy has as an objective the renewal of the bank's services and premises. At the same time, it targets the beginning of segmentation of the bank's clients, responding to the dynamic evolution of the market. BISTP has simultaneously followed a policy of technological innovation, which constitutes one of its strategic goals.

The bank has 130 employees, and over the last few years has experienced an increase in highly qualified staff, with a concentration in the range of between 30 and 39 years old.

Timor

Banco Nacional Ultramarino (BNU) was the first bank to establish itself in the geographical area of Indonesia known as Timor. It still is the oldest bank operating in the territory.

At the beginning, CGD set up a representative office with headquarters in Companhia de Timor (1902). Its first banking branch was formed in 1912 in Dili, the capital.

When Indonesia's sovereign rule of Timor ended in 1999, CGD reassumed its active participation in the country's reconstruction.

BNU was incorporated into CGD in 2001, and the joint company opened its first subsidiary in Timor in the same year.

CGD operates in two market segments: individuals and enterprises. In the individuals segment it is worth highlighting the existence of financing lines to support a better social and familiar environment; namely, credit lines related to the acquisition of goods for domestic purposes, automobiles, health support, and education financing, together with household improvements.

As far as the enterprises segment is concerned, CGD offers a comprehensive array of options to comply with the needs of business management and entrepreneurial activity development, characterized by both strong innovation and dynamism.

CGD has a presence in all district capitals, with a network of 13 branches, which covers around 90% of Timor. Its subsidiary has 118 employees, 110 of whom are native born.

Macau

The history of CGD in Macau began in 1901, when a contract was established between the Government of Portugal and BNU, with the purpose of issuing notes and bonds. By the early 1990s, BNU ranked second in Macau's banking system (formed of 21 banks), just after Bank of China.

In March 2001, BNU was incorporated into CGD. Therefore, in July 2001 the subsidiary of BNU in Macau became a subsidiary of CGD with headquarters in Macau, the corresponding capital fully subscribed by CGD.

Nowadays, BNU is still developing its commercial banking activity and the role of money issuance. The contribution of BNU Macau to the CGD Group has assumed great relevance, in particular in terms of raising funds, and its market performance has shown high levels of profitability.

At the end of 2013, BNU's network was built on 18 branches and a representative office in Shanghai. The number of employees had reached 447.

Millennium bcp

After achieving and consolidating a significant position in the Portuguese market, Millennium bcp clearly opted for a strategy of retail business expansion to new geographies. From the very beginning, its internationalization was based on the prospects of growth and profitability in foreign markets with a close historical link to Portugal or with large communities of Portuguese descent. It also targeted markets where there was a strong commercial rationale for the establishment of banking operations supported by business models and technological platforms similar to those used by the bank and of recognized success in the Portuguese market, adapting them to the financial requirements and needs of local customers.

The BCP Group became a reference institution at an international level with a focus on the retail distribution of financial products and services, in Poland (Bank Millennium), Mozambique (Millennium bim), and Angola (Banco Millennium Angola). All three international operations are profitable, self-funded, and self-sustainable, with capital for growth. It also has a private banking platform in Switzerland, which plays an important role in this business area, providing services to group clients in Portugal, Poland, and other geographies. Millennium bcp is also present in Macau, through its onshore branch, which aims to be an international business platform between China/Macau, Portuguese-speaking Africa, and Europe.

Due to the nature of this chapter, where we are interested in Portuguese banks and their expansion in Portuguese-speaking countries, we will focus our attention on two countries: Mozambique and Angola.

Table 9.6 outlines the numbers relevant to this unique international presence focused in the strategic markets of Mozambique and Angola.

In these key strategic markets, Millennium bcp delivered strong earnings growth, as shown in Tables 9.7 and 9.8.

For all three operations abroad (that is, Angola, Mozambique, and Poland), the compound annual growth rate (CAGR) of net income amounted to 7.2% between 2006 and 2010, and reached 16.9% between 2010 and 2014.

Table 9.6 Millennium bcp's presence in Angola and Mozambique

Angola: Banco Millennium Angola	Mozambique: Millennium bim
Market share: 3.4% in loans and 3.4% in deposits	Market share: 29.6% in loans and 30.2% in deposits
Loans to customers (gross): €1,005 million	Loans to customers (gross): €1,481 million
Customer funds: €1,452 million	Customer funds: €1,932 million
Employees: 1,143	Employees: 2,513
Branches: 88	Branches: 166

Table 9.7 Banco Millennium Angola net income (in million euros)

Year	Amount
2006	3
2010	24
2014	51

Table 9.8 Millennium bim net income (in million euros)

Year	Amount
2006	39
2010	53
2014	89

Table 9.9 International presence of BCP

Country	ROE (2014)	LTD (2014)	BV (2014)	BCP Stake
Poland	12%	92%	€2.4bn**	65.5%
Mozambique	23%	74%	€0.4bn	66.7%
Angola	18%	66%	€0.3bn	50.1%

**Market capitalization as at December 31, 2014.
**Source*: IMF-WEO 2014 (average expected annual nominal GDP growth 2014–16).

Adding to the strong growth in earnings obtained abroad, Millennium bcp's international presence can be pictured by the data in Table 9.9, where we have deliberately included Poland to capture a more precise picture.

In Poland the market environment provides a significant upside, and the bank's strengths are as follows:

- Well-distributed branch network.
- Highly recognized brand and top-quality service.
- Modern multichannel infrastructure.
- Risk management and cost control.
- Being self-funded and self-sustainable.

In Mozambique and Angola, the high growth potential has been driven by a sector under penetration and high expected GDP growth. The loan-to-GDP ratio analysis allows the conclusion of under penetrated markets expected to converge to peer levels. This ratio is 30% for Mozambique and 25% for Angola (according to BMI, Bank of Angola, and IMF figures). The real GDP growth (2014–17) analysis gives the idea that market expansion will be supported by high expected GDP growth levels, ahead of most emerging-market peers. According to the International Monetary Fund (IMF), real GDP growth between 2014 and 2017 will average 8% in Mozambique and 5% in Angola.

In conclusion, on the one hand Mozambique and Angola are under penetrated banking markets that are expected to converge to peer levels given their higher expected GDP growth levels. On the other hand, the valuation of emerging-market banks is based on the evolution of earnings per share (EPS) growth.

This section ends with a set of guidelines for the group's activities in both Mozambique and Angola.

Mozambique

Millennium bim is a profitable market leader in a fast-growing country, which can be characterized by the following key highlights:

- Under penetrated banking system.
- High expected GDP growth based on extractive industries, coal and natural gas production – expected to become one of the 10 largest coal exporters in the world and one of the largest exporters of natural gas to Asia, according to Mining Weekly (Mozambique Q2 Mining Report Release) and Frost & Sullivan – infrastructure investment, and credit expansion.
- Affinity market with strong historical, cultural, and economic ties to Portugal.
- Economic and political stability since the end of the civil war in 1992.

Millennium bim shows the following strengths as a bank:

- Market leader.
- Largest branch network.
- High profitability.
- Being self-funded and self-sustainable.

Its strategic plan is built on the targets shown in Table 9.10.

Table 9.10 Millennium bim targets for Mozambique

	2014	2017
ROE	23%	>15%
C/I	44%	<45%
LTD*	74%	<90%

*Net loans/deposits

Millennium bim's main objectives in Mozambique are as follows:

- Reinforce its competitive position in corporate and investment banking to consolidate market leadership.
- Consolidate the prestige segment to support the increasing number of affluent clients.
- Focus on innovation, mobile, and transactional products.

Its shareholder structure is:

- BCP (Portugal): 67%
- State of Mozambique/Social Security: 22%
- Others: 11%

Angola

Banco Millennium Angola maintains high growth, gaining market share while experiencing further increasing profitability. The country is characterized by the following key highlights:

- Under penetrated banking system.
- Third largest economy in Sub-Saharan Africa (equivalent to 57% of Portuguese GDP, according to the IMF).
- High expected GDP growth based on oil production (third largest oil producer in Africa, according to the National Bank of Angola), government effort to diversify the economy (non-oil GDP growth was 11.5% in 2013, according to the US Central Intelligence Agency), and credit expansion.
- Affinity market with strong historical, cultural, and economic ties to Portugal.
- Economic and political stability since the end of the civil war in 2002.

In Angola, Banco Millennium Angola shows the following strengths:

- Modern and innovative infrastructure.
- Expansion plan to improve penetration.
- Highly efficient and compliant.
- Strong brand recognition.
- Being self-funded and self-sustainable.

Its strategic plan is built on the targets shown in Table 9.11.

Table 9.11 Banco Millennium Angola targets for Angola

	2014	2017
ROE	18%	>20%
C/I	51%	<40%
LTD*	66%	<75%

*Net loans/deposits

Banco Millennium Angola's main initiatives in Angola are:

- Improve service quality in affluent segments to increase cross-selling and customer acquisition.
- Create risk management policies and strengthen guarantees in order to mitigate decreasing oil price risks.
- Reevaluate and reinforce branch expansion.
- Continue to focus on innovative products.

Its shareholder structure is:

- BCP (Portugal): 50%
- Sonangol: 30%
- Others: 20%

Conclusion

The study of the literature concerning the foreign presence of Portuguese banks that has just been outlined is a good example of the Portuguese "Diaspora" and of how Portugal has expanded its influence over the five continents of the world.

Acknowledgments

I wish to thank Luís Mira Amaral, José Carlos Mateus, Ricardo Araújo, Filomena Oliveira, and Erik Burns for their valuable information and contribution to this chapter. Any remaining errors are my own.

Index

Note: "n" after a page reference denotes a note on that page.

Printed and bound by CPI Group (UK) Ltd, Croydon, CR0 4YY